50% OFF Online TSI (TSIA2) Prep Course!

Dear Customer,

We consider it an honor and a privilege that you chose our TSI Study Guide. As a way of showing our appreciation and to help us better serve you, we have partnered with Mometrix Test Preparation to offer **50% off their online TSI Prep Course**. Many TSI courses are needlessly expensive and don't deliver enough value. With their course, you get access to the best TSI prep material, and **you only pay half price**.

Mometrix has structured their online course to perfectly complement your printed study guide. The TSI Prep Course contains **in-depth lessons** that cover all the most important topics, **220+ video reviews** that explain difficult concepts, **over 1,300 practice questions** to ensure you feel prepared, and **520+ digital flashcards**, so you can study while you're on the go.

Online TSI Assessment 2.0 Prep Course

Topics Covered:
- Mathematics
    - Quantitative Reasoning
    - Algebraic Reasoning
    - Geometric and Spatial Reasoning
    - Probabilistic and Statistical Reasoning
- English Language Arts and Reading
    - Literary Text Analysis
    - Inferences
    - Conventions of Grammar and Usage
- Essay
    - Body, Paragraphs, & Paragraph Length
    - Sequence Words and Phrases, Transitions, & Conclusion

Course Features:
- TSI Study Guide
    - Get content that complements our best-selling study guide.
- 10 Full-Length Practice Tests
    - With over 1,300 practice questions, you can test yourself again and again.
- Mobile Friendly
    - If you need to study on the go, the course is easily accessible from your mobile device.
- TSI Flashcards
    - Their course includes a flashcard mode consisting of over 520 content cards to help you study.

To receive this discount, simply head to their website: mometrix.com/university/tsi or simply scan this QR code with your smartphone. At the checkout page, enter the discount code: **TPBTSI50**

If you have any questions or concerns, please contact Mometrix at support@mometrix.com.

Sincerely,

 in partnership with

Online Resources

Included with your purchase are multiple online resources. This includes the practice tests in an interactive format and a convenient study timer to help you manage your time.

Instructions for accessing these resources can be found on the last page of this book.

TSI Study Guide 2025-2026

6 TSI Practice Tests and Exam Prep Book for the Texas Success Initiative Assessment [7th Edition]

Lydia Morrison

Copyright © 2025 by TPB Publishing

All rights reserved. No part of this publication may be reproduced, distributed, or transmitted in any form or by any means, including photocopying, recording, or other electronic or mechanical methods, without the prior written permission of the publisher, except in the case of brief quotations embodied in critical reviews and certain other noncommercial uses permitted by copyright law.

Written and edited by TPB Publishing.

TPB Publishing is not associated with or endorsed by any official testing organization. TPB Publishing is a publisher of unofficial educational products. All test and organization names are trademarks of their respective owners. Content in this book is included for utilitarian purposes only and does not constitute an endorsement by TPB Publishing of any particular point of view.

Interested in buying more than 10 copies of our product? Contact us about bulk discounts:
bulkorders@studyguideteam.com

ISBN 13: 9781637755020

Table of Contents

Welcome *1*

Quick Overview *2*

Test-Taking Strategies *3*

Introduction to the TSI Exam *7*

Study Prep Plan for the TSI Exam *9*

Math Reference Sheet *12*

Mathematics *13*

   Quantitative and Algebraic Reasoning 13

   Geometric and Spatial Reasoning 36

   Probabilistic and Statistical Reasoning 49

English Language Arts and Reading *58*

   Reading: Literary Text Analysis 58

   Reading: Informational Text Analysis and Synthesis 63

   Reading: Vocabulary 71

   Writing: Essay Revision and Editing 73

   Writing: Sentence Revision, Editing, and Completion 77

Essay *105*

   Five-Paragraph Persuasive Essay 105

TSI Practice Test #1 .... *107*

   Math 107

   English Language Arts and Reading 111

   Essay 120

Answer Explanations #1 .... *124*

- Math 124
- English Language Arts and Reading 128

TSI Practice Test #2 132
- Math 132
- English Language Arts and Reading 136
- Essay 145

Answer Explanations #2 149
- Math 149
- English Language Arts and Reading 153

TSI Practice Test #3 158
- Math 158
- English Language Arts and Reading 161
- Essay 172

Answer Explanations #3 176
- Math 176
- English Language Arts and Reading 179

TSI Practice Tests #4, #5, and #6 183

Index 184

Online Resources 189

Welcome

Dear Reader,

Welcome to your new Test Prep Books study guide! We are pleased that you chose us to help you prepare for your exam. There are many study options to choose from, and we appreciate you choosing us. Studying can be a daunting task, but we have designed a smart, effective study guide to help prepare you for what lies ahead.

Whether you're a parent helping your child learn and grow, a high school student working hard to get into your dream college, or a nursing student studying for a complex exam, we want to help give you the tools you need to succeed. We hope this study guide gives you the skills and the confidence to thrive, and we can't thank you enough for allowing us to be part of your journey.

In an effort to continue to improve our products, we welcome feedback from our customers. We look forward to hearing from you. Suggestions, success stories, and criticisms can all be communicated by emailing us at info@studyguideteam.com.

Sincerely,
Test Prep Books Team

Quick Overview

As you draw closer to taking your exam, effective preparation becomes more and more important. Thankfully, you have this study guide to help you get ready. Use this guide to help keep your studying on track and refer to it often.

This study guide contains several key sections that will help you be successful on your exam. The guide contains tips for what you should do the night before and the day of the test. Also included are test-taking tips. Knowing the right information is not always enough. Many well-prepared test takers struggle with exams. These tips will help equip you to accurately read, assess, and answer test questions.

A large part of the guide is devoted to showing you what content to expect on the exam and to helping you better understand that content. In this guide are practice test questions so that you can see how well you have grasped the content. Then, answer explanations are provided so that you can understand why you missed certain questions.

Don't try to cram the night before you take your exam. This is not a wise strategy for a few reasons. First, your retention of the information will be low. Your time would be better used by reviewing information you already know rather than trying to learn a lot of new information. Second, you will likely become stressed as you try to gain a large amount of knowledge in a short amount of time. Third, you will be depriving yourself of sleep. So be sure to go to bed at a reasonable time the night before. Being well-rested helps you focus and remain calm.

Be sure to eat a substantial breakfast the morning of the exam. If you are taking the exam in the afternoon, be sure to have a good lunch as well. Being hungry is distracting and can make it difficult to focus. You have hopefully spent lots of time preparing for the exam. Don't let an empty stomach get in the way of success!

When traveling to the testing center, leave earlier than needed. That way, you have a buffer in case you experience any delays. This will help you remain calm and will keep you from missing your appointment time at the testing center.

Be sure to pace yourself during the exam. Don't try to rush through the exam. There is no need to risk performing poorly on the exam just so you can leave the testing center early. Allow yourself to use all of the allotted time if needed.

Remain positive while taking the exam even if you feel like you are performing poorly. Thinking about the content you should have mastered will not help you perform better on the exam.

Once the exam is complete, take some time to relax. Even if you feel that you need to take the exam again, you will be well served by some down time before you begin studying again. It's often easier to convince yourself to study if you know that it will come with a reward!

Test-Taking Strategies

1. Predicting the Answer

When you feel confident in your preparation for a multiple-choice test, try predicting the answer before reading the answer choices. This is especially useful on questions that test objective factual knowledge. By predicting the answer before reading the available choices, you eliminate the possibility that you will be distracted or led astray by an incorrect answer choice. You will feel more confident in your selection if you read the question, predict the answer, and then find your prediction among the answer choices. After using this strategy, be sure to still read all of the answer choices carefully and completely. If you feel unprepared, you should not attempt to predict the answers. This would be a waste of time and an opportunity for your mind to wander in the wrong direction.

2. Reading the Whole Question

Too often, test takers scan a multiple-choice question, recognize a few familiar words, and immediately jump to the answer choices. Test authors are aware of this common impatience, and they will sometimes prey upon it. For instance, a test author might subtly turn the question into a negative, or he or she might redirect the focus of the question right at the end. The only way to avoid falling into these traps is to read the entirety of the question carefully before reading the answer choices.

3. Looking for Wrong Answers

Long and complicated multiple-choice questions can be intimidating. One way to simplify a difficult multiple-choice question is to eliminate all of the answer choices that are clearly wrong. In most sets of answers, there will be at least one selection that can be dismissed right away. If the test is administered on paper, the test taker could draw a line through it to indicate that it may be ignored; otherwise, the test taker will have to perform this operation mentally or on scratch paper. In either case, once the obviously incorrect answers have been eliminated, the remaining choices may be considered. Sometimes identifying the clearly wrong answers will give the test taker some information about the correct answer. For instance, if one of the remaining answer choices is a direct opposite of one of the eliminated answer choices, it may well be the correct answer. The opposite of obviously wrong is obviously right! Of course, this is not always the case. Some answers are obviously incorrect simply because they are irrelevant to the question being asked. Still, identifying and eliminating some incorrect answer choices is a good way to simplify a multiple-choice question.

4. Don't Overanalyze

Anxious test takers often overanalyze questions. When you are nervous, your brain will often run wild, causing you to make associations and discover clues that don't actually exist. If you feel that this may be a problem for you, do whatever you can to slow down during the test. Try taking a deep breath or counting to ten. As you read and consider the question, restrict yourself to the particular words used by the author. Avoid thought tangents about what the author *really* meant, or what he or she was *trying* to say. The only things that matter on a multiple-choice test are the words that are actually in the question. You must avoid reading too much into a multiple-choice question, or supposing that the writer meant something other than what he or she wrote.

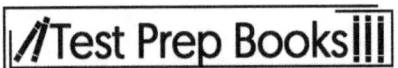

5. No Need for Panic

It is wise to learn as many strategies as possible before taking a multiple-choice test, but it is likely that you will come across a few questions for which you simply don't know the answer. In this situation, avoid panicking. Because most multiple-choice tests include dozens of questions, the relative value of a single wrong answer is small. As much as possible, you should compartmentalize each question on a multiple-choice test. In other words, you should not allow your feelings about one question to affect your success on the others. When you find a question that you either don't understand or don't know how to answer, just take a deep breath and do your best. Read the entire question slowly and carefully. Try rephrasing the question a couple of different ways. Then, read all of the answer choices carefully. After eliminating obviously wrong answers, make a selection and move on to the next question.

6. Confusing Answer Choices

When working on a difficult multiple-choice question, there may be a tendency to focus on the answer choices that are the easiest to understand. Many people, whether consciously or not, gravitate to the answer choices that require the least concentration, knowledge, and memory. This is a mistake. When you come across an answer choice that is confusing, you should give it extra attention. A question might be confusing because you do not know the subject matter to which it refers. If this is the case, don't  eliminate the answer before you have affirmatively settled on another. When you come across an answer choice of this type, set it aside as you look at the remaining choices. If you can confidently assert that one of the other choices is correct, you can leave the confusing answer aside. Otherwise, you will need to take a moment to try to better understand the confusing answer choice. Rephrasing is one way to tease out the sense of a confusing answer choice.

7. Your First Instinct

Many people struggle with multiple-choice tests because they overthink the questions. If you have studied sufficiently for the test, you should be prepared to trust your first instinct once you have carefully and completely read the question and all of the answer choices. There is a great deal of research suggesting that the mind can come to the correct conclusion very quickly once it has obtained all of the relevant information. At times, it may seem to you as if your intuition is working faster even than your reasoning mind. This may in fact be true. The knowledge you obtain while studying may be retrieved from your subconscious before you have a chance to work out the associations that support it. Verify your instinct by working out the reasons that it should be trusted.

8. Key Words

Many test takers struggle with multiple-choice questions because they have poor reading comprehension skills. Quickly reading and understanding a multiple-choice question requires a mixture of skill and experience. To help with this, try jotting down a few key words and phrases on a piece of scrap paper. Doing this concentrates the process of reading and forces the mind to weigh the relative importance of the question's parts. In selecting words and phrases to write down, the test taker thinks about the question more deeply and carefully. This is especially true for multiple-choice questions that are preceded by a long prompt.

9. Subtle Negatives

One of the oldest tricks in the multiple-choice test writer's book is to subtly reverse the meaning of a question with a word like *not* or *except*. If you are not paying attention to each word in the question, you can easily be led astray by this trick. For instance, a common question format is, "Which of the following is...?" Obviously, if the question instead is, "Which of the following is not...?," then the answer will be quite different. Even worse, the test makers are aware of the potential for this mistake and will include one answer choice that would be correct if the question were not negated or reversed. A test taker who misses the reversal will find what he or she believes to be a correct answer and will be so confident that he or she will fail to reread the question and discover the original error. The only way to avoid this is to practice a wide variety of multiple-choice questions and to pay close attention to each and every word.

10. Reading Every Answer Choice

It may seem obvious, but you should always read every one of the answer choices! Too many test takers fall into the habit of scanning the question and assuming that they understand the question because they recognize a few key words. From there, they pick the first answer choice that answers the question they believe they have read. Test takers who read all of the answer choices might discover that one of the latter answer choices is actually *more* correct. Moreover, reading all of the answer choices can remind you of facts related to the question that can help you arrive at the correct answer. Sometimes, a misstatement or incorrect detail in one of the latter answer choices will trigger your memory of the subject and will enable you to find the right answer. Failing to read all of the answer choices is like not reading all of the items on a restaurant menu: you might miss out on the perfect choice.

11. Spot the Hedges

One of the keys to success on multiple-choice tests is paying close attention to every word. This is never truer than with words like *almost, most, some,* and *sometimes*. These words are called "hedges" because they indicate that a statement is not totally true or not true in every place and time. An absolute statement will contain no hedges, but in many subjects, the answers are not always straightforward or absolute. There are always exceptions to the rules in these subjects. For this reason,

you should favor those multiple-choice questions that contain hedging language. The presence of qualifying words indicates that the author is taking special care with his or her words, which is certainly important when composing the right answer. After all, there are many ways to be wrong, but there is only one way to be right! For this reason, it is wise to avoid answers that are absolute when taking a multiple-choice test. An absolute answer is one that says things are either all one way or all another. They often include words like *every, always, best,* and *never*. If you are taking a multiple-choice test in a subject that doesn't lend itself to absolute answers, be on your guard if you see any of these words.

12. Long Answers

In many subject areas, the answers are not simple. As already mentioned, the right answer often requires hedges. Another common feature of the answers to a complex or subjective question are qualifying clauses, which are groups of words that subtly modify the meaning of the sentence. If the question or answer choice describes a rule to which there are exceptions or the subject matter is complicated, ambiguous, or confusing, the correct answer will require many words in order to be expressed clearly and accurately. In essence, you should not be deterred by answer choices that seem excessively long. Oftentimes, the author of the text will not be able to write the correct answer without offering some qualifications and modifications. Your job is to read the answer choices thoroughly and completely and to select the one that most accurately and precisely answers the question.

13. Restating to Understand

Sometimes, a question on a multiple-choice test is difficult not because of what it asks but because of how it is written. If this is the case, restate the question or answer choice in different words. This process serves a couple of important purposes. First, it forces you to concentrate on the core of the question. In order to rephrase the question accurately, you have to understand it well. Rephrasing the question will concentrate your mind on the key words and ideas. Second, it will present the information to your mind in a fresh way. This process may trigger your memory and render some useful scrap of information picked up while studying.

14. True Statements

Sometimes an answer choice will be true in itself, but it does not answer the question. This is one of the main reasons why it is essential to read the question carefully and completely before proceeding to the answer choices. Too often, test takers skip ahead to the answer choices and look for true statements. Having found one of these, they are content to select it without reference to the question above. The savvy test taker will always read the entire question before turning to the answer choices. Then, having settled on a correct answer choice, he or she will refer to the original question and ensure that the selected answer is relevant. The mistake of choosing a correct-but-irrelevant answer choice is especially common on questions related to specific pieces of objective knowledge.

15. No Patterns

One of the more dangerous ideas that circulates about multiple-choice tests is that the correct answers tend to fall into patterns. These erroneous ideas range from a belief that B and C are the most common right answers, to the idea that an unprepared test-taker should answer "A-B-A-C-A-D-A-B-A." It cannot be emphasized enough that pattern-seeking of this type is exactly the WRONG way to approach a multiple-choice test. To begin with, it is highly unlikely that the test maker will plot the correct answers according to some predetermined pattern. The questions are scrambled and delivered in a random order. Furthermore, even if the test maker was following a pattern in the assignation of correct answers, there is no reason why the test taker would know which pattern he or she was using. Any attempt to discern a pattern in the answer choices is a waste of time and a distraction from the real work of taking the test. A test taker would be much better served by extra preparation before the test than by reliance on a pattern in the answers.

Introduction to the TSI Exam

Function of the Test

The Texas Success Initiative Assessment (TSI) is used to measure a student's readiness for college-level coursework. The TSI assesses incoming freshmen in the state of Texas in the subject areas of English language arts and reading (ELAR) as well as mathematics. The results of this test are used to place an incoming student into the appropriate college-level course and determine the type of intervention, if any, a student needs.

Many students can be exempt from the TSI if they meet the minimum score on the SAT, ACT, or statewide high school test. If students have already completed college-level English and math courses, they will be exempt. Other ways to be exempt from taking the TSI include current enrollment in a Level-One certificate program (fewer than 43 semester credit hours), not seeking a college degree, or students currently or formerly enrolled in the military. Those students that are not exempt will be asked to take two tests, one in each of the subject areas of mathematics and ELAR. A diagnostic test may be given in addition to these tests in a particular subject area if deemed necessary.

The TSI is meant to give an institute detailed information on a student's strengths and weaknesses. Before taking the TSI, a candidate must take the Pre-Assessment activity. The activity includes an explanation of the TSI, practice questions and feedback, an explanation of developmental educational options if a minimum score is not met, and campus and community resources.

Test Administration

There are testing centers located at universities for the TSI assessment. Retesting is acceptable, and there are no restrictions as to when a retest can be done. However, students are encouraged to study and prepare before retaking the TSI. Some colleges and universities also host workshops to better prepare a student to retake the TSI. It is advised to contact the local university or college where a candidate wishes to take the test to receive more information on retesting and workshops. Advisors and counselors at a particular institution can better help a candidate with any further questions they may have.

Test Format

The TSI has two different components: one in mathematics and one in English language arts and reading. All sections are multiple choice with an additional essay section for writing. The table below outlines the concepts tested in each of the sections.

Mathematics	ELAR
Quantitative Reasoning	Literary Text Analysis
Algebraic Reasoning	Informational Text Analysis and Synthesis
Geometric and Spatial Reasoning	Essay Revision and Editing
Probabilistic and Statistical Reasoning	Sentence Revision, Editing, and Completion

The essay section is a five-paragraph persuasive essay on a controversial issue or current event topic. The essay should be 300–600 words and must clearly state a main idea with supporting evidence. Proper English language conventions are expected, and no dictionaries or resources may be used. Scratch paper

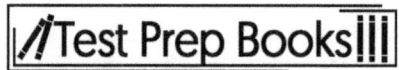

Introduction to the TSI Exam

and essay paper will be provided at the testing center. Students are not allowed to use their own calculators, but a pop-up calculator will be available on select questions.

Section	Number of Items on College Readiness Classification Test*	Number of Items on Diagnostic Test
Mathematics	20	48
ELAR	30	48

*Note that the College Readiness Classification (CRC) Test is the standard test that is taken by most test candidates. The Diagnostic Test is usually required for those candidates who fail to meet the college-readiness cut score in any of the domains after taking the CRC. Results from the Diagnostic Test can then be used to help place the student in an appropriate developmental or readiness course.

Scoring

For each section of the test, a classification score ranging from 910 to 990 is given at the end of the CRC Test. If a score is high enough, a classification of "college ready" is given. If a score in one section is not high enough, a Diagnostic Test for that section is then administered. After the Diagnostic Test, an Educational Functioning Level (EFL) is given, ranging from level 2 through level 6, with level 6 being the highest. For Math, a CRC score above the cut-off or a CRC score below the cut-off with an EFL of 6 is required to receive "college ready" classification. For ELAR, a CRC score above the cut-off or a CRC score below the cut-off with an EFL of at least a 4 will lead to the essay test. After the essay, a CRC score above the cut-off or an EFL of at least a 5 is required to receive "college ready" classification. At the end, test takers will either receive a "college ready" classification or a diagnostic classification, which will have their EFL Level and scores on the different concepts in that section.

Recent Developments

In October 2020, the College Board revised the TSI and made the Texas Success Initiative Assessment 2 (TSIA2). This new edition combined the previous edition's Reading and Writing sections into a single ELAR section. The TSIA2 also changed the scoring system. For each section there is now one classification score (range 910–990) and two categories ("college ready" or "not college ready" with a diagnostic classification). The essay section remains unchanged.

Study Prep Plan for the TSI Exam

1 **Schedule** - Use one of our study schedules below or come up with one of your own.

2 **Relax** - Test anxiety can hurt even the best students. There are many ways to reduce stress. Find the one that works best for you.

3 **Execute** - Once you have a good plan in place, be sure to stick to it.

One Week Study Schedule

Day 1	Mathematics
Day 2	Geometric and Spatial Reasoning
Day 3	Probabilistic and Statistical Reasoning
Day 4	Reading: Vocabulary
Day 5	TSI Practice Test #1
Day 6	TSI Practice Test #2
Day 7	Take Your Exam!

Two Week Study Schedule

Day 1	Mathematics	Day 8	Conventions of Punctuation
Day 2	Quadratic Functions	Day 9	Essay
Day 3	Geometric and Spatial Reasoning	Day 10	TSI Practice Test #1
Day 4	Probabilistic and Statistical Reasoning	Day 11	TSI Practice Test #2
Day 5	English Language Arts and Reading	Day 12	TSI Practice Test #3
Day 6	Reading: Vocabulary	Day 13	TSI Practice Test #4
Day 7	Conventions of Grammar and Usage	Day 14	Take Your Exam!

One Month Study Schedule

Day 1	Mathematics	Day 11	Probabilistic and Statistical Reasoning	Day 21	TSI Practice Test #1
Day 2	Forms of Linear Equations	Day 12	Linear Data Fitting	Day 22	Answer Explanations #1
Day 3	Linear Systems of Equations	Day 13	English Language Arts and Reading	Day 23	TSI Practice Test #2
Day 4	Polynomials	Day 14	Reading: Informational Text Analysis and Synthesis	Day 24	Answer Explanations #2
Day 5	Quadratic Functions	Day 15	Author's Craft	Day 25	TSI Practice Test #3
Day 6	Exponents and Roots	Day 16	Reading: Vocabulary	Day 26	Answer Explanations #3
Day 7	Rational Expressions	Day 17	Conventions of Grammar and Usage	Day 27	TSI Practice Test #4
Day 8	Geometric and Spatial Reasoning	Day 18	Conventions of Punctuation	Day 28	TSI Practice Test #5
Day 9	Dilation	Day 19	Conventions of Spelling and Capitalization	Day 29	TSI Practice Test #6
Day 10	Volumes and Surface Areas	Day 20	Essay	Day 30	Take Your Exam!

Build your own prep plan by visiting:

testprepbooks.com/prep

As you study for your test, we'd like to take the opportunity to remind you that you are capable of great things! With the right tools and dedication, you truly can do anything you set your mind to. The fact that you are holding this book right now shows how committed you are. In case no one has told you lately, you've got this! Our intention behind including this coloring page is to give you the chance to take some time to engage your creative side when you need a little brain-break from studying. As a company, we want to encourage people like you to achieve their dreams by providing good quality study materials for the tests and certifications that improve careers and change lives. As individuals, many of us have taken such tests in our careers, and we know how challenging this process can be. While we can't come alongside you and cheer you on personally, we can offer you the space to recall your purpose, reconnect with your passion, and refresh your brain through an artistic practice. We wish you every success, and happy studying!

Math Reference Sheet

Symbol	Phrase
+	added to, increased by, sum of, more than
-	decreased by, difference between, less than, take away
×	multiplied by, 3 (4, 5 ...) times as large, product of
÷	divided by, quotient of, half (third, etc.) of
=	is, the same as, results in, as much as
x, t, n, etc.	a variable which is an unknown value or quantity
<	is under, is below, smaller than, beneath
>	is above, is over, bigger than, exceeds
≤	no more than, at most, maximum; less than or equal to
≥	no less than, at least, minimum; greater than or equal to
√	square root of, exponent divided by 2

Geometry	Description
$P = 2l + 2w$	for perimeter of a rectangle
$P = 4 \times s$	for perimeter of a square
$P = a + b + c$	for perimeter of a triangle
$A = \frac{1}{2} \times b \times h = \frac{bh}{2}$	for area of a triangle
$A = b \times h$	for area of a parallelogram
$A = \frac{1}{2} \times h(b_1 + b_2)$	for area of a trapezoid
$A = \frac{1}{2} \times a \times P$	for area of a regular polygon
$C = 2 \times \pi \times r$	for circumference (perimeter) of a circle
$A = \pi \times r^2$	for area of a circle
$c^2 = a^2 + b^2; c = \sqrt{a^2 + b^2}$	for finding the hypotenuse of a right triangle
$SA = 2xy + 2yz + 2xz$	for finding surface area
$V = \frac{1}{3}xyh$	for finding volume of a rectangular pyramid
$V = \frac{4}{3}\pi r^3; \frac{1}{3}\pi r^2 h; \pi r^2 h$	for volume of a sphere; a cone; and a cylinder

Radical Expressions	Description
$\sqrt[n]{a} = a^{\frac{1}{n}}, \sqrt[n]{a^m} = (\sqrt[n]{a})^m = a^{\frac{m}{n}}$	a is the radicand, n is the index, m is the exponent
$\sqrt{x^2} = (x^2)^{\frac{1}{2}} = x$	to convert square root to exponent
$a^m \times a^n = a^{m+n}$	multiplying radicands with exponents
$(a^m)^n = a^{m \times n}$	multiplying exponents
$(a \times b)^m = a^m \times b^m$	parentheses with exponents

Property	Addition	Multiplication
Commutative	$a + b = b + a$	$a \times b = b \times a$
Associative	$(a + b) + c = a + (b + c)$	$(a \times b) \times c = a \times (b \times c)$
Identity	$a + 0 = a; 0 + a = a$	$a \times 1 = a; 1 \times a = a$
Inverse	$a + (-a) = 0$	$a \times \frac{1}{a} = 1; a \neq 0$
Distributive		$a(b + c) = ab + ac$

Data	Description
Mean	equal to the total of the values of a data set, divided by the number of elements in the data set
Median	middle value in an odd number of ordered values of a data set, or the mean of the two middle values in an even number of ordered values in a data set
Mode	the value that appears most often
Range	the difference between the highest and the lowest values in the set

Graphing	Description
(x, y)	ordered pair, plot points in a graph
$y = mx + b$	slope-intercept form; m represents the slope of the line and b represents the y-intercept
$f(x)$	read as f of x, which means it is a function of x
(x_2, y_2) and (x_2, y_2)	two ordered pairs used to determine the slope of a line
$m = \frac{y_2 - y_1}{x_2 - x_1}$	to find the slope of the line, m, for ordered pairs
$Ax + By = C$	standard form of an equation, also for solving a system of equations through the elimination method
$M = (\frac{x_1 + x_2}{2}, \frac{y_1 + y_2}{2})$	for finding the midpoint of an ordered pair
$y = ax^2 + bx + c$	quadratic function for a parabola
$y = a(x - h)^2 + k$	quadratic function for a parabola with vertex
$y = ab^x; y = a \times b^x$	function for exponential curve
$y = ax^2 + bx + c$	standard form of a quadratic function
$x = \frac{-b}{2a}$	for finding axis of symmetry in a parabola; given quadratic formula in standard form
$f = \sqrt{\frac{\Sigma(x - \bar{x})^2}{n - 1}}$	function for standard deviation of the sample; where $\bar{x}$ = sample mean and n = sample size

Proportions and Percentage	Description
$\frac{gallons}{cost} = \frac{gallons}{cost} : \frac{7\ gallons}{\$14.70} = \frac{x}{\$20}$	written as equal ratios with a variable representing the missing quantity
$\frac{y_1}{x_1} = \frac{y_2}{x_2}$	for direct proportions
$(y_1)(x_1) = (y_2)(x_2)$	for indirect proportions
$\frac{change}{original\ value} \times 100 = percent\ change$	for finding percentage change in value
$\frac{new\ quantity - old\ quantity}{old\ quantity} \times 100$	for calculating the increase or decrease in percentage

Mathematics

Quantitative and Algebraic Reasoning

Relations and Functions

First, it's important to understand the definition of a **relation**. Given two variables, x and y, which stand for unknown numbers, a *relation* between x and y is an object that splits all of the pairs (x, y) into those for which the relation is true and those for which it is false. For example, consider the relation of:

$$x^2 = y^2$$

This relationship is true for the pair $(1, 1)$ and for the pair $(-2, 2)$, but false for $(2, 3)$. Another example of a relation is $x \leq y$. This is true whenever x is less than or equal to y.

A **function** is a special kind of relation where, for each value of x, there is only a single value of y that satisfies the relation. So:

$$x^2 = y^2$$

is *not* a function because in this case, if x is 1, y can be either 1 or -1: the pair $(1, 1)$ and $(1, -1)$ both satisfy the relation. More generally, for this relation, any pair of the form $(a, \pm a)$ will satisfy it. On the other hand, consider the following relation:

$$y = x^2 + 1$$

This is a function because for each value of x, there is a unique value of y that satisfies the relation. Notice, however, there are multiple values of x that give us the same value of y. This is perfectly acceptable for a function. Therefore, y is a function of x.

To determine if a relation is a function, check to see if every x value has a unique corresponding y value.

A function can be viewed as an object that has x as its input and outputs a unique y-value. It is sometimes convenient to express this using **function notation**, where the function itself is given a name, often f. To emphasize that f takes x as its input, the function is written as $f(x)$. In the above example, the equation could be rewritten as:

$$f(x) = x^2 + 1$$

To write the value that a function yields for some specific value of x, that value is put in place of x in the function notation. For example, $f(3)$ means the value that the function outputs when the input value is 3. If $f(x) = x^2 + 1$ then,

$$f(3) = 3^2 + 1 = 10$$

A function can also be viewed as a table of pairs (x, y), which lists the value for y for each possible value of x.

The set of all possible values for x in $f(x)$ is called the **domain** of the function, and the set of all possible outputs is called the **range** of the function. Note that usually the domain is assumed to be all real

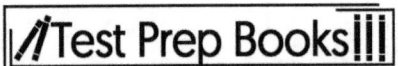

numbers, except those for which the expression for $f(x)$ is not defined, unless the problem specifies otherwise. An example of how a function might not be defined is in the case of:

$$f(x) = \frac{1}{x+1}$$

which is not defined when $x = -1$ (which would require dividing by zero). Therefore, in this case the domain would be all real numbers except $x = -1$.

If y is a function of x, then x is the **independent variable** and y is the **dependent variable**. This is because in many cases, the problem will start with some value of x and then see how y changes depending on this starting value.

Evaluating Functions

To evaluate functions, plug in the given value everywhere the variable appears in the expression for the function. For example, find $g(-2)$ where:

$$g(x) = 2x^2 - \frac{4}{x}$$

To complete the problem, plug in -2 in the following way:

$$g(-2) = 2(-2)^2 - \frac{4}{-2}$$

$$2 \times 4 + 2 = 8 + 2 = 10$$

Defining Linear Equations

A function is called **linear** if it can take the form of the equation:

$$f(x) = ax + b$$

or

$$y = ax + b$$

For any two numbers a and b.

Mathematics

A linear equation forms a straight line when graphed on the coordinate plane. An example of a linear function is shown below on the graph.

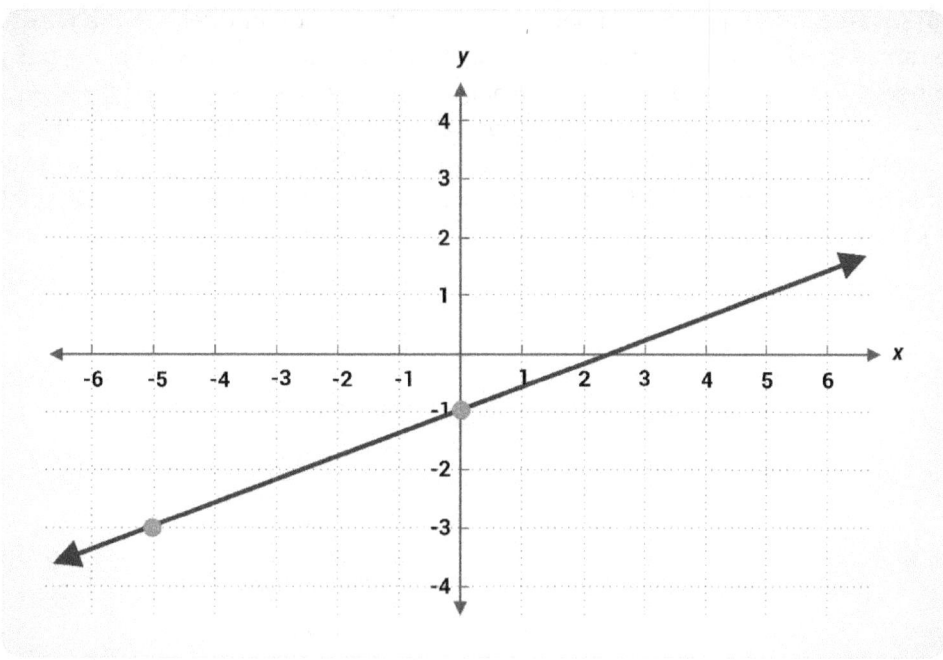

This is a graph of the following function: $y = \frac{2}{5}x - 1$. A table of values that satisfies this function is shown below.

x	y
-5	-3
0	-1
5	1
10	3

These points can be found on the graph using the form (x, y). For more on graphing in the coordinate plane, refer to the Graphing section below.

Graphing Functions and Relations

To graph relations and functions, the Cartesian plane is used. This means to think of the plane as being given a grid of squares, with one direction being the x-axis and the other direction the y-axis. Any point on the plane can be specified by saying how far to go along the x-axis and how far along the y-axis with a pair of numbers (x, y). Specific values for these pairs can be given names such as $C = (-1, 3)$. Negative values mean to move left or down; positive values mean to move right or up. The point where the axes cross one another is called the **origin**. The origin has coordinates $(0, 0)$ and is usually called O when given a specific label. An illustration of the Cartesian plane, along with the plotted points $(2, 1)$ and $(-1, -1)$, is below.

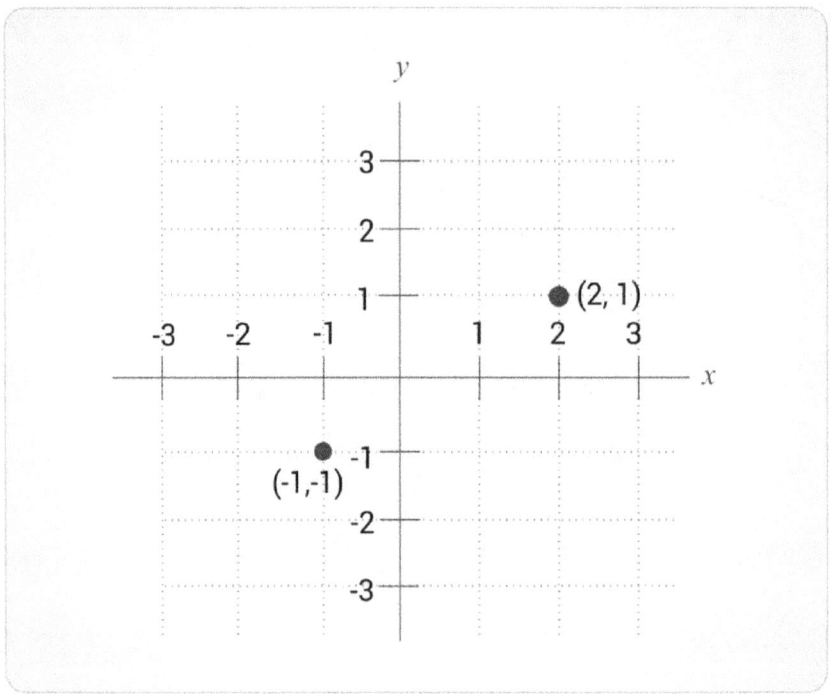

Relations also can be graphed by marking each point whose coordinates satisfy the relation. If the relation is a function, then there is only one value of y for any given value of x. This leads to the **vertical line test**: if a relation is graphed, then the relation is a function if any possible vertical line drawn anywhere along the graph would only touch the graph of the relation in no more than one place. Conversely, when graphing a function, then any possible vertical line drawn will not touch the graph of the function at any point or will touch the function at just one point. This test is made from the definition of a function, where each x-value must be mapped to one and only one y-value.

Forms of Linear Equations

When graphing a linear function, note that the ratio of the change of the y-coordinate to the change in the x-coordinate is constant between any two points on the resulting line, no matter which two points are chosen. In other words, in a pair of points on a line, (x_1, y_1) and (x_2, y_2), with $x_1 \neq x_2$ so that the two points are distinct, then the ratio $\frac{y_2 - y_1}{x_2 - x_1}$ will be the same, regardless of which particular pair of

Mathematics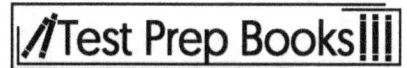

points are chosen. The ratio $\frac{y_2-y_1}{x_2-x_1}$ is called the **slope** of the line and is frequently denoted with the letter m. If slope m is positive, then the line goes upward when moving to the right, while if slope m is negative, then the line goes downward when moving to the right. If the slope is 0, then the line is called **horizontal**, and the y coordinate is constant along the entire line. In lines where the x coordinate is constant along the entire line, y is not actually a function of x. For such lines, the slope is not defined. These lines are called **vertical lines**.

Linear functions may take forms other than $y = ax + b$. The most common forms of linear equations are explained below:

1. **Standard Form**: $Ax + By = C$, in which the slope is given by $m = \frac{-A}{B}$, and the y-intercept is given by $\frac{C}{B}$.

2. **Slope-Intercept Form**: $y = mx + b$, where the slope is m and the y-intercept is b.

3. **Point-Slope Form**: $y - y_1 = m(x - x_1)$, where the slope is m and (x_1, y_1) is any point on the chosen line.

4. **Two-Point Form**: $\frac{y-y_1}{x-x_1} = \frac{y_2-y_1}{x_2-x_1}$, where (x_1, y_1) and (x_2, y_2) are any two distinct points on the chosen line. Note that the slope is given by $m = \frac{y_2-y_1}{x_2-x_1}$.

5. **Intercept Form**: $\frac{x}{x_1} + \frac{y}{y_1} = 1$, in which x_1 is the x-intercept and y_1 is the y-intercept.

These five ways to write linear equations are all useful in different circumstances. Depending on the given information, it may be easier to write one of the forms over another.

If $y = mx$, y is directly proportional to x. In this case, changing x by a factor changes y by that same factor. If $y = \frac{m}{x}$, y is inversely proportional to x. For example, if x is increased by a factor of 3, then y will be decreased by the same factor, 3.

Solving Linear Equations

Sometimes, rather than a situation where there's an equation such as $y = ax + b$ and finding y for some value of x is requested, the result is given and finding x is requested.

The key to solving any equation is to remember that from one true equation, another true equation can be found by adding, subtracting, multiplying, or dividing both sides by the same quantity. In this case, it's necessary to manipulate the equation so that one side only contains x. Then, the other side will show what x is equal to.

For example, in solving $3x - 5 = 2$ adding 5 to each side results in:

$$3x = 7$$

Next, dividing both sides by 3 results in:

$$x = \frac{7}{3}$$

To ensure the calculated results of x is correct, this calculated value can be substituted into the original equation and solved to see if it makes a true statement. For example,

$$3\left(\frac{7}{3}\right) - 5 = 2$$

This can be simplified by cancelling out the two 3s. This yields $7 - 5 = 2$, which is a true statement.

Sometimes an equation may have more than one x-term. For example, consider the following equation:

$$3x + 2 = x - 4$$

Moving all of the x-terms to one side by subtracting x from both sides results in:

$$2x + 2 = -4$$

Next, subtract 2 from both sides so that there is no constant term on the left side. This yields:

$$2x = -6$$

Finally, divide both sides by 2, which leaves $x = -3$.

Solving Linear Inequalities

Solving linear inequalities is very similar to solving equations, except for one rule: when multiplying or dividing an inequality by a negative number, the inequality symbol changes direction. Given the following inequality, solve for x:

$$-2x + 5 < 13$$

The first step in solving this equation is to subtract 5 from both sides. This leaves the inequality:

$$-2x < 8$$

The last step is to divide both sides by -2. By using the rule, the answer to the inequality is:

$$x > -4$$

Since solutions to inequalities include more than one value, number lines are often used to model the answer. For the previous example, the answer is modelled on the number line below. It shows that any number greater than -4, not including -4, satisfies the inequality.

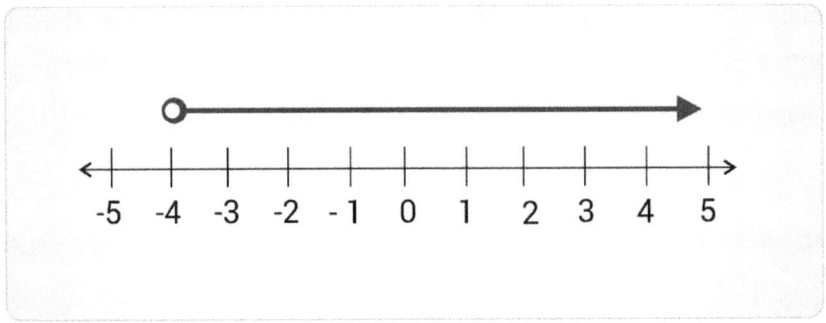

Mathematics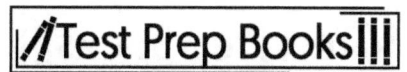

Linear Systems of Equations

A problem sometimes involves multiple variables and multiple equations. These are called **systems of equations**. In this case, try to manipulate them until an expression is found that provides the value of one of the variables. There are a couple of different approaches to this, and some of them can be used together in some cases. The three basic rules to keep in mind are the following.

1. Manipulate a set of equations by doing the same operation to both equations, just as is done when working with just one equation.

2. If one of the equations can be changed so that it expresses one variable in terms of the others, then that expression can be substituted into the other equations and the variable can be eliminated. This means the other equations will have one less variable in them. This is called the method of substitution.

3. If two equations of the form $a = b, c = d$ are included, then a new equation can be formed by adding the left sides and adding the right sides, $a + c = b + d$, or $a - c = b - d$. This enables the elimination of one of the variables from an equation. This is called the method of elimination.

The simplest case is the case of a **linear system of equations**. Although the equations may be written in more complicated forms, linear systems of equations with two variables can always be written in the form:

$$ax + by = c$$

$$dx + ey = f$$

The two basic approaches to solving these systems are substitution and elimination.

Consider the system $3x - y = 2$ and $2x + 2y = 3$. This can be solved in two ways:

1. By substitution: start by solving the first equation for y. First, subtract $3x$ from both sides to obtain:

$$-y = 2 - 3x$$

Next, divide both sides by -1, to obtain $y = 3x - 2$. Then substitute this value for y into the second equation. This yields:

$$2x + 2(3x - 2) = 3$$

This can be simplified to $2x + 6x - 4 = 3$, or $8x = 7$, which means $x = \frac{7}{8}$. By plugging in this value for x into $y = 3x - 2$, the result is:

$$y = 3\left(\frac{7}{8}\right) - 2 = \frac{21}{8} - \frac{16}{8} = \frac{5}{8}$$

So, this results in $x = \frac{7}{8}, y = \frac{5}{8}$.

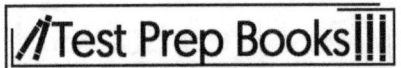

2. By elimination: first, multiply the first equation by 2. This results in $-2y$, which could cancel out the $+2y$ in the second equation. Multiplying both sides of the first equation by 2 gives results in $2(3x - y) = 2(2)$, or $6x - 2y = 4$. Adding the left sides and the right sides of the two equations and setting the results equal to one another results in:

$$(6x + 2x) + (-2y + 2y) = 4 + 3$$

This simplifies to $8x = 7$, so again $x = \frac{7}{8}$. Plug this back into either of the original equations and the result is $3\left(\frac{7}{8}\right) - y = 2$ or:

$$y = 3\left(\frac{7}{8}\right) - 2 = \frac{21}{8} - \frac{16}{8} = \frac{5}{8}$$

This again yields $x = \frac{7}{8}, y = \frac{5}{8}$.

As this shows, both methods will give the same answer. However, one method is sometimes preferred over another simply because of the amount of work required. To check the answer, the values can be substituted into the given system to make sure they form two true statements.

Algebraic Expressions and Equations

Algebraic expressions look similar to equations, but they do not include the equal sign. Algebraic expressions are comprised of numbers, variables, and mathematical operations. Some examples of algebraic expressions are:

$$8x + 7y - 12z$$

$$3a^2$$

And

$$5x^3 - 4y^4$$

Algebraic expressions and equations can be used to represent real-life situations and model the behavior of different variables. For example, $2x + 5$ could represent the cost to play games at an arcade. In this case, 5 represents the price of admission to the arcade, and 2 represents the cost of each game played. To calculate the total cost, use the number of games played for x, multiply it by 2, and add 5.

Word Problems and Applications

In word problems, multiple quantities are provided with a request to find some kind of relation between them. This often will mean that one variable (the dependent variable whose value needs to be found) can be written as a function of another variable (the independent variable whose value can be figured from the given information). The usual procedure for solving these problems is to start by giving each quantity in the problem a variable, and then figuring the relationship between these variables.

For example, suppose a car gets 25 miles per gallon. How far will the car travel if it uses 2.4 gallons of fuel? In this case, y would be the distance the car has traveled in miles, and x would be the amount of fuel burned in gallons (2.4). Then the relationship between these variables can be written as an algebraic equation, $y = 25x$. In this case, the equation is:

$$y = 25 \times 2.4 = 60$$

So, the car has traveled 60 miles.

Some word problems require more than just one simple equation to be written and solved. Consider the following situations and the linear equations used to model them.

Suppose Margaret is 2 miles to the east of John at noon. Margaret walks to the east at 3 miles per hour. How far apart will they be at 3 p.m.? To solve this, x would represent the time in hours past noon, and y would represent the distance between Margaret and John. Now, noon corresponds to the equation where x is 0, so the y-intercept is going to be 2. It's also known that the slope will be the rate at which the distance is changing, which is 3 miles per hour. This means that the slope will be 3 (be careful at this point: if units were used, other than miles and hours, for x and y variables, a conversion of the given information to the appropriate units would be required first). The simplest way to write an equation given the y-intercept, and the slope is the slope-intercept form, which is:

$$y = mx + b$$

Recall that m here is the slope and b is the y intercept. So, $m = 3$ and $b = 2$. Therefore, the equation will be $y = 3x + 2$. The word problem asks how far to the east Margaret will be from John at 3 p.m., which means when x is 3. So, substitute $x = 3$ into this equation to obtain:

$$y = 3 \times 3 + 2 = 9 + 2 = 11$$

Therefore, she will be 11 miles to the east of him at 3 p.m.

For another example, suppose that a box with 4 cans in it weighs 6 lbs., while a box with 8 cans in it weighs 12 lbs. Find out how much a single can weighs. To do this, let x denote the number of cans in the box, and y denote the weight of the box with the cans in lbs. This line touches two pairs: $(4, 6)$ and $(8, 12)$.

A formula for this relation could be written using the two-point form, with:

$$x_1 = 4$$

$$y_1 = 6$$

$$x_2 = 8$$

$$y_2 = 12$$

This would yield:

$$\frac{y-6}{x-4} = \frac{12-6}{8-4}$$

or

$$\frac{y-6}{x-4} = \frac{6}{4} = \frac{3}{2}$$

However, only the slope is needed to solve this problem, since the slope will be the weight of a single can. From the computation, the slope is $\frac{3}{2}$. Therefore, each can weighs $\frac{3}{2}$ lb.

Polynomials

An expression of the form ax^n, where n is a non-negative integer, is called a **monomial** because it contains one term. A sum of monomials is called a **polynomial**. For example:

$$-4x^3 + x$$

This is a polynomial, while $5x^7$ is a monomial. A function equal to a polynomial is called a **polynomial function**. The monomials in a polynomial are also called the **terms of the polynomial**. The constants that precede the variables are called **coefficients**.

The highest value of the exponent of x in a polynomial is called the **degree of the polynomial**. So, $-4x^3 + x$ has a degree of 3, while $-2x^5 + x^3 + 4x + 1$ has a degree of 5. When multiplying polynomials, the degree of the result will be the sum of the degrees of the two polynomials being multiplied.

To add polynomials, add the coefficients of like powers of x. For example:

$$(-2x^5 + x^3 + 4x + 1) + (-4x^3 + x)$$

$$-2x^5 + (1-4)x^3 + (4+1)x + 1$$

$$-2x^5 - 3x^3 + 5x + 1$$

Likewise, subtraction of polynomials is performed by subtracting coefficients of like powers of x. So:

$$(-2x^5 + x^3 + 4x + 1) - (-4x^3 + x)$$

$$-2x^5 + (1+4)x^3 + (4-1)x + 1$$

$$-2x^5 + 5x^3 + 3x + 1$$

To multiply two polynomials, multiply each term of the first polynomial by each term of the second polynomial and add the results. For example:

$$(4x^2 + x)(-x^3 + x)$$

$$4x^2(-x^3) + 4x^2(x) + x(-x^3) + x(x)$$

$$-4x^5 + 4x^3 - x^4 + x^2$$

Mathematics

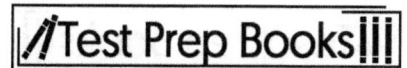

In the case where each polynomial has two terms, like in this example, some students find it helpful to remember this as multiplying the First terms, then the Outer terms, then the Inner terms, and finally the Last terms, with the mnemonic **FOIL**. For longer polynomials, the multiplication process is the same, but there will be, of course, more terms, and there is no common mnemonic to remember each combination.

Factors for polynomials are similar to factors for integers—they are numbers, variables, or polynomials that, when multiplied together, give a product equal to the polynomial in question. One polynomial is a factor of a second polynomial if the second polynomial can be obtained from the first by multiplying by a third polynomial. $6x^6 + 13x^4 + 6x^2$ can be obtained by multiplying together:

$$(3x^4 + 2x^2)(2x^2 + 3)$$

This means:

$$2x^2 + 3$$

and

$$3x^4 + 2x^2$$

Both are factors of:

$$6x^6 + 13x^4 + 6x^2$$

In general, finding the factors of a polynomial can be tricky. However, there are a few types of polynomials that can be factored in a straightforward way.

If a certain monomial is in each term of a polynomial, it can be factored out. There are several common forms polynomials take, which if you recognize, you can solve. The first example is a perfect square trinomial. To factor this polynomial, first expand the middle term of the expression:

$$x^2 + 2xy + y^2$$
$$x^2 + xy + xy + y^2$$

Factor out a common term in each half of the expression (in this case x from the left and y from the right):

$$x(x + y) + y(x + y)$$

Then, the same can be done again, treating $(x + y)$ as the common factor:

$$(x + y)(x + y) = (x + y)^2$$

Therefore, the formula for this polynomial is:

$$x^2 + 2xy + y^2 = (x + y)^2$$

Next is another example of a perfect square trinomial. The process is the similar, but notice the difference in sign:

$$x^2 - 2xy + y^2$$

23

$$x^2 - xy - xy + y^2$$

Factor out the common term on each side:

$$x(x - y) - y(x - y)$$

Factoring out the common term again:

$$(x - y)(x - y) = (x - y)^2$$

Thus,

$$x^2 - 2xy + y^2 = (x - y)^2$$

The next is known as a difference of squares. This process is effectively the reverse of binomial multiplication:

$$x^2 - y^2$$

$$x^2 - xy + xy - y^2$$

$$x(x - y) + y(x - y)$$

$$(x + y)(x - y)$$

Therefore,

$$x^2 - y^2 = (x + y)(x - y)$$

The following two polynomials are known as the sum or difference of cubes. These are special polynomials that take the form of:

$$x^3 + y^3$$

or

$$x^3 - y^3$$

The following formula factors the sum of cubes:

$$x^3 + y^3 = (x + y)(x^2 - xy + y^2)$$

Next is the difference of cubes, but note the change in sign. The formulas for both are similar, but the order of signs for factoring the sum or difference of cubes can be remembered by using the acronym **SOAP**, which stands for "same, opposite, always positive." The first sign is the same as the sign in the first expression, the second is opposite, and the third is always positive. The next formula factors the difference of cubes:

$$x^3 - y^3 = (x - y)(x^2 + xy + y^2)$$

The following two examples are expansions of cubed binomials. Similarly, these polynomials always follow a pattern:

$$x^3 + 3x^2y + 3xy^2 + y^3 = (x + y)^3$$

$$x^3 - 3x^2y + 3xy^2 - y^3 = (x - y)^3$$

These rules can be used in many combinations with one another. For example, the expression $3x^3 - 24$ has a common factor of 3, which becomes:

$$3(x^3 - 8)$$

A difference of cubes still remains which can then be factored out:

$$3(x - 2)(x^2 + 2x + 4)$$

There are no other terms to be pulled out, so this expression is completely factored.

When factoring polynomials, a good strategy is to multiply the factors to check the result. Let's try another example.

$$4x^3 + 16x^2$$

Both sides of the expression can be divided by 4, and both contain x^2, because $4x^3$ can be thought of as $4x^2(x)$, so the common term can simply be factored out:

$$4x^2(x + 4)$$

It sometimes can be necessary to rewrite the polynomial in some clever way before applying the above rules. Consider the problem of factoring $x^4 - 1$. This does not immediately look like any of the previous polynomials. However, it's possible to think of this polynomial as:

$$x^4 - 1 = (x^2)^2 - (1^2)^2$$

Now, it can be treated as a difference of squares to simplify this:

$$(x^2)^2 - (1^2)^2$$

$$(x^2)^2 - x^2 1^2 + x^2 1^2 - (1^2)^2$$

$$x^2(x^2 - 1^2) + 1^2(x^2 - 1^2)$$

$$(x^2 + 1^2)(x^2 - 1^2)$$

$$(x^2 + 1)(x^2 - 1)$$

Quadratic Functions

A polynomial of degree 2 is called **quadratic**. Every quadratic function can be written in the form:

$$ax^2 + bx + c$$

The graph of a quadratic function, $y = ax^2 + bx + c$, is called a **parabola**. Parabolas are vaguely U-shaped.

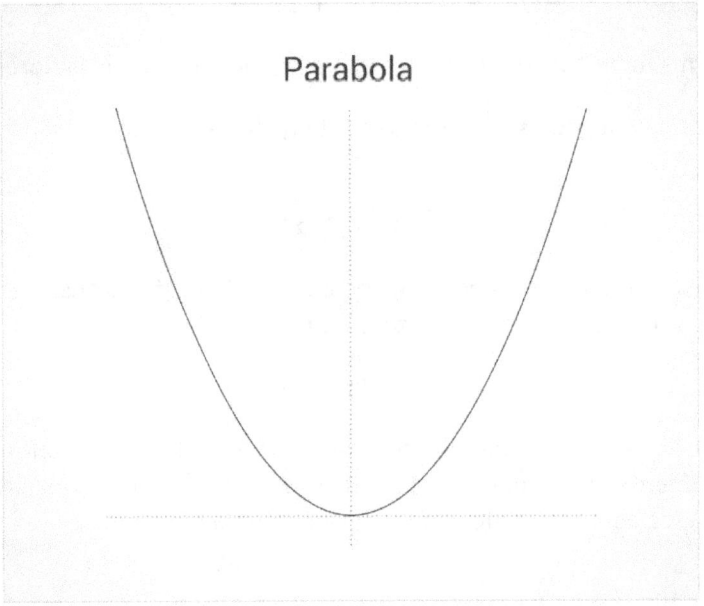

Parabola

Whether the parabola opens upward or downward depends on the sign of a. If a is positive, then the parabola will open upward. If a is negative, then the parabola will open downward. The value of a will also affect how wide the parabola is. If the absolute value of a is large, then the parabola will be fairly skinny. If the absolute value of a is small, then the parabola will be quite wide.

Changes to the value of b affect the parabola in different ways, depending on the sign of a. For positive values of a, increasing b will move the parabola to the left, and decreasing b will move the parabola to the right. On the other hand, if a is negative, the effects will be the opposite: increasing b will move the parabola to the right, while decreasing b will move the parabola to the left.

Changes to the value of c move the parabola vertically. The larger that c is, the higher the parabola gets. This does not depend on the value of a.

The quantity $D = b^2 - 4ac$ is called the **discriminant** of the parabola. When the discriminant is positive, then the parabola has two real zeros, or x-intercepts. However, if the discriminant is negative, then there are no real zeros, and the parabola will not cross the x-axis. The highest or lowest point of the parabola is called the **vertex**. If the discriminant is zero, then the parabola's highest or lowest point is on the x-axis, and it will have a single real zero. The x-coordinate of the vertex can be found using the equation:

$$x = -\frac{b}{2a}$$

Mathematics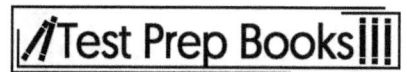

Plug this x-value into the equation and find the y-coordinate.

A quadratic equation is often used to model the path of an object thrown into the air. The x-value can represent the time in the air, while the y-value can represent the height of the object. In this case, the maximum height of the object would be the y-value found when the x-value is $-\frac{b}{2a}$.

Solving Quadratic Equations

A **quadratic equation** is an equation in the form:

$$ax^2 + bx + c = 0$$

There are several methods to solve such equations. The easiest method will depend on the quadratic equation in question.

Sometimes, it is possible to solve quadratic equations by manually **factoring** them. This means rewriting them in the form:

$$(x + A)(x + B) = 0$$

If this is done, then they can be solved by remembering that when $ab = 0$, either a or b must be equal to zero. Therefore, to have $(x + A)(x + B) = 0$:

$$(x + A) = 0$$

Or $(x + B) = 0$ is needed.

These equations have the solutions $x = -A$ and $x = -B$, respectively.

In order to factor a quadratic equation, note that:

$$(x + A)(x + B) = x^2 + (A + B)x + AB$$

So, if an equation is in the form:

$$x^2 + bx + c$$

Two numbers, A and B, need to be found that will add up to give us b, and multiply together to give us c.

As an example, consider solving the equation:

$$-3x^2 + 6x + 9 = 0$$

Start by dividing both sides by -3, leaving:

$$x^2 - 2x - 3 = 0$$

Now, notice that $1 - 3 = -2$, and also that $(1)(-3) = -3$. This means the equation can be factored into:

$$(x + 1)(x - 3) = 0$$

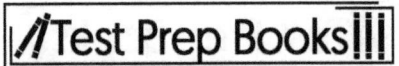

Now, solve $(x + 1) = 0$ and $(x - 3) = 0$ to get $x = -1$ and $x = 3$ as the solutions.

It is useful when trying to factor to remember that:

$$x^2 + 2xy + y^2 = (x + y)^2$$

$$x^2 - 2xy + y^2 = (x - y)^2$$

and

$$x^2 - y^2 = (x + y)(x - y)$$

However, factoring by hand is often hard to do. If there are no obvious ways to factor the quadratic equation, solutions can still be found by using the **quadratic formula**.

The quadratic formula is:

$$x = \frac{-b \pm \sqrt{b^2 - 4ac}}{2a}$$

This method will always work, although it sometimes can take longer than factoring by hand, if the factors are easy to guess. Using the standard form:

$$ax^2 + bx + c = 0$$

Plug the values of a, b, and c from the equation into the formula and solve for x. There will either be two answers, one answer, or no real answer. No real answer comes when the value of the discriminant, the number under the square root, is a negative number. Since there are no real numbers that square to get a negative, the answer will be no real roots.

Here is an example of solving a quadratic equation using the quadratic formula. Suppose the equation to solve is:

$$-2x^2 + 3x + 1 = 0$$

There is no obvious way to factor this, so the quadratic formula is used, with $a = -2, b = 3, c = 1$. After substituting these values into the quadratic formula, it yields this:

$$x = \frac{-3 \pm \sqrt{3^2 - 4(-2)(1)}}{2(-2)}$$

Mathematics

This can be simplified to obtain:

$$\frac{3 \pm \sqrt{9+8}}{4}$$

or

$$\frac{3 \pm \sqrt{17}}{4}$$

Challenges can be encountered when asked to find a quadratic equation with specific roots. Given roots A and B, a quadratic function can be constructed with those roots by taking $(x - A)(x - B)$. So, in constructing a quadratic equation with roots $x = -2, 3$, it would result in:

$$(x + 2)(x - 3) = x^2 - x - 6$$

Multiplying this by a constant also could be done without changing the roots.

Exponents and Roots

An **exponent** is written as a^b. In this expression, a is called the **base** and b is called the **exponent**. It is properly stated that a is raised to the nth power. Therefore, in the expression 2^3, the exponent is 3, while the base is 2. Such an expression is called an **exponential expression**. Note that when the exponent is 2, it is called **squaring** the base, and when it is 3, it is called **cubing** the base.

When the exponent is a positive integer, this indicates the base is multiplied by itself the number of times written in the exponent. So, in the expression 2^3, multiply 2 by itself with 3 copies of 2:

$$2^3 = 2 \times 2 \times 2 = 8$$

One thing to notice is that, for positive integers n and m, $a^n a^m = a^{n+m}$ is a rule. In order to make this rule be true for an integer of 0, $a^0 = 1$, so that:

$$a^n a^0 = a^{n+0} = a^n$$

And, in order to make this rule be true for negative exponents, $a^{-n} = \frac{1}{a^n}$.

Another rule for simplifying expressions with exponents is shown by the following equation:

$$(a^m)^n = a^{mn}$$

This is true for fractional exponents as well. So, for a positive integer, define $a^{\frac{1}{n}}$ to be the number that, when raised to the nth power, provides a. In other words:

$$(a^{\frac{1}{n}})^n = a$$

This is the desired equation.

It should be noted that $a^{\frac{1}{n}}$ is the nth root of a. This also can be written as:

$$a^{\frac{1}{n}} = \sqrt[n]{a}$$

The symbol on the right-hand side of this equation is called a **radical**. If the root is left out, assume that the 2nd root should be taken, also called the **square root**:

$$a^{\frac{1}{2}} = \sqrt[2]{a} = \sqrt{a}$$

Additionally, $\sqrt[3]{a}$ is also called the **cube root**.

Note that when multiple roots exist, $a^{\frac{1}{n}}$ is defined to be the **positive root**. So, $4^{\frac{1}{2}} = 2$. Also note that negative numbers do not have even roots in the real numbers.

This also enables finding exponents for any rational number:

$$a^{\frac{m}{n}} = (a^{\frac{1}{n}})^m = (a^m)^{\frac{1}{n}}$$

In fact, the exponent can be any real number. In general, the following rules for exponents should be used for any numbers a, b, m, and n.

- $a^1 = a$
- $1^a = 1$
- $a^0 = 1$
- $a^m a^n = a^{m+n}$
- $\frac{a^m}{a^n} = a^{m-n}$
- $(a^m)^n = a^{m \times n}$
- $(ab)^m = a^m b^m$
- $\left(\frac{a}{b}\right)^m = \frac{a^m}{b^m}$

As an example of applying these rules, consider the problem of simplifying the expression:

$$(3x^2y)^3(2xy^4)$$

Start by simplifying the left term using the sixth rule listed. Applying this rule yields the following expression:

$$27x^6y^3(2xy^4)$$

The exponents can now be combined with base x and the exponents with base y. Multiply the coefficients to yield:

$$54x^7y^7$$

Order of Operations

When working with complicated expressions, parentheses are used to indicate in which order to perform operations. However, to avoid having too many parentheses in an expression, here are some basic rules concerning the proper order to perform operations when not otherwise specified.

Mathematics

1. Parentheses: always perform operations inside parentheses first, regardless of what those operations are
2. Exponents
3. Multiplication and Division
4. Addition and Subtraction

For #3 & #4, work these from left to right. So, if there a subtraction problem and then an addition problem, the subtraction problem will be worked first.

Note that multiplication and division are performed from left to right as they appear in the expression or equation. Addition and subtraction also are performed from left to right as they appear.

As an aid to memorizing this, some students like to use the mnemonic **PEMDAS**. Furthermore, this acronym can be associated with a mnemonic phrase such as "Pirates Eat Many Donuts At Sea."

Solving Equations with Exponents and Roots

Here are some of the most important properties of exponents and roots: if n is an integer, and if:

$$a^n = b^n$$

Then, $a = b$ if n is odd; but $a = \pm b$ if n is even. Similarly, if the roots of two things are equal:

$$\sqrt[n]{a} = \sqrt[n]{b}$$

Then, $a = b$.

This means that when starting with a true equation, both sides of that equation can be raised to a given power to obtain another true equation. Beware that when an even-powered root is taken on both sides of the equation, a $\pm$ in the result. For example, given the equation $x^2 = 16$, take the square root of both sides to solve for x. This results in the answer $x = \pm 4$ because $(-4)^2 = 16$ and $(4)^2 = 16$.

Another property is that if $a^n = a^m$, then $n = m$. This is true for any real numbers n and m.

For solving the equation:

$$\sqrt{x+2} - 1 = 3$$

Start by moving the -1 over to the right-hand side. This is performed by adding 1 to both sides, which yields:

$$\sqrt{x+2} = 4$$

Now, square both sides, but remember that by squaring both sides, the signs are irrelevant. This yields:

$$x + 2 = 16$$

This simplifies to give $x = 14$.

Now consider the problem:

$$(x+1)^4 = 16$$

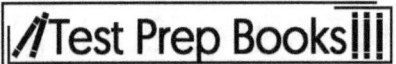

To solve this, take the 4th root of both sides, which means an ambiguity in the sign will be introduced because it is an even root:

$$\sqrt[4]{(x+1)^4} = \pm\sqrt[4]{16}$$

The right-hand side is 2, since:

$$2^4 = 16$$

Therefore,

$$x + 1 = \pm 2$$

or

$$x = -1 \pm 2$$

Thus, the two possible solutions are $x = -3$ and $x = 1$.

Remember, when solving equations, the answer can be checked by plugging the solution back into the problem to make a true statement.

Rational Expressions

A **rational expression** is a fraction where the numerator and denominator are both polynomials. Some examples of rational expressions include the following:

$$\frac{4x^3y^5}{3z^4}$$

$$\frac{4x^3 + 3x}{x^2}$$

$$\frac{x^2 + 7x + 10}{x + 2}$$

Since these refer to expressions and not equations, they can be simplified but not solved. Using the rules in the previous Exponents and Roots sections, some rational expressions with monomials can be simplified. Other rational expressions such as the last example take more steps to be simplified:

$$\frac{x^2 + 7x + 10}{x + 2}$$

First, the polynomial on top can be factored from:

$$x^2 + 7x + 10$$

into

$$(x + 5)(x + 2)$$

Then, the common factors can be canceled and the expression can be simplified to $(x + 5)$.

Consider this problem as an example of using rational expressions. Reggie wants to lay sod in his rectangular backyard. The length of the yard is given by the expression $4x + 2$, and the width is unknown. The area of the yard is $20x + 10$. Reggie needs to find the width of the yard. Knowing that the area of a rectangle is length multiplied by width, an expression can be written to find the width:

$$\frac{20x + 10}{4x + 2}$$

This is the area divided by length. Simplifying this expression by factoring out 10 on the top and 2 on the bottom leads to this expression:

$$\frac{10(2x + 1)}{2(2x + 1)}$$

By cancelling out the $2x + 1$, that results in $\frac{10}{2} = 5$. The width of the yard is found to be 5 by simplifying a rational expression.

Rational Equations

A **rational equation** can be as simple as an equation with a ratio of polynomials:

$$\frac{p(x)}{q(x)}$$

set equal to a value, where $p(x)$ and $q(x)$ are both polynomials. Notice that a rational equation has an equal sign, which is different from expressions. This leads to solutions, or numbers that make the equation true.

It is possible to solve rational equations by trying to get all of the x-terms out of the denominator and then isolate them on one side of the equation. For example, to solve the equation:

$$\frac{3x + 2}{2x + 3} = 4$$

Start by multiplying both sides by $(2x + 3)$. This will cancel on the left side to yield:

$$3x + 2 = 4(2x + 3)$$

Then,

$$3x + 2 = 8x + 12$$

Now, subtract $8x$ from both sides, which yields:

$$-5x + 2 = 12$$

Subtracting 2 from both sides results in $-5x = 10$. Finally, divide both sides by -5 to obtain $x = -2$.

Sometimes, when solving rational equations, it can be easier to try to simplify the rational expression by factoring the numerator and denominator first, then cancelling out common factors.

For example, to solve:

$$\frac{2x^2 - 8x + 6}{x^2 - 3x + 2} = 1$$

Start by factoring:

$$2x^2 - 8x + 6 = 2(x^2 - 4x + 3) = 2(x - 1)(x - 3)$$

Then, factor:

$$x^2 - 3x + 2$$

into

$$(x - 1)(x - 2)$$

This turns the original equation into:

$$\frac{2(x - 1)(x - 3)}{(x - 1)(x - 2)} = 1$$

The common factor of $(x - 1)$ can be canceled, leaving us with:

$$\frac{2(x - 3)}{x - 2} = 1$$

Now the same method used in the previous example can be followed. Multiplying both sides by $x - 1$ and performing the multiplication on the left yields:

$$2x - 6 = x - 2$$

This can be simplified to $x = 4$.

Rational Functions

A **rational function** is similar to an equation, but it includes two variables. In general, a rational function is in the form:

$$f(x) = \frac{p(x)}{q(x)}$$

$p(x)$ and $q(x)$ are polynomials. Refer to the previous Functions section for a more detailed definition of functions. Rational functions are defined everywhere except where the denominator is equal to zero. When the denominator is equal to zero, this indicates either a hole in the graph or an asymptote. An asymptote can be either vertical, horizontal, or slant. A hole occurs when both the numerator and denominator are equal to 0 for a given value of x. A rational function can have at most one vertical asymptote and one horizontal or slant asymptote. An asymptote is a line such that the distance between the curve and the line tends toward 0, but never reaches it, as the line heads toward infinity. Examples of these types of functions are shown below. The first graph shows a rational function with a vertical asymptote at $x = 0$. This can be found by setting the denominator equal to 0.

In this case it is just $x = 0$.

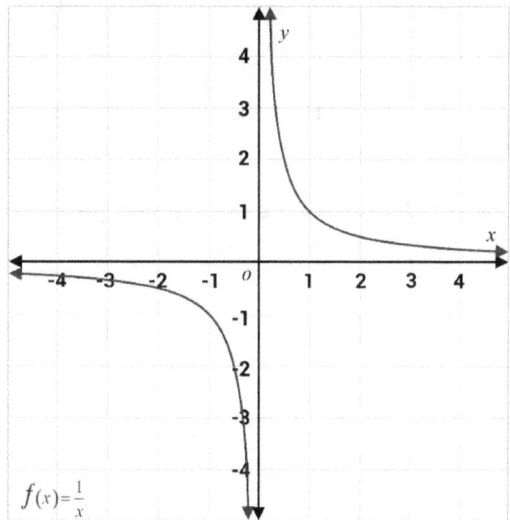

The second graph shows a rational function with a vertical asymptote at $x = -0.5$. Again, this can be found by just setting the denominator equal to 0. So:

$$2x^2 + x = 0, 2x + 1 = 0, 2x = -1, x = -0.5$$

This graph also has a hole in the graph at $x = 0$. This is because both the numerator and denominator are equal to 0 when $x = 0$.

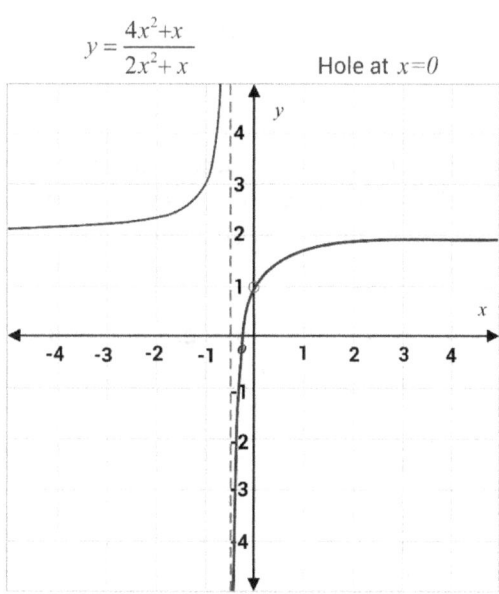

Geometric and Spatial Reasoning

Plane Geometry

Locations on the plane that have no width or breadth are called **points**. These points usually will be denoted with capital letters such as P.

Any pair of points A, B on the plane will determine a unique straight line between them. This line is denoted AB. Sometimes to emphasize a line is being considered, this will be written as $\overleftrightarrow{AB}$.

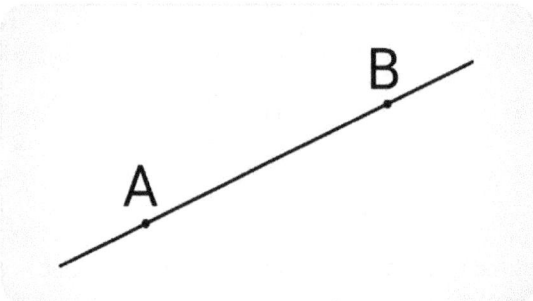

If the Cartesian coordinates for A and B are known, then the distance $d(A, B)$ along the line between them can be measured using the **Distance formula**, which states that if:

$$A = (x_1, y_1) \text{ and } B = (x_2, y_2)$$

The distance between them is:

$$d(A, B) = \sqrt{(x_2 - x_1)^2 + (y_2 - y_1)^2}$$

The part of a line that lies between A and B is called a **line segment**. It has two endpoints, one at A and one at B. **Rays** also can be formed. Given points A and B, a *ray* is the portion of a line that starts at one of these points, passes through the other, and keeps on going. Therefore, a ray has a single endpoint, but the other end goes off to infinity.

Given a pair of points A and B, a circle centered at A and passing through B can be formed. This is the set of points whose distance from A is exactly $d(A, B)$. The radius of this circle will be $d(A, B)$.

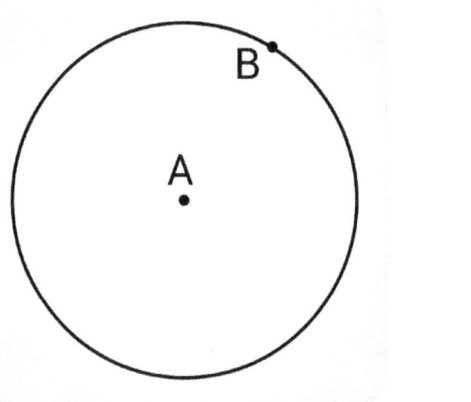

Mathematics

The **circumference** of a circle is the distance traveled by following the edge of the circle for one complete revolution, and the length of the circumference is given by $2\pi r$, where r is the radius of the circle. The formula for circumference is $C = 2\pi r$.

When two lines cross, they form an **angle**. The point where the lines cross is called the **vertex** of the angle. The angle can be named by either just using the vertex, $\angle A$, or else by listing three points $\angle BAC$, as shown in the diagram below.

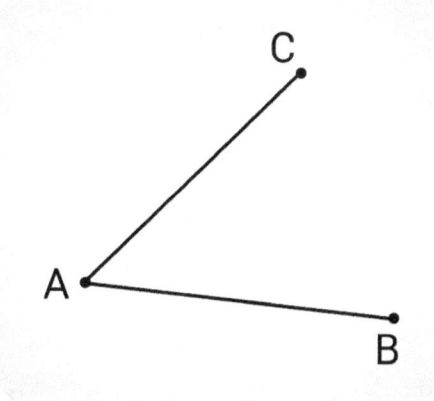

The measurement of an angle can be given in degrees or in radians. In degrees, a full circle is 360 degrees, written 360°. In radians, a full circle is 2π radians.

Given two points on the circumference of a circle, the path along the circle between those points is called an **arc** of the circle. For example, the arc between B and C is denoted by a thinner line:

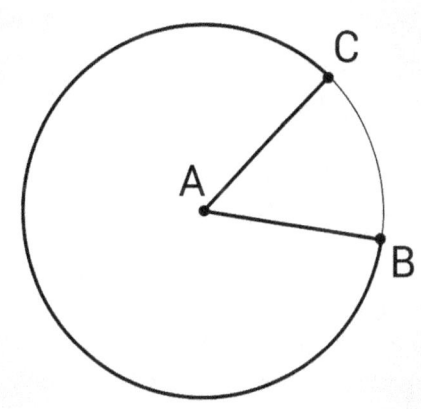

The length of the path along an arc is called the **arc length**. If the circle has radius r, then the arc length is given by multiplying the measure of the angle in radians by the radius of the circle.

Two lines are said to be **parallel** if they never intersect. If the lines are AB and CD, then this is written as $AB \parallel CD$.

If two lines cross to form four quarter-circles, that is, 90° angles, the two lines are **perpendicular**. If the point at which they cross is B, and the two lines are AB and BC, then this is written as $AB \perp BC$.

A **polygon** is a closed figure (meaning it divides the plane into an inside and an outside) consisting of a collection of line segments between points. These points are called the **vertices** of the polygon. These line segments must not overlap one another. Note that the number of sides is equal to the number of angles, or vertices of the polygon. The angles between line segments meeting one another in the polygon are called **interior angles**.

A **regular polygon** is a polygon whose edges are all the same length and whose interior angles are all of equal measure.

A **triangle** is a polygon with three sides. A **quadrilateral** is a polygon with four sides.

A **right triangle** is a triangle that has one 90° angle.

The sum of the interior angles of any triangle must add up to 180°.

An **isosceles triangle** is a triangle in which two of the sides are the same length. In this case, it will always have two congruent interior angles. If a triangle has two congruent interior angles, it will always be isosceles.

An **equilateral triangle** is a triangle whose sides are all the same length and whose angles are all equivalent to one another, equal to 60°. Equilateral triangles are examples of regular polygons. Note that equilateral triangles are also isosceles.

A **rectangle** is a quadrilateral whose interior angles are all 90°. A rectangle has two sets of sides that are equal to one another.

A **square** is a rectangle whose width and height are equal. Therefore, squares are regular polygons.

A **parallelogram** is a quadrilateral in which the opposite sides are parallel and equivalent to each other.

Transformations of a Plane

Given a figure drawn on a plane, many changes can be made to that figure, including *rotation*, *translation*, and *reflection*. **Rotations** turn the figure about a point, translations slide the figure, and reflections flip the figure over a specified line. When performing these transformations, the original figure is called the **pre-image**, and the figure after transformation is called the **image**.

More specifically, **translation** means that all points in the figure are moved in the same direction by the same distance. In other words, the figure is slid in some fixed direction. Of course, while the entire figure is slid by the same distance, this does not change any of the measurements of the figures involved. The result will have the same distances and angles as the original figure.

In terms of Cartesian coordinates, a translation means a shift of each of the original points (x, y) by a fixed amount in the x and y directions, to become:

$$(x + a, y + b)$$

Another procedure that can be performed is called **reflection**. To do this, a line in the plane is specified, called the **line of reflection**. Then, take each point and flip it over the line so that it is the same distance from the line but on the opposite side of it. This does not change any of the distances or angles involved, but it does reverse the order in which everything appears.

Mathematics

To reflect something over the x-axis, the points (x, y) are sent to $(x, -y)$. To reflect something over the y-axis, the points (x, y) are sent to the points $(-x, y)$. Flipping over other lines is not something easy to express in Cartesian coordinates. However, by drawing the figure and the line of reflection, the distance to the line and the original points can be used to find the reflected figure.

Example: Reflect this triangle with vertices $(-1, 0)$, $(2, 1)$, and $(2, 0)$ over the y-axis. The pre-image is shown below.

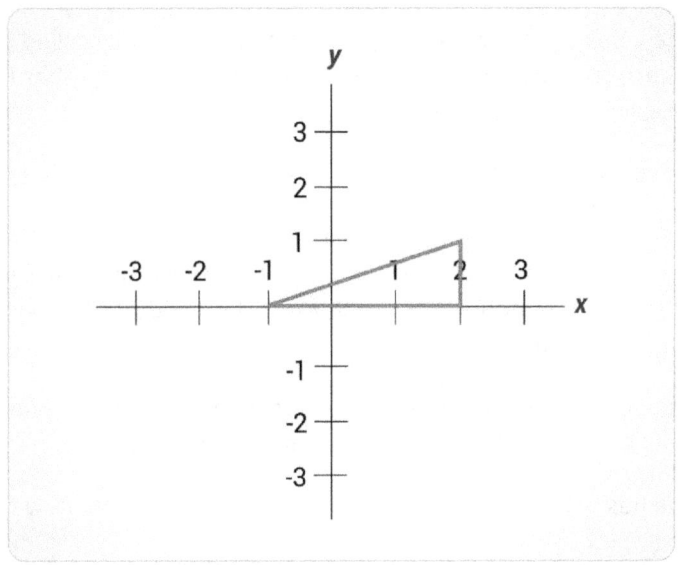

To do this, flip the x-values of the points involved to the negatives of themselves, while keeping the y-values the same. The image is shown here.

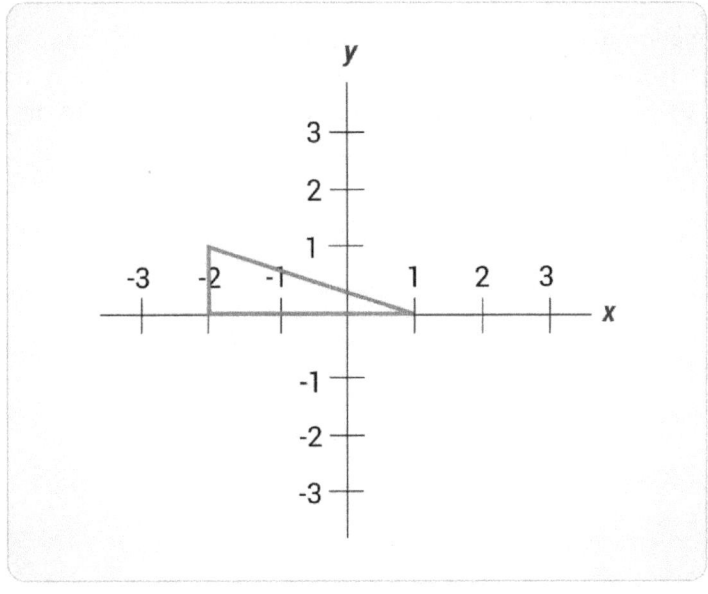

The new vertices will be (1, 0), (-2, 1), and (-2, 0).

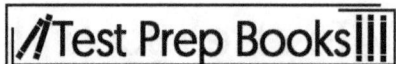

Another procedure that does not change the distances and angles in a figure is **rotation**. In this procedure, pick a center point, then rotate every vertex along a circle around that point by the same angle. This procedure is also not easy to express in Cartesian coordinates, and this is not a requirement on this test. However, as with reflections, it's helpful to draw the figures and see what the result of the rotation would look like. This transformation can be performed using a compass and protractor.

Each one of these transformations can be performed on the coordinate plane without changes to the original dimensions or angles.

If two figures in the plane involve the same distances and angles, they are called **congruent figures**. In other words, two figures are congruent when they go from one form to another through reflection, rotation, and translation, or a combination of these.

Remember, rotation and translation will give back a new figure that is identical to the original figure, but reflection will give back a mirror image of it.

To recognize that a figure has undergone a rotation, check to see that the figure has not been changed into a mirror image, but that its orientation has changed (that is, whether the parts of the figure now form different angles with the x and y axes).

To recognize that a figure has undergone a translation, check to see that the figure has not been changed into a mirror image, and that the orientation remains the same.

To recognize that a figure has undergone a reflection, check to see that the new figure is a mirror image of the old figure.

Keep in mind that sometimes a combination of translations, reflections, and rotations may be performed on a figure.

Dilation

A **dilation** is a transformation that preserves angles, but not distances. This can be thought of as stretching or shrinking a figure. If a dilation makes figures larger, it is called an **s**. If a dilation makes figures smaller, it is called a **reduction**. The easiest example is to dilate around the origin. In this case, multiply the x- and y-coordinates by a **scale factor**, k, sending points (x, y) to (kx, ky).

As an example, draw a dilation of the following triangle, whose vertices will be the points $(-1, 0)$, $(1, 0)$, and $(1, 1)$.

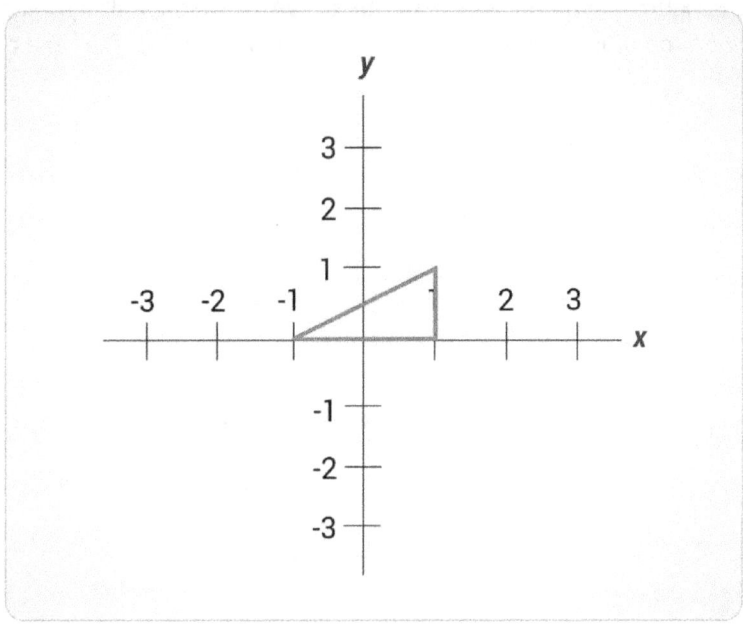

For this problem, dilate by a scale factor of 2, so the new vertices will be $(-2, 0)$, $(2, 0)$, and $(2, 2)$.

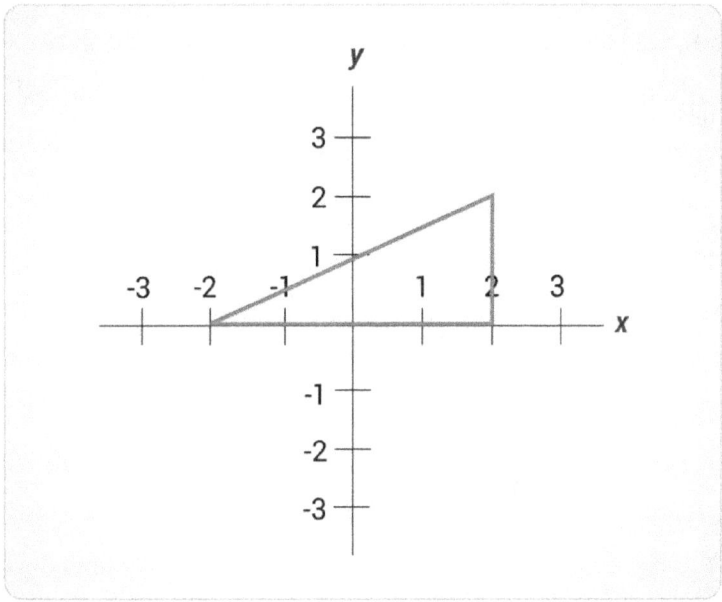

Note that after a dilation, the distances between the vertices of the figure will have changed, but the angles will remain the same. The two figures that are obtained by dilation, along with possibly translation, rotation, and reflection, are all *similar* to one another. Another way to think of this is that similar figures have the same number of vertices and edges, and their angles are all the same. Similar figures have the same basic shape, but are different in size.

Symmetry

Using the types of transformations above, if an object can undergo these changes and not appear to have changed, then the figure is symmetrical. If an object can be split in half by a line and flipped over that line to lie directly on top of itself, it is said to have **line symmetry**. An example of both types of figures is seen below.

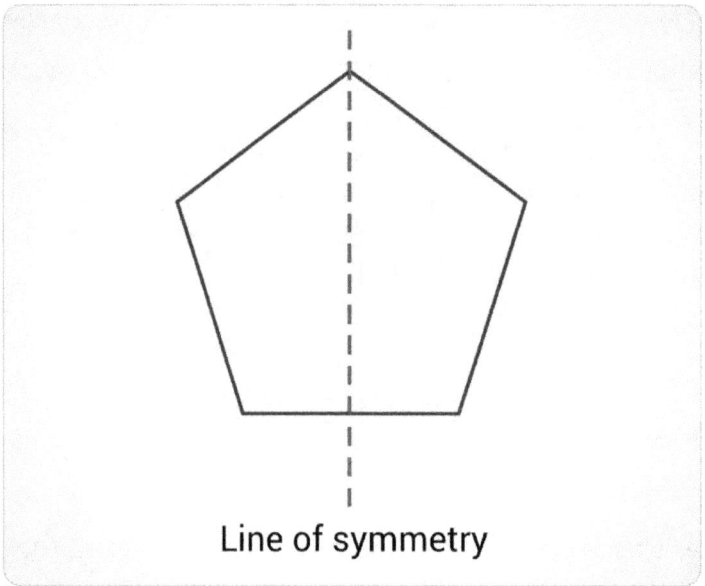

Line of symmetry

If an object can be rotated about its center to any degree smaller than 360, and it lies directly on top of itself, the object is said to have **rotational symmetry**. An example of this type of symmetry is shown below. The pentagon has an order of 5.

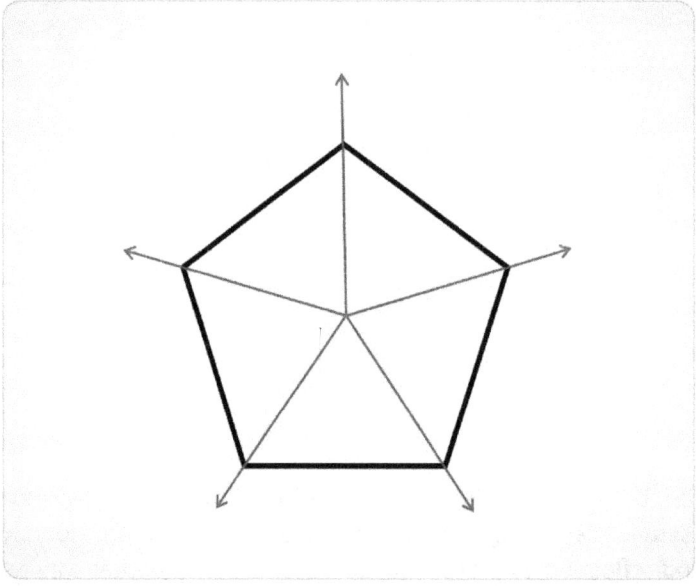

The rotational symmetry lines in the figure above can be used to find the angles formed at the center of the pentagon. Knowing that all of the angles together form a full circle, at 360 degrees, the figure can be split into 5 angles equally. By dividing the 360° by 5, each angle is 72°.

Given the length of one side of the figure, the perimeter of the pentagon can also be found using rotational symmetry. If one side length was 3 cm, that side length can be rotated onto each other side length four times. This would give a total of 5 side lengths equal to 3 cm. To find the perimeter, or distance around the figure, multiply 3 by 5. The perimeter of the figure would be 15 cm.

If a line cannot be drawn anywhere on the object to flip the figure onto itself or rotated less than or equal to 180 degrees to lay on top of itself, the object is asymmetrical. Examples of these types of figures are shown below.

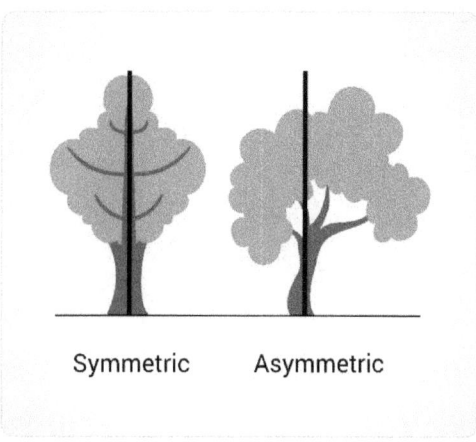

Perimeters and Areas

The **perimeter** of a polygon is the total length of a trip around the whole polygon, starting and ending at the same point. It is found by adding up the lengths of each line segment in the polygon. For a rectangle with sides of length x and y, the perimeter will be:

$$2x + 2y$$

The **area of a polygon** is the area of the region that it encloses. Regarding the area of a rectangle with sides of length x and y, the area is given by xy. For a triangle with a base of length b and a height of length h, the area is $\frac{1}{2}bh$.

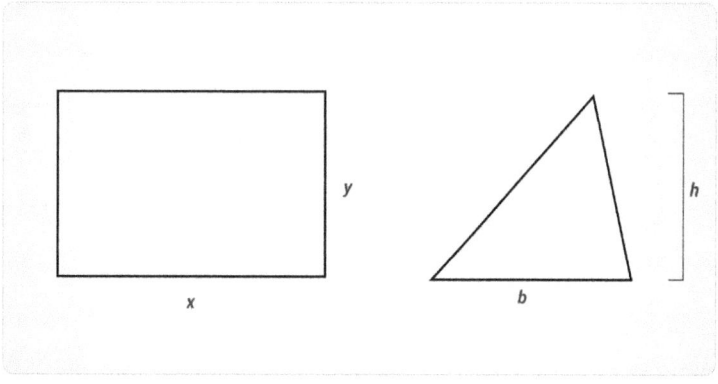

To find the areas of more general polygons, it is usually easiest to break up the polygon into rectangles and triangles. For example, find the area of the following figure whose vertices are $(-1, 0)$, $(-1, 2)$, $(1, 3)$, and $(1, 0)$.

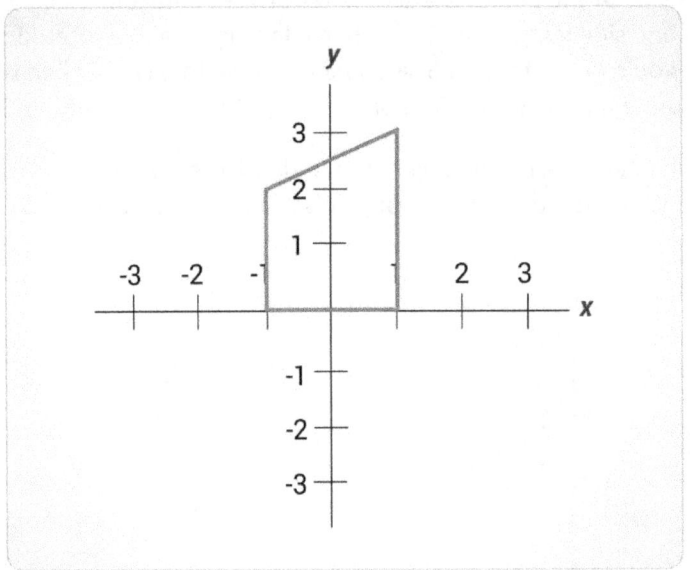

Separate this into a rectangle and a triangle as shown:

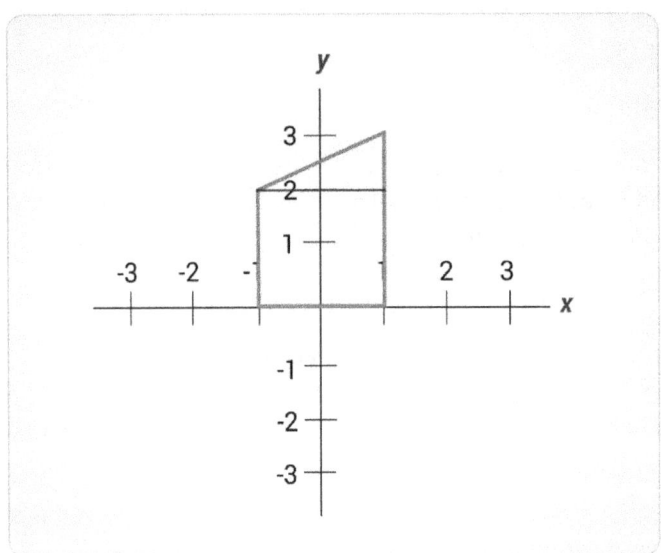

The rectangle has a height of 2 and a width of 2, so it has a total area of $2 \times 2 = 4$. The triangle has a width of 2 and a height of 1, so it has an area of:

$$\frac{1}{2} 2 \times 1 = 1$$

Therefore, the entire quadrilateral has an area of $4 + 1 = 5$.

As another example, suppose someone wants to tile a rectangular room that is 10 feet by 6 feet using triangular tiles that are 12 inches by 6 inches. How many tiles would be needed? To figure this, first find the area of the room, which will be:

$$10 \times 6 = 60 \text{ square feet}$$

The dimensions of the triangle are 1 foot by $\frac{1}{2}$ foot, so the area of each triangle is:

$$\frac{1}{2} \times 1 \times \frac{1}{2} = \frac{1}{4} \text{ square feet}$$

Notice that the dimensions of the triangle had to be converted to the same units as the rectangle. Now, take the total area divided by the area of one tile to find the answer:

$$\frac{60}{\frac{1}{4}} = 60 \times 4 = 240 \text{ tiles required}$$

Volumes and Surface Areas

Geometry in three dimensions is similar to geometry in two dimensions. The main new feature is that three points now define a unique **plane** that passes through each of them. Three dimensional objects can be made by putting together two-dimensional figures in different surfaces. Below, some of the possible three-dimensional figures will be provided, along with formulas for their volumes and surface areas.

A **rectangular prism** is a box whose sides are all rectangles meeting at 90° angles. Such a box has three dimensions: length, width, and height. If the length is x, the width is y, and the height is z, then the volume is given by $V = xyz$.

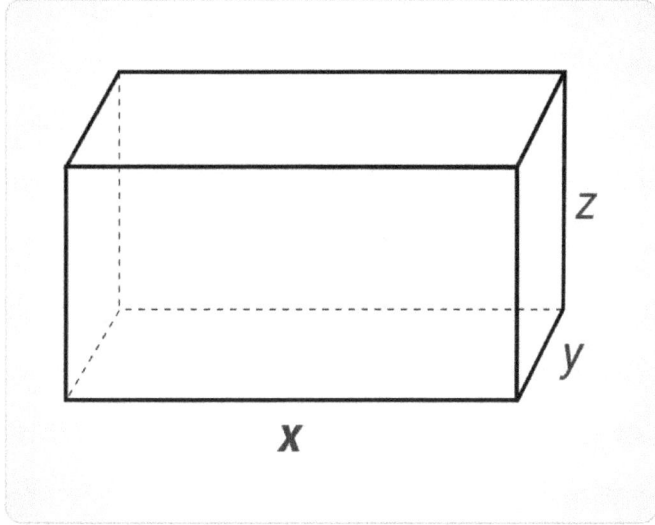

The surface area will be given by computing the surface area of each rectangle and adding them together. There are a total of six rectangles. Two of them have sides of length x and y, two have sides of length y and z, and two have sides of length x and z. Therefore, the total surface area will be given by:

$$SA = 2xy + 2yz + 2xz$$

A **rectangular pyramid** is a figure with a rectangular base and four triangular sides that meet at a single vertex. If the rectangle has sides of length x and y, then the volume will be given by:

$$V = \frac{1}{3}xyh$$

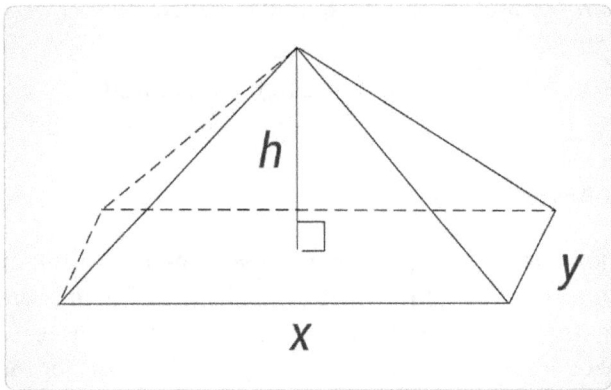

To find the surface area, the dimensions of each triangle need to be known. However, these dimensions can differ depending on the problem in question. Therefore, there is no general formula for calculating total surface area.

A **sphere** is a set of points all of which are equidistant from some central point. It is like a circle, but in three dimensions. The volume of a sphere of radius r is given by:

$$V = \frac{4}{3}\pi r^3$$

The surface area is given by:

$$A = 4\pi r^2$$

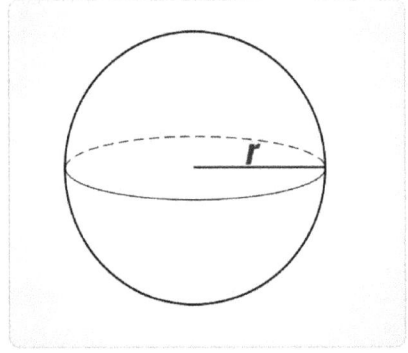

The Pythagorean Theorem

The **Pythagorean theorem** is an important concept in geometry. It states that for right triangles, the sum of the squares of the two shorter sides will be equal to the square of the longest side (also called the **hypotenuse**). The longest side will always be the side opposite to the 90° angle. If this side is called c, and the other two sides are a and b, then the Pythagorean theorem states that $c^2 = a^2 + b^2$. Since lengths are always positive, this also can be written as:

$$c = \sqrt{a^2 + b^2}$$

A diagram to show the parts of a triangle using the Pythagorean theorem is below.

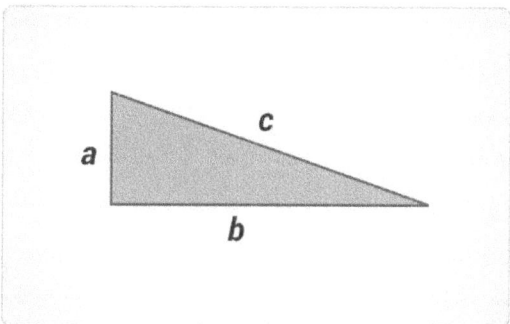

As an example of the theorem, suppose that Shirley has a rectangular field that is 5 feet wide and 12 feet long, and she wants to split it in half using a fence that goes from one corner to the opposite corner. How long will this fence need to be? To figure this out, note that this makes the field into two right triangles, whose hypotenuse will be the fence dividing it in half. Therefore, the fence length will be given by:

$$\sqrt{5^2 + 12^2} = \sqrt{169} = 13 \text{ feet long}$$

Similar Figures and Proportions

Sometimes, two figures are similar, meaning they have the same basic shape and the same interior angles, but they have different dimensions. If the ratio of two corresponding sides is known, then that ratio, or scale factor, holds true for all of the dimensions of the new figure.

Here is an example of applying this principle. Suppose that Lara is 5 feet tall and is standing 30 feet from the base of a light pole, and her shadow is 6 feet long. How high is the light on the pole? To figure this, it helps to make a sketch of the situation:

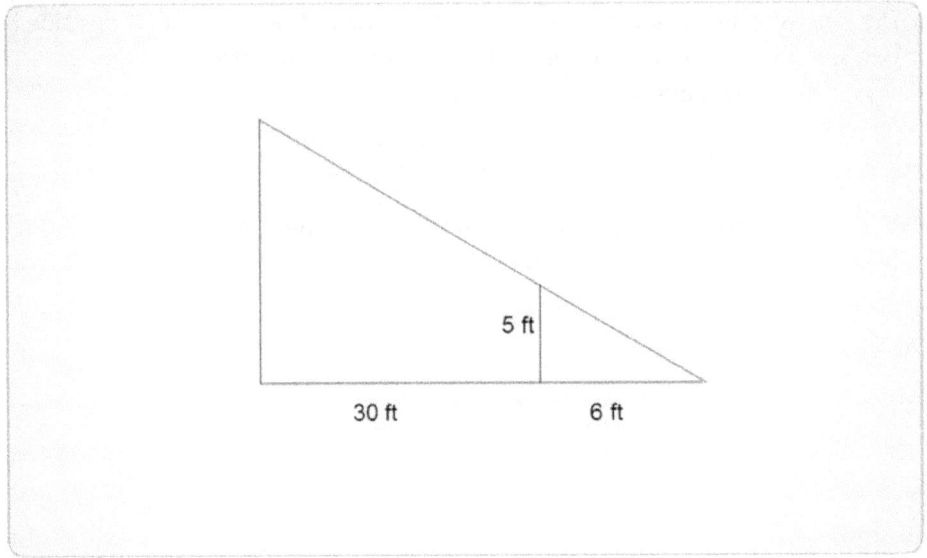

The light pole is the left side of the triangle. Lara is the 5-foot vertical line. Notice that there are two right triangles here, and that they have all the same angles as one another. Therefore, they form similar triangles. So, the ratio of proportionality between them must be determined.

The bases of these triangles are known. The small triangle, formed by Lara and her shadow, has a base of 6 feet. The large triangle formed by the light pole along with the line from the base of the pole out to the end of Lara's shadow is:

$$30 + 6 = 36 \text{ feet long}$$

So, the ratio of the big triangle to the little triangle will be $\frac{36}{6} = 6$. The height of the little triangle is 5 feet. Therefore, the height of the big triangle will be:

$$6 \times 5 = 30 \text{ ft}$$

This means that the light is 30 feet up the pole.

Notice that the perimeter of a figure changes by the ratio of proportionality between two similar figures, but the area changes by the *square* of the ratio. This is because if the length of one side is doubled, the area is quadrupled.

As an example, suppose two rectangles are similar, but the edges of the second rectangle are three times longer than the edges of the first rectangle. The area of the first rectangle is 10 square inches. How much more area does the second rectangle have than the first?

To answer this, note that the area of the second rectangle is $3^2 = 9$ times the area of the first rectangle, which is 10 square inches. Therefore, the area of the second rectangle is going to be $9 \times 10 = 90$ square inches. This means it has $90 - 10 = 80$ square inches more area than the first rectangle.

Mathematics

As a second example, suppose X and Y are similar right triangles. The hypotenuse of X is 4 inches. The area of Y is $\frac{1}{4}$ the area of X. What is the hypotenuse of Y?

First, realize the area has changed by a factor of $\frac{1}{4}$. The area changes by a factor that is the *square* of the ratio of changes in lengths, so the ratio of the lengths is the square root of the ratio of areas. That means that the ratio of lengths must be is $\sqrt{\frac{1}{4}} = \frac{1}{2}$, and the hypotenuse of Y must be $\frac{1}{2} \times 4 = 2$ inches.

Volumes between similar solids change like the cube of the change in the lengths of their edges. Likewise, if the ratio of the volumes between similar solids is known, the ratio between their lengths is known by finding the cube root of the ratio of their volumes.

For example, suppose there are two similar rectangular pyramids X and Y. The base of X is 1 inch by 2 inches, and the volume of X is 8 inches. The volume of Y is 64 inches. What are the dimensions of the base of Y?

To answer this, first find the ratio of the volume of Y to the volume of X. This will be given by $\frac{64}{8} = 8$. Now the ratio of lengths is the cube root of the ratio of volumes, or $\sqrt[3]{8} = 2$. So, the dimensions of the base of Y must be 2 inches by 4 inches.

Probabilistic and Statistical Reasoning

What are Statistics?

The field of statistics describes relationships between quantities that are related, but not necessarily in a deterministic manner. For example, a graduating student's salary will often be higher when the student graduates with a higher GPA, but this is not always the case. Likewise, people who smoke tobacco are more likely to develop lung cancer, but, in fact, it is possible for non-smokers to develop the disease as well. **Statistics** describes these kinds of situations, where the likelihood of some outcome depends on the starting data.

Descriptive statistics involves analyzing a collection of data to describe its broad properties such average (or mean), what percent of the data falls within a given range, and other such properties. An example of this would be taking all of the test scores from a given class and calculating the average test score. **Inferential statistics** attempts to use data about a subset of some population to make inferences about the rest of the population. An example of this would be taking a collection of students who received tutoring and comparing their results to a collection of students who did not receive tutoring, then using that comparison to try to predict whether the tutoring program in question is beneficial.

To be sure that inferences have a high probability of being true for the whole population, the subset that is analyzed needs to resemble a miniature version of the population as closely as possible. For this reason, statisticians like to choose random samples from the population to study, rather than picking a specific group of people based on some similarity. For example, studying the incomes of people who live in Portland does not reveal anything useful about the incomes of people who live in Tallahassee.

Mean, Median, and Mode

Mean

Suppose that you have a set of data points and some description of the general properties of this data need to be found.

The first property that can be defined for this set of data is the **mean**. This is the same as the average. To find the mean, add up all the data points, then divide by the total number of data points. For example, suppose that in a class of 10 students, the scores on a test were 50, 60, 65, 65, 75, 80, 85, 85, 90, 100. Therefore, the average test score will be:

$$\frac{50 + 60 + 65 + 65 + 75 + 80 + 85 + 85 + 90 + 100}{10} = 75.5$$

The mean is a useful number if the distribution of data is normal (more on this later), which means that the frequency of different outcomes has a single peak and is roughly equally distributed on both sides of that peak. However, it is less useful in some cases where the data might be split or where there are some **outliers**. Outliers are data points that are far from the rest of the data. For example, suppose there are 10 executives and 90 employees at a company. The executives make $1,000 per hour, and the employees make $10 per hour.

Therefore, the average pay rate will be:

$$\frac{\$1{,}000 \times 10 + \$10 \times 90}{100} = \$109 \text{ per hour}$$

In this case, this average is not very descriptive since it's not close to the actual pay of the executives or the employees.

Median

Another useful measurement is the **median**. In a data set, the median is the point in the middle. The middle refers to the point where half the data comes before it and half comes after, when the data is recorded in numerical order. For instance, these are the speeds of the fastball of a pitcher during the last inning that he pitched (in order from least to greatest):

90, 92, 93, 93, 95, 96, 97, 97, 97

There are nine total numbers, so the middle or *median* number is the 5th one, which is 95.

In cases where the number of data points is an even number, then the average of the two middle points is taken. In the previous example of test scores, the two middle points are 75 and 80. Since there is no single point, the average of these two scores needs to be found. The average is:

$$\frac{75 + 80}{2} = 77.5$$

The median is generally a good value to use if there are a few outliers in the data. It prevents those outliers from affecting the "middle" value as much as when using the mean.

Since an outlier is a data point that is far from most of the other data points in a data set, this means an outlier also is any point that is far from the median of the data set. The outliers can have a substantial effect on the mean of a data set, but they usually do not change the median or mode, or do not change them by a large quantity. For example, consider the data set (3, 5, 6, 6, 6, 8). This has a median of 6 and a mode of 6, with a mean of $\frac{34}{6} \approx 5.67$. Now, suppose a new data point of 1,000 is added so that the data set is now (3, 5, 6, 6, 6, 8, 1,000). The median and mode, which are both still 6, remain unchanged. However, the average is now $\frac{1,034}{7}$, which is approximately 147.7. In this case, the median and mode will be better descriptions for most of the data points.

Outliers in a given data set are sometimes the result of an error by the experimenter, but oftentimes, they are perfectly valid data points that must be taken into consideration.

Mode

One additional measure to describe a set of data is the **mode**. This is the data point that appears most frequently. If two or more data points all tie for the most frequent appearance, then each of them is considered a mode. In the case of the test scores, where the numbers were 50, 60, 65, 65, 75, 80, 85, 85, 90, 100, there are two modes: 65 and 85.

Quartiles and Percentiles

The **first quartile** of a set of data refers to the number under which the first 25% of the data points fall (when written in ascending order). This usually means taking the median of the first half of the data points (excluding the median itself if there are an odd number of data points). The term also has a slightly different use: when it is said that a data point lies **in the first quartile**, it means it is less than or equal to the median of the first half of the data points. Conversely, if it lies **at the first quartile**, then it is the median of the first half of the data points.

When it is said that a data point lies in the **second quartile**, it means it is between the first quartile and the median.

The **third quartile** refers to the median of the second half of the data points in a set. Data points in the **third quartile** include all of the data that lie between the median and the median of the top half of the data.

Data that lies in the **fourth quartile** refers to all of the data above the third quartile.

Percentiles may be defined in a similar manner to quartiles. Generally, this is defined in the following manner:

If a data point lies **in the nth percentile**, this means it lies in the range of the first *n%* of the data.

If a data point lies **at the nth percentile**, then it means that *n%* of the data lies below this data point.

Standard Deviation

Given a data set X consisting of data points $(x_1, x_2, x_3, \ldots x_n)$, the **variance** of X is defined to be:

$$\frac{\sum_{i=1}^{n}(x_i - \bar{X})^2}{n}$$

This means that the variance of X is the average of the squares of the differences between each data point and the mean of X. In the formula, $\bar{X}$ is the mean of the values in the data set, and x_i represents

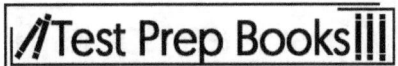

each individual value in the data set. The sigma notation indicates that the sum should be found with n being the number of values to add together. $i = 1$ means that the values should begin with the first value.

Given a data set X consisting of data points $(x_1, x_2, x_3, \ldots x_n)$, the **standard deviation** of X is defined to be:

$$s_x = \sqrt{\frac{\sum_{i=1}^{n}(x_i - \bar{X})^2}{n}}$$

In other words, the standard deviation is the square root of the variance.

Both the variance and the standard deviation are measures of how much the data tend to be spread out. When the standard deviation is low, the data points are mostly clustered around the mean. When the standard deviation is high, this generally indicates that the data are quite spread out or that there are a few substantial outliers.

As a simple example, compute the standard deviation for the data set (1, 3, 3, 5). First, compute the mean, which will be:

$$\frac{1+3+3+5}{4} = \frac{12}{4} = 3$$

Now, find the variance of X with the formula:

$$\sum_{i=1}^{4}(x_i - \bar{X})^2 = (1-3)^2 + (3-3)^2 + (3-3)^2 + (5-3)^2$$

$$-2^2 + 0^2 + 0^2 + 2^2 = 8$$

Therefore, the variance is $\frac{8}{4} = 2$. Taking the square root, the standard deviation will be $\sqrt{2}$.

Note that the standard deviation only depends upon the mean, not upon the median or mode(s). Generally, if there are multiple modes that are far apart from one another, the standard deviation will be high. A high standard deviation does not always mean there are multiple modes, however.

Fitting Functions to Data

Sometimes, when data are measured, it is not simply measuring the frequency of a given outcome, but rather measuring a relationship between two different quantities. In these cases, there is usually one variable that is controlled, the **independent variable**, and one that depends on this variable, the **dependent variable**. If there is a relationship between the two variables, then they are said to be **correlated**.

There are two caveats to these terms. First, the independent variable is not necessarily controlled by the experimenters. It is simply the one chosen to organize the data. In other words, the data are divided up based on the value of an independent variable. Second, finding a significant relationship between the dependent variable and the independent variable does not necessarily imply that there is a causal relationship between the two variables. It only means that once the independent variable is known, a

Mathematics

fairly accurate prediction of the dependent variable can be made. This is often expressed with the phrase *correlation does not imply causation*. In other words, just because there is a relationship between two variables does not mean that one is the cause of the other. There could be other factors involved that are the real cause.

Consider some examples. An experimenter could do an experiment in which the independent variable is the number of hours that a student studies for a given test, and the dependent variable is the score the student receives when he or she actually takes the test. Such an experiment would attempt to measure whether there is a relationship between the time spent studying and the score a student receives when taking the test. The expectation would be that the larger value of the independent variable would yield a larger value for the dependent variable. Another experimenter might do an experiment with runners, where the independent variable is the length of the runner's leg, and the dependent variable is the time it takes for the runner to run a fixed distance. In this experiment, as the independent variable increases, the dependent variable would be expected to decrease.

As an example of the phenomenon that correlation does not imply causation, consider an experiment where the independent variable is the value of a person's house, and the dependent variable is their income. Although people in more expensive houses are expected to make more money, it is clear that their expensive houses are not the cause of them making more money. This illustrates one example of why it is important for experimenters to be careful when drawing conclusions about causation from their data.

Linear Data Fitting

The simplest type of correlation between two variables is a **linear correlation**. If the independent variable is x and the dependent variable is y, then a linear correlation means $y = mx + b$. If m is positive, then y will increase as x increases. While if m is negative, then y decreases while x increases. The variable b represents the value of y when x is 0.

As one example of such a correlation, consider a manufacturing plant. Suppose x is the number of units produced by the plant, and y is the cost to the company. In this example, b will be the cost of the plant itself. The plant will cost money even if it is never used, just by buying the machinery. For each unit produced, there will be a cost for the labor and the material. Let m represent this cost to produce one unit of the product.

For a more concrete example, suppose a computer factory costs $100,000. It requires $100 of parts and $50 of labor to make one computer. How much will it cost for a company to make 1,000 computers? To figure this, let y be the amount of money the company spends, and let x be the number of computers. The cost of the factory is $100,000, so $b = 100,000$. On the other hand, the cost of producing a computer is the parts plus labor, or $150, so $m = 150$. Therefore:

$$y = 150x + 100,000$$

Substitute 1,000 for x and get:

$$y = 150 \times 1,000 + 100,000 = 150,000 + 1,000 = 250,000$$

It will cost the company $250,000 to make 1,000 computers.

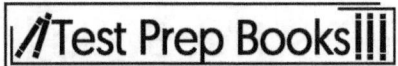

Probabilities

Given a set of possible outcomes X, a **probability distribution** on X is a function that assigns a probability to each possible outcome. If the outcomes are $(x_1, x_2, x_3, \ldots x_n)$, and the probability distribution is p, then the following rules are applied.

- $0 \leq p(x_i) \leq 1$, for any i.
- $\sum_{i=1}^{n} p(x_i) = 1$.

In other words, the probability of a given outcome must be between zero and 1, while the total probability must be 1.

If $p(x_i)$ is constant, then this is called a **uniform probability distribution**, and $p(x_i) = \frac{1}{n}$. For example, on a six-sided die, the probability of each of the six outcomes will be $\frac{1}{6}$.

If seeking the probability of an outcome occurring in some specific range A of possible outcomes, written $P(A)$, add up the probabilities for each outcome in that range. For example, consider a six-sided die, and figure the probability of getting a 3 or lower when it is rolled. The possible rolls are 1, 2, 3, 4, 5, and 6. So, to get a 3 or lower, a roll of 1, 2, or 3 must be completed. The probabilities of each of these is $\frac{1}{6}$, so add these to get:

$$p(1) + p(2) + p(3) = \frac{1}{6} + \frac{1}{6} + \frac{1}{6} = \frac{1}{2}$$

Conditional Probabilities

An outcome occasionally lies within some range of possibilities B, and the probability that the outcomes also lie within some set of possibilities A needs to be figured. This is called a **conditional probability**. It is written as $P(A|B)$, which is read "the probability of A given B." The general formula for computing conditional probabilities is:

$$P(A|B) = \frac{P(A \cap B)}{P(B)}$$

However, when dealing with uniform probability distributions, simplify this a bit. Write $|A|$ to indicate the number of outcomes in A. Then, for uniform probability distributions, write:

$$P(A|B) = \frac{|A \cap B|}{|B|}$$

Recall that $A \cap B$ means "A intersect B," and consists of all of the outcomes that lie in both A and B. This means that all possible outcomes do not need to be known. To see why this formula works, suppose that the set of outcomes X is $(x_1, x_2, x_3, \ldots x_n)$, so that $|X| = n$. Then, for a uniform probability distribution:

$$P(A) = \frac{|A|}{n}$$

However, this means:

$$(A|B) = \frac{P(A \cap B)}{P(B)} = \frac{\frac{|A \cap B|}{n}}{\frac{|B|}{n}} = \frac{|A \cap B|}{|B|}$$

The n's cancel out.

For example, suppose a die is rolled, and it is known that it will land between 1 and 4. However, how many sides the die has is unknown. Figure the probability that the die is rolled higher than 2. To figure this, $P(3)$ or $P(4)$ does not need to be determined, or any of the other probabilities, since it is known that a fair die has a uniform probability distribution. Therefore, apply the formula $\frac{|A \cap B|}{|B|}$. So, in this case B is (1, 2, 3, 4) and $A \cap B$ is (3, 4). Therefore:

$$\frac{|A \cap B|}{|B|} = \frac{2}{4} = \frac{1}{2}$$

Conditional probability is an important concept because, in many situations, the likelihood of one outcome can differ radically depending on how something else comes out. The probability of passing a test given that one has studied all of the material is generally much higher than the probability of passing a test given that one has not studied at all. The probability of a person having heart trouble is much lower if that person exercises regularly. The probability that a college student will graduate is higher when their SAT scores are higher, and so on. For this reason, there are many people who are interested in conditional probabilities.

Note that in some practical situations, changing the order of the conditional probabilities can make the outcome very different. For example, the probability that a person with heart trouble has exercised regularly is quite different than the probability that a person who exercises regularly will have heart trouble. The probability of a person receiving a military-only award, given that he or she is or was a soldier, is generally not very high, but the probability that a person being or having been a soldier, given that he or she received a military-only award, is 1.

However, in some cases, the outcomes do not influence one another this way. If the probability of A is the same regardless of whether B is given; that is, if $P(A|B) = P(A)$, then A and B are considered *independent*. In this case:

$$P(A|B) = \frac{P(A \cap B)}{P(B)} = P(A)$$

So,

$$P(A \cap B) = P(A)P(B)$$

In fact, if $P(A \cap B) = P(A)P(B)$ it can be determined that:

$$P(A|B) = P(A)$$

and

$$P(A|B) = P(B)$$

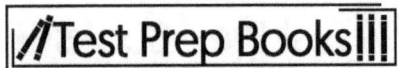

by working backward. Therefore, B is also independent of A.

An example of something being independent can be seen in rolling dice. In this case, consider a red die and a green die. It is expected that when the dice are rolled, the outcome of the green die should not depend in any way on the outcome of the red die. Or, to take another example, if the same die is rolled repeatedly, then the next number rolled should not depend on which numbers have been rolled previously. Similarly, if a coin is flipped, then the next flip's outcome does not depend on the outcomes of previous flips.

This can sometimes be counter-intuitive, since when rolling a die or flipping a coin, there can be a streak of surprising results. If, however, it is known that the die or coin is fair, then these results are just the result of the fact that over long periods of time, it is very likely that some unlikely streaks of outcomes will occur. Therefore, avoid making the mistake of thinking that when considering a series of independent outcomes, a particular outcome is "due to happen" simply because a surprising series of outcomes has already been seen.

There is a second type of common mistake that people tend to make when reasoning about statistical outcomes: the idea that when something of low probability happens, this is surprising. It would be surprising that something with low probability happened after just one attempt. However, with so much happening all at once, it is easy to see at least something happen in a way that seems to have a very low probability. In fact, a lottery is a good example. The odds of winning a lottery are very small, but the odds that somebody wins the lottery each week are actually fairly high. Therefore, no one should be surprised when some low probability things happen.

Addition Rule

The **addition rule for probabilities** states that the probability of A or B happening is $P(A \cup B) = P(A) + P(B) - P(A \cap B)$. Note that the subtraction of $P(A \cap B)$ must be performed, or else it would result in double counting any outcomes that lie in both A and in B. For example, suppose that a 20-sided die is being rolled. Fred bets that the outcome will be greater than 10, while Helen bets that it will be greater than 4 but less than 15. What is the probability that at least one of them is correct?

We apply the rule $P(A \cup B) = P(A) + P(B) - P(A \cap B)$, where A is that outcome x is in the range $x > 10$, and B is that outcome x is in the range $4 < x < 15$.

$$P(A) = 10 \times \frac{1}{20} = \frac{1}{2}$$

$$P(B) = 10 \times \frac{1}{20} = \frac{1}{2}$$

$P(A \cap B)$ can be computed by noting that $A \cap B$ means the outcome x is in the range $10 < x < 15$, so:

$$P(A \cap B) = 4 \times \frac{1}{20} = \frac{1}{5}$$

Mathematics

Therefore,

$$P(A \cup B) = P(A) + P(B) - P(A \cap B)$$

$$\frac{1}{2} + \frac{1}{2} - \frac{1}{5} = \frac{4}{5}$$

Multiplication Rule

As mentioned, the **multiplication rule for probabilities** for independent events states the probability of A and B both happening is:

$$P(A \cap B) = P(A) \times P(B)$$

The multiplication rule for probabilities for dependent events states the probability of A and B both happening is:

As an example, suppose that when Jamie wears black pants, there is a $\frac{1}{2}$ probability that she wears a black shirt as well, and that she wears black pants $\frac{3}{4}$ of the time. What is the probability that she is wearing both a black shirt and black pants?

To figure this, use the above formula, where A will be "Jamie is wearing black pants," while B will be "Jamie is wearing a black shirt." It is known that $P(A)$ is $\frac{3}{4}$. It is also known that:

$$P(B|A) = \frac{1}{2}$$

Multiplying the two, the probability that she is wearing both black pants and a black shirt is:

$$P(A)P(B|A) = \frac{3}{4} \times \frac{1}{2} = \frac{3}{8}$$

English Language Arts and Reading

Reading: Literary Text Analysis

Explicit Information

Identify Passage Characteristics

Writing can be classified under four passage types: narrative, expository, descriptive (sometimes called technical), and persuasive. Though these types are not mutually exclusive, one form tends to dominate the rest. By recognizing the *type* of passage you're reading, you gain insight into *how* you should read. When reading a narrative intended to entertain, sometimes you can read more quickly through the passage if the details are discernible. A technical document, on the other hand, might require a close read because skimming the passage might cause the reader to miss salient details.

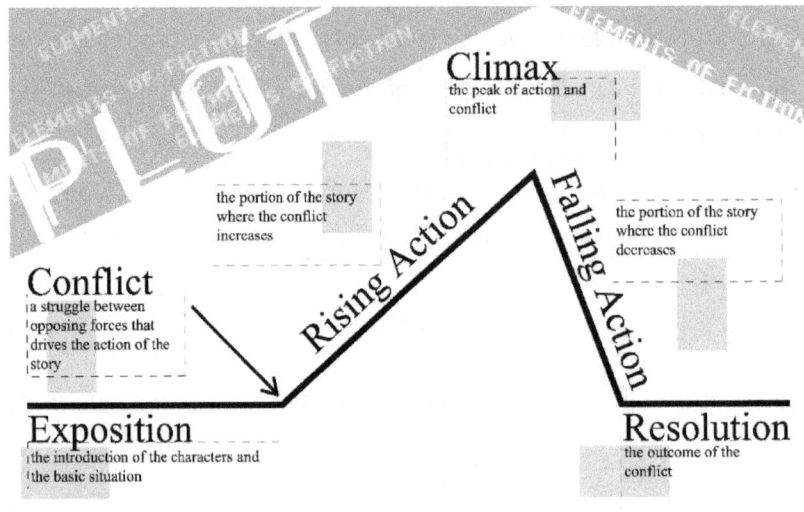

1. **Narrative writing**, at its core, is the art of storytelling. For a narrative to exist, certain elements must be present. First, it must have characters. While many characters are human, characters could be defined as anything that thinks, acts, and talks like a human. For example, many recent movies, such as *Lord of the Rings* and *The Chronicles of Narnia*, include animals, fantasy creatures, and even trees that behave like humans. Narratives also must have a plot or sequence of events. Typically, those events follow a standard plot diagram, but recent trends start *in medias res* or in the middle (nearer the climax). In this instance, foreshadowing and flashbacks often fill in plot details. Finally, along with characters and a plot, there must also be conflict. Conflict is usually divided into two types: internal and external. Internal conflict indicates the character is in turmoil. Think of an angel on one shoulder and the devil on the other, arguing it out. Internal conflicts are presented through the character's thoughts. External conflicts are visible. Types of external conflict include person versus person, person versus nature, person versus technology, person versus the supernatural, or person versus fate.

2. **Expository writing** is detached and to the point, while other types of writing — persuasive, narrative, and descriptive — are livelier. Since expository writing is designed to instruct or inform, it usually involves directions and steps written in second person ("you" voice) and lacks any persuasive or

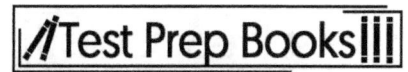

narrative elements. Sequence words such as *first*, *second*, and *third*, or *in the first place*, *secondly*, and *lastly* are often given to add fluency and cohesion. Common examples of expository writing include instructor's lessons, cookbook recipes, and repair manuals.

3. Due to its empirical nature, **technical writing** is filled with steps, charts, graphs, data, and statistics. The goal of technical writing is to advance understanding in a field through the scientific method. Experts such as teachers, doctors, or mechanics use words unique to the profession in which they operate. These words, which often incorporate acronyms, are called **jargon**. Technical writing is a type of expository writing but is not meant to be understood by the general public. Instead, technical writers assume readers have received a formal education in a particular field of study and need no explanation as to what the jargon means. Imagine a doctor trying to understand a diagnostic reading for a car or a mechanic trying to interpret lab results. Only professionals with proper training will fully comprehend the text.

4. **Persuasive writing** is designed to change opinions and attitudes. The topic, stance, and arguments are found in the thesis, positioned near the end of the introduction. Later supporting paragraphs offer relevant quotations, paraphrases, and summaries from primary or secondary sources, which are then interpreted, analyzed, and evaluated. The goal of persuasive writers is not to stack quotes but to develop original ideas by using sources as a starting point. Good persuasive writing makes powerful arguments with valid sources and thoughtful analysis. Poor persuasive writing is riddled with bias and logical fallacies. Sometimes logical and illogical arguments are sandwiched together in the same text. Therefore, readers should display skepticism when reading persuasive arguments.

Inferences

Readers should be able to make **inferences**. Making an inference requires the reader to read between the lines and look for what is implied rather than what is explicitly stated. That means, using information that is known from the text, the reader is able to make a logical assumption about information that is not explicitly stated but is probably true. Read the following passage:

"Hey, do you want to meet my new puppy?" Jonathan asked.

"Oh, I'm sorry but please don't—" Jacinta began to protest, but before she could finish, Jonathan had already opened the passenger side door of his car and a perfect white ball of fur came bouncing towards Jacinta.

"Isn't he the cutest?" beamed Jonathan.

"Yes—achoo!—he's pretty—aaaachooo!!—adora—aaa—aaaachoo!" Jacinta managed to say in between sneezes. "But if you don't mind, I—I—achoo!—need to go inside."

Which of the following can be inferred from Jacinta's reaction to the puppy?
   a. She hates animals.
   b. She is allergic to dogs.
   c. She prefers cats to dogs.
   d. She is angry at Jonathan.

An inference requires the reader to consider the information presented and then form their own idea about what is probably true. Based on the details in the passage, what is the best answer to the question? Important details to pay attention to in the passage include the tone of Jacinta's dialogue, as

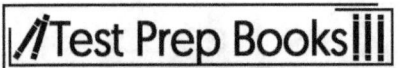

English Language Arts and Reading

well as her reaction itself, which is a long string of sneezes. Answer choices (a) and (d) both express strong emotions ("hates" and "angry") that are not evident in Jacinta's speech or actions. Answer choice (c) mentions cats, but there is nothing in the passage to indicate Jacinta's feelings about cats. Answer choice (b), "she is allergic to dogs," is the most logical choice. Based on the fact she began sneezing as soon as a fluffy dog approached her, it makes sense to guess that Jacinta might be allergic to dogs. Using the clues in the passage, it is reasonable to guess that this is true even though Jacinta never directly states, "Sorry, I'm allergic to dogs!"

Making inferences is crucial because literary texts often avoid presenting complete and direct information to readers about characters' thoughts or feelings, or they present the information in an unclear way, leaving it up to the reader to interpret clues given in the text. In order to make inferences while reading, readers should ask themselves:

- What details are being presented in the text?
- Is there any important information that seems to be missing?
- Based on the information that the author *does* include, what else is probably true?
- Is this inference reasonable based on what is already known?

Author's Craft

Authors utilize a wide range of techniques to tell a story or communicate information. Readers should be familiar with the most common of these techniques. Techniques of writing are also commonly known as **rhetorical devices**.

Figurative Language

Figurative language, like the use of similes and metaphors, is a type of rhetorical device commonly found in literature. In addition to rhetorical devices that play on the **meanings** of words, there are also rhetorical devices that use the *sounds* of words. These devices are most often found in poetry but may also be found in other types of literature and in nonfiction writing like speech texts.

Alliteration and **assonance** are both varieties of sound repetition. Other types of sound repetition include: **anaphora**, repetition that occurs at the beginning of the sentences; **epiphora**, repetition occurring at the end of phrases; **antimetabole**, repetition of words in reverse order; and **antiphrasis**, a form of denial of an assertion in a text.

Alliteration refers to the repetition of the first sound of each word. Recall Robert Burns' opening line:

> My love is like a red, red rose

This line includes two instances of alliteration: "love" and "like" (repeated *L* sound), as well as "red" and "rose" (repeated *R* sound). Next, assonance refers to the repetition of vowel sounds and can occur anywhere within a word (not just the opening sound). Here is the opening of a poem by John Keats:

> When I have fears that I may cease to be
>
> Before my pen has glean'd my teeming brain

Assonance can be found in the words "fears," "cease," "be," "glean'd," and "teeming," all of which stress the long *E* sound. Both alliteration and assonance create a harmony that unifies the writer's language.

English Language Arts and Reading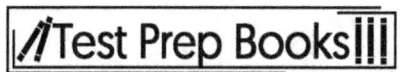

Another sound device is **onomatopoeia**, or words whose spelling mimics the sound they describe. Words such as "crash," "bang," and "sizzle" are all examples of onomatopoeia. Use of onomatopoetic language adds auditory imagery to the text.

Readers are probably most familiar with the technique of **pun**. A pun is a play on words, taking advantage of two words that have the same or similar pronunciation. Puns can be found throughout Shakespeare's plays, for instance:

> Now is the winter of our discontent
> Made glorious summer by this son of York

These lines from *Richard III* contain a play on words. Richard III refers to his brother, the newly crowned King Edward IV, as the "son of York," referencing their family heritage from the house of York. However, while drawing a comparison between the political climate and the weather (times of political trouble were the "winter," but now the new king brings "glorious summer"), Richard's use of the word "son" also implies another word with the same pronunciation, "sun"—so Edward IV is also like the sun, bringing light, warmth, and hope to England. Puns are a clever way for writers to suggest two meanings at once.

Style, Tone, and Mood

Style, tone, and mood are often thought to be the same thing. Though they're closely related, there are important differences to keep in mind. The easiest way to do this is to remember that style "creates and affects" tone and mood. More specifically, style is how the writer uses words to create the desired tone and mood for their writing.

Style

Style can include any number of technical writing choices. A few examples of style choices include:

- Sentence Construction: When presenting facts, does the writer use shorter sentences to create a quicker sense of the supporting evidence, or do they use longer sentences to elaborate and explain the information?

- Technical Language: Does the writer use jargon to demonstrate their expertise in the subject, or do they use ordinary language to help the reader understand things in simple terms?

- Formal Language: Does the writer refrain from using contractions such as *won't* or *can't* to create a more formal tone, or do they use a colloquial, conversational style to connect to the reader?

- Formatting: Does the writer use a series of shorter paragraphs to help the reader follow a line of argument, or do they use longer paragraphs to examine an issue in great detail and demonstrate their knowledge of the topic?

On the test, examine the writer's style and how their writing choices affect the way the text comes across.

Tone

Tone refers to the writer's attitude toward the subject matter. Tone conveys how the writer feels about characters, situations, events, ideas, etc.

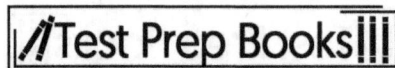

A lot of nonfiction writing has a neutral tone, which is an important tone for the writer to take. A **neutral tone** demonstrates that the writer is presenting a topic impartially and letting the information speak for itself. On the other hand, nonfiction writing can be just as effective and appropriate if the tone isn't neutral. For instance, take this example involving seat belts:

> Seat belts save more lives than any other automobile safety feature. Many studies show that airbags save lives as well; however, not all cars have airbags. For instance, some older cars don't. Furthermore, air bags aren't entirely reliable. For example, studies show that in 15% of accidents airbags don't deploy as designed, but, on the other hand, seat belt malfunctions are extremely rare. The number of highway fatalities has plummeted since laws requiring seat belt usage were enacted.

In this passage, the writer mostly chooses to retain a neutral tone when presenting information. If the writer would instead include their own personal experience of losing a friend or family member in a car accident, the tone would change dramatically. The tone would no longer be neutral and would show that the writer has a personal stake in the content, allowing them to interpret the information in a different way. When analyzing tone, consider what the writer is trying to achieve in the text and how they *create* the tone using style.

Mood

Mood refers to the feelings and atmosphere that the writer's words create for the reader. Like tone, many nonfiction texts can have a neutral mood. To return to the previous example, if the writer would choose to include information about a person they know being killed in a car accident, the text would suddenly carry an emotional component that is absent in the previous example. Depending on how they present the information, the writer can create a sad, angry, or even hopeful mood. When analyzing the mood, consider what the writer wants to accomplish and whether the best choice was made to achieve that end.

Consistency

Whatever style, tone, and mood the writer uses, good writing should remain consistent throughout. If the writer chooses to include the tragic, personal experience above, it would affect the style, tone, and mood of the entire text. It would seem out of place for such an example to be used in the middle of a neutral, measured, and analytical text. To adjust the rest of the text, the writer needs to make additional choices to remain consistent. For example, the writer might decide to use the word *tragedy* in place of the more neutral *fatality*, or they could describe a series of car-related deaths as an *epidemic*. Adverbs and adjectives such as *devastating* or *horribly* could be included to maintain this consistent attitude toward the content. When analyzing writing, look for sudden shifts in style, tone, and mood, and consider whether the writer would be wiser to maintain the prevailing strategy.

Identify the Position and Purpose

When it comes to an author's writing, readers should always identify a position or stance. No matter how objective a text may seem, readers should assume the author has preconceived beliefs. One can reduce the likelihood of accepting an invalid argument by looking for multiple articles on the topic, including those with varying opinions. If several opinions point in the same direction and are backed by reputable peer-reviewed sources, it's more likely the author has a valid argument. Positions that run contrary to widely held beliefs and existing data should invite scrutiny. There are exceptions to the rule, so be a careful consumer of information.

Though themes, symbols, and motifs are buried deep within the text and can sometimes be difficult to infer, an author's purpose is usually obvious from the beginning. There are four purposes of writing: to inform, to persuade, to describe, and to entertain. **Informative writing** presents facts in an accessible way. **Persuasive writing** appeals to emotions and logic to inspire the reader to adopt a specific stance. Be wary of this type of writing, as it can mask a lack of objectivity with powerful emotion. **Descriptive writing** is designed to paint a picture in the reader's mind, while texts that entertain are often narratives designed to engage and delight the reader.

The various writing styles are usually blended, with one purpose dominating the rest. A persuasive text, for example, might begin with a humorous tale to make readers more receptive to the persuasive message, or a recipe in a cookbook designed to inform might be preceded by an entertaining anecdote that makes the recipes more appealing.

Interpret Influences of Historical Context

Studying historical literature is fascinating. It reveals a snapshot in time of people, places, and cultures; a collective set of beliefs and attitudes that no longer exist. Writing changes as attitudes and cultures evolve. Beliefs previously considered immoral or wrong may be considered acceptable today. Researching the historical period of an author gives the reader perspective. The dialogue in Jane Austen's *Pride and Prejudice*, for example, is indicative of social class during the Regency era. Similarly, the stereotypes and slurs in *The Adventures of Huckleberry Finn* were a result of common attitudes and beliefs in the late 1800s, attitudes now found to be reprehensible.

Recognizing Cultural Themes

Regardless of culture, place, or time, certain themes are universal to the human condition. Because humans experience joy, rage, jealousy, and pride, certain themes span centuries. For example, Shakespeare's *Macbeth*, as well as modern works like *The 50th Law* by rapper 50 Cent and Robert Greene or the Netflix series *House of Cards* all feature characters who commit atrocious acts because of ambition. Similarly, *The Adventures of Huckleberry Finn*, published in the 1880s, and *The Catcher in the Rye*, published in the 1950s, both have characters who lie, connive, and survive on their wits.

Moviegoers know whether they are seeing an action, romance or horror film, and are often disappointed if the movie doesn't fit into the conventions of a particular category. Similarly, categories or genres give readers a sense of what to expect from a text. Some of the most basic genres in literature include books, short stories, poetry, and drama. Many genres can be split into sub-genres. For example, the sub-genres of historical fiction, realistic fiction, and fantasy all fit under the fiction genre.

Each genre has a unique way of approaching a particular theme. Books and short stories use plot, characterization, and setting, while poems rely on figurative language, sound devices, and symbolism. Dramas reveal plot through dialogue and the actor's voice and body language.

Reading: Informational Text Analysis and Synthesis

Main Ideas and Supporting Details

Topic Versus the Main Idea

It is very important to know the difference between the topic and the main idea of the text. Even though these two are similar because they both present the central point of a text, they have distinctive differences. A **topic** is the subject of the text; This can usually be described in a concise one- to two-word phrase. On the other hand, the **main idea** is more detailed and provides the author's central point of the text. It can be expressed through a complete sentence and can be found in the beginning, middle, or end of a paragraph. In most nonfiction books, the first sentence of the passage usually (but not always) states the main idea. Take a look at the passage below to review the topic versus the main idea:

Cheetahs

Cheetahs are one of the fastest mammals on land, reaching up to 70 miles an hour over short distances. Even though cheetahs can run as fast as 70 miles an hour, they usually only have to run half that speed to catch up with their choice of prey. Cheetahs cannot maintain a fast pace over long periods of time because they will overheat their bodies. After a chase, cheetahs need to rest for approximately 30 minutes prior to eating or returning to any other activity.

In the example above, the topic of the passage is "Cheetahs" simply because that is the subject of the text. The main idea of the text is "Cheetahs are one of the fastest mammals on land but can only maintain this fast pace for short distances." While it covers the topic, it is more detailed and refers to the text in its entirety.

Supporting Details

Supporting details help readers better develop and understand the main idea. Supporting details answer questions like *who, what, where, when, why,* and *how*. Different types of supporting details include examples, facts and statistics, anecdotes, and sensory details.

Persuasive and informative texts often use supporting details. In persuasive texts, authors attempt to make readers agree with their point of view, and supporting details are often used as "selling points." If authors make a statement, they should support the statement with evidence in order to adequately persuade readers. Informative texts use supporting details such as examples and facts to inform readers. Take another look at the previous "Cheetahs" passage to find examples of supporting details:

Cheetahs

Cheetahs are one of the fastest mammals on land, reaching up to 70 miles an hour over short distances. Even though cheetahs can run as fast as 70 miles an hour, they usually only have to run half that speed to catch up with their choice of prey. Cheetahs cannot maintain a fast pace over long periods of time because they will overheat their bodies. After a chase, cheetahs need to rest for approximately 30 minutes prior to eating or returning to any other activity.

In the example above, supporting details include:

- Cheetahs reach up to 70 miles per hour over short distances.
- They usually only have to run half that speed to catch up with their prey.
- Cheetahs will overheat their bodies if they exert a high speed over longer distances.
- Cheetahs need to rest for 30 minutes after a chase.

Look at the diagram below (applying the cheetah example) to help determine the hierarchy of topic, main idea, and supporting details.

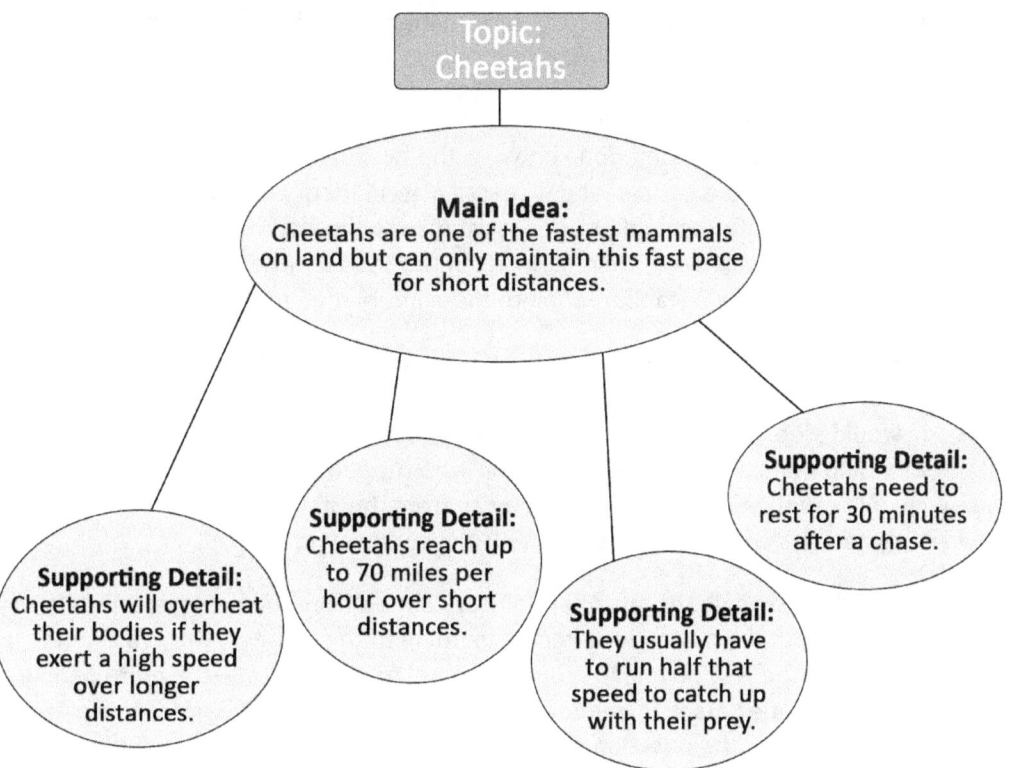

Inferences

Directly Stated Information Versus Implications

Engaged readers should constantly self-question while reviewing texts to help them form conclusions. Self-questioning is when readers review a paragraph, page, passage, or chapter and ask themselves, "Did I understand what I read?," "What was the main event in this section?," "Where is this taking place?," and so on. Authors can provide clues or pieces of evidence throughout a text or passage to guide readers toward a conclusion. This is why active and engaged readers should read the text or passage in its entirety before forming a definitive conclusion. If readers do not gather all the pieces of evidence needed, then they may jump to an illogical conclusion.

At times, authors directly state conclusions while others simply imply them. Of course, it is easier if authors outwardly provide conclusions to readers because it does not leave any information open to interpretation. On the other hand, implications are things that authors do not directly state but can be assumed based off of information they provided. If authors only imply what may have happened, readers can form a menagerie of ideas for conclusions. For example, look at the following statement: "Once we heard the sirens, we hunkered down in the storm shelter." In this statement, the author does not directly state that there was a tornado, but clues such as "sirens" and "storm shelter" provide insight to the readers to help form that conclusion.

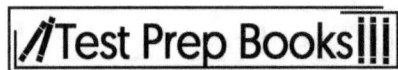

Apply Information

A natural extension of making inferences is also being able to apply that information to new contexts. This is especially useful in nonfiction or informative writing. Considering the facts and details presented in the text, readers should consider how the same information might be relevant in a different situation. The following is an example of applying an inferential conclusion to a different context:

> Often, individuals behave differently in large groups than they do as individuals. One example of this is the psychological phenomenon known as the bystander effect. According to the bystander effect, the more people who witness an accident or crime occur, the less likely each individual bystander is to respond or offer assistance to the victim. A classic example of this is the murder of Kitty Genovese in New York City in the 1960s. Although there were over thirty witnesses to her killing by a stabber, none of them intervened to help Kitty or contact the police.

Considering the phenomenon of the bystander effect, what would probably happen if somebody tripped on the stairs in a crowded subway station?
a. Everybody would stop to help the person who tripped
b. Bystanders would point and laugh at the person who tripped
c. Someone would call the police after walking away from the station
d. Few if any bystanders would offer assistance to the person who tripped

This question asks readers to apply the information they learned from the passage, which is an informative paragraph about the bystander effect. According to the passage, this is a concept in psychology that describes the way people in groups respond to an accident—the more people that are present, the less likely any one person is to intervene. While the passage illustrates this effect with the example of a woman's murder, the question asks readers to apply it to a different context—in this case, someone falling down the stairs in front of many subway passengers. Although this specific situation is not discussed in the passage, readers should be able to apply the general concepts described in the paragraph. The definition of the bystander effect includes any instance of an accident or crime in front of a large group of people. The question asks about a situation that falls within the same definition, so the general concept should still hold true: in the midst of a large crowd, few individuals are likely to actually respond to an accident. In this case, answer choice (d) is the best response.

Outlining

An **outline** is a system used to organize writing. When reading texts, outlining is important because it helps readers organize important information in a logical pattern using roman numerals. Usually, outlines start with the main idea(s) and then branch out into subgroups or subsidiary thoughts of subjects. Not only do outlines provide a visual tool for readers to reflect on how events, characters, settings, or other key parts of the text or passage relate to one another, but they can also lead readers to a stronger conclusion.

English Language Arts and Reading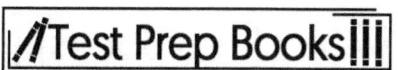

The sample below demonstrates what a general outline looks like.

I. Main Topic 1
    a. Subtopic 1
    b. Subtopic 2
        1. Detail 1
        2. Detail 2
II. Main Topic 2
    a. Subtopic 1
    b. Subtopic 2
        1. Detail 1
        2. Detail 2

Summarizing

At the end of a text or passage, it is important to summarize what the readers read. **Summarizing** is a strategy in which readers determine what is important throughout the text or passage, shorten those ideas, and rewrite or retell it in their own words. A summary should identify the main idea of the text or passage. Important details or supportive evidence should also be accurately reported in the summary. If writers provide irrelevant details in the summary, it may cloud the greater meaning of the summary in the text. When summarizing, writers should not include their opinions, quotes, or what they thought the author should have said. A clear summary provides clarity of the text or passage to the readers. Let's review the checklist of items writers should include in their summary.

Summary Checklist
- Title of the story
- Someone: Who is or are the main character(s)?
- Wanted: What did the character(s) want?
- But: What was the problem?
- So: How did the character(s) solve the problem?
- Then: How did the story end? What was the resolution?

Paraphrasing

Another strategy readers can use to help them fully comprehend a text or passage is paraphrasing. **Paraphrasing** is when readers take the author's words and put them into their own words. When readers and writers paraphrase, they should avoid copying the text—that is plagiarism. It is also important to include as many details as possible when restating the facts. Not only will this help readers and writers recall information, but by putting the information into their own words, they demonstrate whether or not they fully comprehend the text or passage. Look at the example below showing an original text and how to paraphrase it.

Original Text: Fenway Park is home to the beloved Boston Red Sox. The stadium opened on April 20, 1912. The stadium currently seats over 37,000 fans, many of whom travel from all over the country to experience the iconic team and nostalgia of Fenway Park.

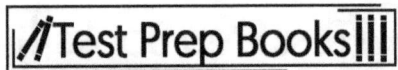

Paraphrased: On April 20, 1912, Fenway Park opened. Home to the Boston Red Sox, the stadium now seats over 37,000 fans. Many spectators travel to watch the Red Sox and experience the spirit of Fenway Park.

Paraphrasing, summarizing, and quoting can often cross paths with one another. Review the chart below showing the similarities and differences between the three strategies.

Paraphrasing	Summarizing	Quoting
Uses own words	Puts main ideas into own words	Uses words that are identical to text
References original source	References original source	Requires quotation marks
Uses own sentences	Shows important ideas of source	Uses author's own words and ideas

Author's Craft

Types of Appeals

In nonfiction writing, authors employ argumentative techniques to present their opinion to readers in the most convincing way. Persuasive writing usually includes at least one type of appeal: an appeal to logic (**logos**), emotion (**pathos**), or credibility and trustworthiness (**ethos**). When a writer appeals to logic, they are asking readers to agree with them based on research, evidence, and an established line of reasoning. An author's argument might also appeal to readers' emotions, perhaps by including personal stories and **anecdotes** (a short narrative of a specific event). A final type of appeal, appeal to authority, asks the reader to agree with the author's argument on the basis of their expertise or credentials. Consider three different approaches to arguing the same opinion:

Logic (Logos)
This is an example of an appeal to logic:

> Our school should abolish its current ban on campus cell phone use. The ban was adopted last year as an attempt to reduce class disruptions and help students focus more on their lessons. However, since the rule was enacted, there has been no change in the number of disciplinary problems in class. Therefore, the rule is ineffective and should be done away with.

The author uses evidence to disprove the logic of the school's rule (the rule was supposed to reduce discipline problems, but the number of problems has not been reduced; therefore, the rule is not working) and call for its repeal.

Emotion (Pathos)
An author's argument might also appeal to readers' emotions, perhaps by including personal stories and anecdotes. The next example presents an appeal to emotion. By sharing the personal anecdote of one student and speaking about emotional topics like family relationships, the author invokes the reader's empathy in asking them to reconsider the school rule.

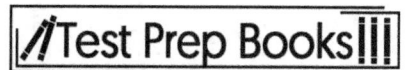

Our school should abolish its current ban on campus cell phone use. If students aren't able to use their phones during the school day, many of them feel isolated from their loved ones. For example, last semester, one student's grandmother had a heart attack in the morning. However, because he couldn't use his cell phone, the student didn't know about his grandmother's accident until the end of the day—when she had already passed away, and it was too late to say goodbye. By preventing students from contacting their friends and family, our school is placing undue stress and anxiety on students.

Credibility (Ethos)
Finally, an appeal to authority includes a statement from a relevant expert. In this case, the author uses a doctor in the field of education to support the argument. All three examples begin from the same opinion—the school's phone ban needs to change—but rely on different argumentative styles to persuade the reader.

Our school should abolish its current ban on campus cell phone use. According to Dr. Bartholomew Everett, a leading educational expert, "Research studies show that cell phone usage has no real impact on student attentiveness. Rather, phones provide a valuable technological resource for learning. Schools need to learn how to integrate this new technology into their curriculum." Rather than banning phones altogether, our school should follow the advice of experts and allow students to use phones as part of their learning.

Rhetorical Questions
Another commonly used argumentative technique is asking **rhetorical questions**, questions that do not actually require an answer but that push the reader to consider the topic further.

I wholly disagree with the proposal to ban restaurants from serving foods with high sugar and sodium contents. Do we really want to live in a world where the government can control what we eat? I prefer to make my own food choices.

Here, the author's rhetorical question prompts readers to put themselves in a hypothetical situation and imagine how they would feel about it.

Counterarguments

If an author presents a differing opinion or a **counterargument** in order to refute it, the reader should consider how and why the information is being presented. It is meant to strengthen the original argument and shouldn't be confused with the author's intended conclusion, but it should also be considered in the reader's final evaluation.

Authors can exhibit bias if they ignore the opposing viewpoint or present their side in an unbalanced way. A strong argument considers the opposition and finds a way to refute it. Critical readers should look for an unfair or one-sided presentation of the argument and be skeptical, as a bias may be present. Even if this bias is unintentional, if it exists in the writing, the reader should be wary of the validity of the argument. Readers should also look for the use of stereotypes, which refer to specific groups. **Stereotypes** are often negative connotations about a person or place and should always be avoided. When a critical reader finds stereotypes in a piece of writing, they should be critical of the argument and consider the validity of anything the author presents. Stereotypes reveal a flaw in the writer's thinking and may suggest a lack of knowledge or understanding about the subject.

Synthesis

Drawing Conclusions

When drawing conclusions about texts or passages, readers should use two main things: the information that they already know and the information they have learned from the text or passage. Authors write with an intended purpose, and it is the reader's responsibility to understand and form logical conclusions of authors' ideas. It is important to remember that the reader's conclusions should be supported by information directly from the text. Readers cannot form conclusions based only off of information they already know.

There are several ways readers can draw conclusions from authors' ideas, such as note taking, text evidence, text credibility, writing a response to text, directly stated information versus implications, outlining, summarizing, and paraphrasing. Let's take a look at each important strategy to help readers draw logical conclusions.

Note Taking

When readers take notes throughout texts or passages, they are jotting down important facts or points that the author makes. Note taking is a useful record of information that helps readers understand the text or passage and respond to it. When taking notes, readers should keep lines brief and filled with pertinent information so that they are not rereading a large amount of text, but rather just key points, elements, or words. After readers have completed a text or passage, they can refer to their notes to help them form a conclusion about the author's ideas in the text or passage.

Text Evidence

Text evidence is the information readers find in a text or passage that supports the main idea or point(s) in a story. In turn, text evidence can help readers draw conclusions about the text or passage. The information should be taken directly from the text or passage and placed in quotation marks. Text evidence provides readers with information to support ideas about the text so that they do not rely simply on their own thoughts. Details should be precise, descriptive, and factual. Statistics are a great piece of text evidence because they provide readers with exact numbers and not just a generalization. For example, instead of saying "Asia has a larger population than Europe," authors could provide detailed information such as, "In Asia there are over 4 billion people, whereas in Europe there are a little over 750 million." More definitive information provides better evidence to readers to help support their conclusions about texts or passages.

Text Credibility

Credible sources are important when drawing conclusions because readers need to be able to trust what they are reading. Authors should always use credible sources to help gain the trust of their readers. A text is **credible** when it is believable and the author is objective and unbiased. If readers do not trust an author's words, they may simply dismiss the text completely. For example, if an author writes a persuasive essay, he or she is outwardly trying to sway readers' opinions to align with their own. Readers may agree or disagree with the author, which may, in turn, lead them to believe that the author is credible or not credible. Also, readers should keep in mind the source of the text. If readers review a journal about astronomy, would a more reliable source be a NASA employee or a medical doctor? Overall, text credibility is important when drawing conclusions, because readers want reliable sources that support the decisions they have made about the author's ideas.

English Language Arts and Reading

Writing a Response to Text

Once readers have determined their opinions and validated the credibility of a text, they can then reflect on the text. Writing a response to a text is one way readers can reflect on the given text or passage. When readers write responses to a text, it is important for them to rely on the evidence within the text to support their opinions or thoughts. Supporting evidence such as facts, details, statistics, and quotes directly from the text are key pieces of information readers should reflect upon or use when writing a response to text.

Reading: Vocabulary

There will be many occasions in one's reading career in which an unknown word or a word with multiple meanings will pop up. There are ways of determining what these words or phrases mean that do not require the use of the dictionary, which is especially helpful during a test where one may not be available. Even outside of the exam, knowing how to derive an understanding of a word via context clues will be a critical skill in the real world. The context is the circumstances in which a story or a passage is happening, and can usually be found in the series of words directly before or directly after the word or phrase in question. The clues are the words that hint towards the meaning of the unknown word or phrase.

There may be questions that ask about the meaning of a particular word or phrase within a passage. There are a couple ways to approach these kinds of questions:

Define the word or phrase in a way that is easy to comprehend (using context clues)

Try out each answer choice in place of the word.

To demonstrate, here's an example from *Alice in Wonderland*:

> Alice was beginning to get very tired of sitting by her sister on the bank, and of having nothing to do: once or twice, she peeped into the book her sister was reading, but it had no pictures or conversations in it, "and what is the use of a book," thought Alice, "without pictures or conversations?"

Q: As it is used in the selection, the word peeped means:

Using the first technique, before looking at the answers, define the word *peeped* using context clues and then find the matching answer. Then, analyze the entire passage in order to determine the meaning, not just the surrounding words.

To begin, imagine a blank where the word should be and put a synonym or definition there: "once or twice, she _____ into the book her sister was reading." The context clue here is the book. It may be tempting to put *read* where the blank is, but notice the preposition word, *into*. One does not read *into* a book, one simply reads a book, and since reading a book requires that it is seen with a pair of eyes, then *look* would make the most sense to put into the blank: "once or twice, she looked into the book her sister was reading."

Once an easy-to-understand word or synonym has been supplanted, readers should check to make sure it makes sense with the rest of the passage. What happened after she looked into the book? She

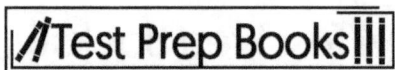

English Language Arts and Reading

thought to herself how a book without pictures or conversations is useless. This situation in its entirety makes sense.

Now check the answer choices for a match:
  a. To make a high-pitched cry
  b. To smack
  c. To look curiously
  d. To pout

Since the word was already defined, Choice *C* is the best option.

Using the second technique, replace the figurative blank with each of the answer choices and determine which one is the most appropriate. Remember to look further into the passage to clarify that they work, because they could still make sense out of context.
  a. Once or twice, she <u>made a high pitched cry</u> into the book her sister was reading
  b. Once or twice, she <u>smacked</u> into the book her sister was reading
  c. Once or twice, she <u>looked curiously</u> into the book her sister was reading
  d. Once or twice, she <u>pouted</u> into the book her sister was reading

For Choice *A*, it does not make much sense in any context for a person to yell into a book, unless maybe something terrible has happened in the story. Given that afterward Alice thinks to herself how useless a book without pictures is, this option does not make sense within context.

For Choice *B*, smacking a book someone is reading may make sense if the rest of the passage indicates a reason for doing so. If Alice was angry or her sister had shoved it in her face, then maybe smacking the book would make sense within context. However, since whatever she does with the book causes her to think, "what is the use of a book without pictures or conversations?" then answer Choice *B* is not an appropriate answer. Answer Choice *C* fits well within context, given her subsequent thoughts on the matter. Answer Choice *D* does not make sense in context or grammatically, as people do not *pout into* things.

This is a simple example to illustrate the techniques outlined above. There may, however, be a question in which all of the definitions are correct and also make sense out of context, in which the appropriate context clues will really need to be honed in on in order to determine the correct answer. For example, here is another passage from *Alice in Wonderland*:

> ... but when the Rabbit actually took a watch out of its waistcoat pocket, and looked at it, and then hurried on, Alice <u>started</u> to her feet, for it flashed across her mind that she had never before seen a rabbit with either a waistcoat-pocket or a watch to take out of it, and burning with curiosity, she ran across the field after it, and was just in time to see it pop down a large rabbit-hole under the hedge.

Q: As it is used in the passage, the word <u>started</u> means _____.
  a. to turn on
  b. to begin
  c. to move quickly
  d. to be surprised

All of these words qualify as a definition of *start*, but using context clues, the correct answer can be identified using one of the two techniques above. It's easy to see that one does not turn on, begin, or be

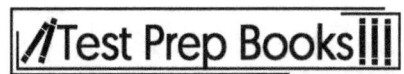

surprised to one's feet. The selection also states that she "ran across the field after it," indicating that she was in a hurry. Therefore, to move quickly would make the most sense in this context.

The same strategies can be applied to vocabulary that may be completely unfamiliar. In this case, focus on the words before or after the unknown word in order to determine its definition. Take this sentence, for example:

> Sam was such a <u>miser</u> that he forced Andrew to pay him twelve cents for the candy, even though he had a large inheritance and he knew his friend was poor.

Unlike with assertion questions, for vocabulary questions, it may be necessary to apply some critical thinking skills when something isn't explicitly stated within the passage. Think about the implications of the passage, or what the text is trying to say. With this example, it is important to realize that it is considered unusually stingy for a person to demand so little money from someone instead of just letting their friend have the candy, especially if this person is already wealthy. Hence, a <u>miser</u> is a greedy or stingy individual.

Questions about complex vocabulary may not be explicitly asked, but this is a useful skill to know. If there is an unfamiliar word while reading a passage and its definition goes unknown, it is possible to miss out on a critical message that could inhibit the ability to appropriately answer the questions. Practicing this technique in daily life will sharpen this ability to derive meanings from context clues with ease.

Writing: Essay Revision and Editing

Development
Leaving a few minutes at the end to revise and proofread offers an opportunity for writers to polish things up. Putting one's self in the reader's shoes and focusing on what the essay actually says helps writers identify problems—it's a movement from the mindset of writer to the mindset of editor. The goal is to have a clean, clear copy of the essay. The following areas should be considered when proofreading:

- Sentence fragments
- Awkward sentence structure
- Run-on sentences
- Incorrect word choice
- Grammatical agreement errors
- Spelling errors
- Punctuation errors
- Capitalization errors

Organization
Good writing is not merely a random collection of sentences. No matter how well written, sentences must relate and coordinate appropriately with one another. If not, the writing seems random, haphazard, and disorganized. Therefore, good writing must be organized, where each sentence fits a larger context and relates to the sentences around it.

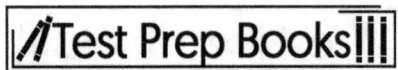

English Language Arts and Reading

Transition Words

The writer should act as a guide, showing the reader how all the sentences fit together. Consider the seat belt example again:

> Seat belts save more lives than any other automobile safety feature. Many studies show that airbags save lives as well. Not all cars have airbags. Many older cars don't. Air bags aren't entirely reliable. Studies show that in 15% of accidents, airbags don't deploy as designed. Seat belt malfunctions are extremely rare.

There's nothing wrong with any of these sentences individually, but together they're disjointed and difficult to follow. The best way for the writer to communicate information is through the use of transition words. Here are examples of transition words and phrases that tie sentences together, enabling a more natural flow:

- To show causality: *as a result*, *therefore*, and *consequently*
- To compare and contrast: *however*, *but*, and *on the other hand*
- To introduce examples: *for instance*, *namely*, and *including*
- To show order of importance: *foremost*, *primarily*, *secondly*, and *lastly*

NOTE: This is not a complete list of transitions. There are many more that can be used; however, most fit into these or similar categories. The important point is that the words should clearly show the relationship between sentences, supporting information, and the main idea.

Here is an update to the previous example using transition words. These changes make it easier to read and bring clarity to the writer's points:

> Seat belts save more lives than any other automobile safety feature. Many studies show that airbags save lives as well; however, not all cars have airbags. For instance, some older cars don't. Furthermore, air bags aren't entirely reliable. For example, studies show that in 15% of accidents, airbags don't deploy as designed, but, on the other hand, seat belt malfunctions are extremely rare.

Also be prepared to analyze whether the writer is using the best transition word or phrase for the situation. Take this sentence for example: "As a result, seat belt malfunctions are extremely rare." This sentence doesn't make sense in the context above because the writer is trying to show the contrast between seat belts and airbags, not the causality.

Logical Sequence

Even if the writer includes plenty of information to support their point, the writing is only coherent when the information is in a logical order. First, the writer should introduce the main idea, whether for a paragraph, a section, or the entire piece. Second, they should present evidence to support the main idea by using transitional language. This shows the reader how the information relates to the main idea and to the sentences around it. The writer should then take time to interpret the information, making sure necessary connections are obvious to the reader. Finally, the writer can summarize the information in a closing section.

Though most writing follows this pattern, it isn't a set rule. Sometimes writers change the order for effect. For example, the writer can begin with a surprising piece of supporting information to grab the reader's attention, and then transition to the main idea. Thus, if a passage doesn't follow the logical order, don't immediately assume it's wrong. However, most writing usually settles into a logical sequence after a nontraditional beginning.

Introductions and Conclusions
Examining the writer's strategies for introductions and conclusions puts the reader in the right mindset to interpret the rest of the text. Look for methods the writer might use for introductions such as:

- Stating the main point immediately, followed by outlining how the rest of the piece supports this claim.

- Establishing important, smaller pieces of the main idea first, and then grouping these points into a case for the main idea.

- Opening with a quotation, anecdote, question, seeming paradox, or other piece of interesting information, and then using it to lead to the main point.

Whatever method the writer chooses, the introduction should make their intention clear, establish their voice as a credible one, and encourage a person to continue reading.

Conclusions tend to follow a similar pattern. In them, the writer restates their main idea a final time, often after summarizing the smaller pieces of that idea. If the introduction uses a quote or anecdote to grab the reader's attention, the conclusion often makes reference to it again. Whatever way the writer chooses to arrange the conclusion, the final restatement of the main idea should be clear and simple for the reader to interpret. Finally, conclusions shouldn't introduce any new information.

Effective Language Use and Standard English Conventions

Precision
People often think of precision in terms of math, but precise word choice is another key to successful writing. Since language itself is imprecise, it's important for the writer to find the exact word or words to convey the full, intended meaning of a given situation. For example:

> The number of deaths has gone down since seat belt laws started.

There are several problems with this sentence. First, the word *deaths* is too general. From the context, it's assumed that the writer is referring only to deaths caused by car accidents. However, without clarification, the sentence lacks impact and is probably untrue. The phrase "gone down" might be accurate, but a more precise word could provide more information and greater accuracy. Did the numbers show a slow and steady decrease of highway fatalities or a sudden drop? If the latter is true, the writer is missing a chance to make their point more dramatically. Instead of "gone down" they could substitute *plummeted, fallen drastically*, or *rapidly diminished* to bring the information to life. Also, the phrase "seat belt laws" is unclear. Does it refer to laws requiring cars to include seat belts or to laws requiring drivers and passengers to use them? Finally, *started* is not a strong verb. Words like *enacted* or *adopted* are more direct and make the content more real. When put together, these changes create a far more powerful sentence:

> The number of highway fatalities has plummeted since laws requiring seat belt usage were enacted.

However, it's important to note that precise word choice can sometimes be taken too far. If the writer of the sentence above takes precision to an extreme, it might result in the following:

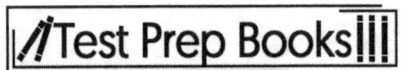

The incidence of high-speed, automobile accident related fatalities has decreased 75% and continued to remain at historical lows since the initial set of federal legislations requiring seat belt use were enacted in 1992.

This sentence is extremely precise, but it takes so long to achieve that precision that it suffers from a lack of clarity. Precise writing is about finding the right balance between information and flow. This is also an issue of conciseness (discussed in the next section).

The last thing to consider with precision is a word choice that's not only unclear or uninteresting, but also confusing or misleading. For example:

The number of highway fatalities has become hugely lower since laws requiring seat belt use were enacted.

In this case, the reader might be confused by the word *hugely*. Huge means large, but here the writer uses *hugely* to describe something small. Though most readers can decipher this, doing so disconnects them from the flow of the writing and makes the writer's point less effective.

Conciseness
"Less is more" is a good rule to follow when writing a sentence. Unfortunately, writers often include extra words and phrases that seem necessary at the time, but add nothing to the main idea. This confuses the reader and creates unnecessary repetition. Writing that lacks conciseness is usually guilty of excessive wordiness and redundant phrases. Here's an example containing both of these issues:

> When legislators decided to begin creating legislation making it mandatory for automobile drivers and passengers to make use of seat belts while in cars, a large number of them made those laws for reasons that were political reasons.

There are several empty or "fluff" words here that take up too much space. These can be eliminated while still maintaining the writer's meaning. For example:

- "Decided to begin" could be shortened to "began"
- "Making it mandatory for" could be shortened to "requiring"
- "Make use of" could be shortened to "use"
- "A large number" could be shortened to "many"

In addition, there are several examples of redundancy that can be eliminated:

- "Legislators decided to begin creating legislation" and "made those laws"
- "Automobile drivers and passengers" and "while in cars"
- "Reasons that were political reasons"

These changes are incorporated as follows:

> When legislators began requiring drivers and passengers to use seat belts, many of them did so for political reasons.

There are many general examples of redundant phrases, such as "add an additional," "complete and total," "time schedule," and "transportation vehicle." If asked to identify a redundant phrase on the test, look for words that are close together with the same (or similar) meanings.

English Language Arts and Reading

Writing: Sentence Revision, Editing, and Completion

Conventions of Grammar and Usage

The English language has eight parts of speech, each serving a different grammatical function.

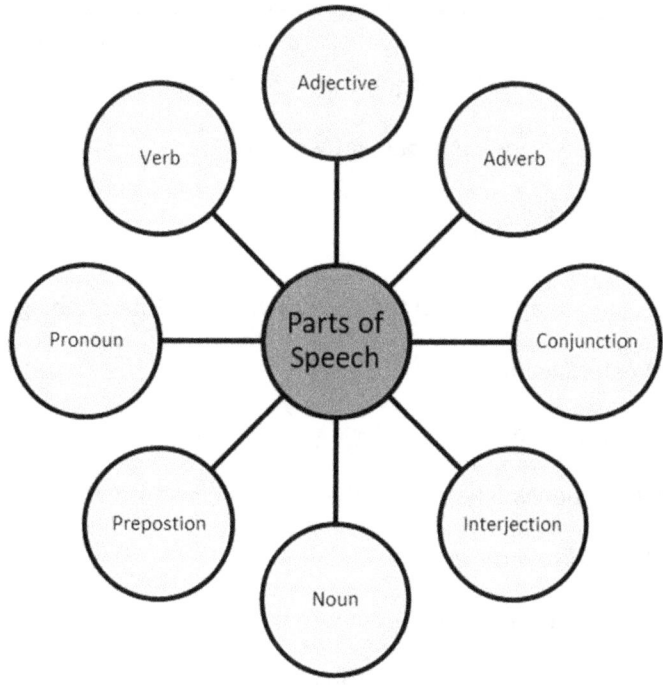

Verbs

A **verb** is the part of speech that describes an action, state of being, or occurrence.

A verb forms the main part of a predicate of a sentence. This means that the verb explains what the noun (which will be discussed shortly) is doing. A simple example is *time flies*. The verb *flies* explains what the action of the noun, *time*, is doing. This example is a *main* verb.

Helping (auxiliary) verbs are words like *have, do, be, can, may, should, must,* and *will*. "I *should* go to the store." Helping verbs assist main verbs in expressing tense, ability, possibility, permission, or obligation.

Particles are minor function words like *not, in, out, up,* or *down* that become part of the verb itself. "I might *not*."

Participles are words formed from verbs that are often used to modify a noun, noun phrase, verb, or verb phrase.

The *running* teenager collided with the cyclist.

Participles can also create compound verb forms.

He is *speaking*.

Verbs have five basic forms: the **base** form, the **-s** form, the **-ing** form, the **past** form, and the **past participle** form.

77

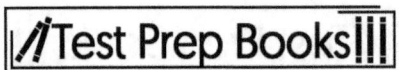

The past forms are either **regular** (*love/loved; hate/hated*) or **irregular** because they don't end by adding the common past tense suffix "-ed" (*go/went; fall/fell; set/set*).

Verb Forms

Shifting verb forms entails **conjugation,** which is used to indicate tense, voice, or mood.

Verb tense is used to show when the action in the sentence took place. There are several different verb tenses, and it is important to know how and when to use them. Some verb tenses can be achieved by changing the form of the verb, while others require the use of helping verbs (e.g., *is, was,* or *has*).

Present tense shows the action is happening currently or is ongoing:

> I walk to work every morning.

> She is stressed about the deadline.

Past tense shows that the action happened in the past or that the state of being is in the past:

> I walked to work yesterday morning.

> She was stressed about the deadline.

Future tense shows that the action will happen in the future or is a future state of being:

> I will walk to work tomorrow morning.

> She will be stressed about the deadline.

Present perfect tense shows action that began in the past, but continues into the present:

> I have walked to work all week.

> She has been stressed about the deadline.

Past perfect tense shows an action was finished before another took place:

> I had walked all week until I sprained my ankle.

> She had been stressed about the deadline until we talked about it.

Future perfect tense shows an action that will be completed at some point in the future:

> By the time the bus arrives, I will have walked to work already.

Voice

Verbs can be in the active or passive voice. When the subject completes the action, the verb is in **active voice.** When the subject receives the action of the sentence, the verb is in **passive voice.**

> Active: Jamie ate the ice cream.

> Passive: The ice cream was eaten by Jamie.

In active voice, the subject (*Jamie*) is the "do-er" of the action (*ate*). In passive voice, the subject *ice cream* receives the action of being eaten.

While passive voice can add variety to writing, active voice is the generally preferred sentence structure.

Nouns

A **noun** is a person, place, thing, or idea. All nouns fit into one of two types, common or proper.

A **common noun** is a word that identifies any of a class of people, places, or things. Examples include numbers, objects, animals, feelings, concepts, qualities, and actions. *A, an,* or *the* usually precedes the common noun. These parts of speech are called *articles*. Here are some examples of sentences using nouns preceded by articles.

A building is under construction.
The girl would like to move to *the* city.

A **proper noun** (also called a **proper name**) is used for the specific name of an individual person, place, or organization. The first letter in a proper noun is capitalized. "My name is *Mary*." "I work for *Walmart*."

Nouns sometimes serve as adjectives (which themselves describe nouns), such as "hockey player" and "state government."

An **abstract noun** is an idea, state, or quality. It is something that can't be touched, such as happiness, courage, evil, or humor.

A **concrete noun** is something that can be experienced through the senses (touch, taste, hear, smell, see). Examples of concrete nouns are birds, skateboard, pie, and car.

A **collective noun** refers to a collection of people, places, or things that act as one. Examples of collective nouns are as follows: team, class, jury, family, audience, and flock.

Pronoun

A word used in place of a noun is known as a **pronoun**. Pronouns are words like *I, mine, hers,* and *us*.

Pronouns can be split into different classifications (see below) which make them easier to learn; however, it's not important to memorize the classifications.

- **Personal pronouns**: refer to people, places, things, etc.

- **First person**: we, I, our, mine

- **Second person**: you, yours

- **Third person**: he, them

- **Possessive pronouns**: demonstrate ownership (mine, his, hers, its, ours, theirs, yours)

- **Interrogative pronouns**: ask questions (what, which, who, whom, whose)

- **Relative pronouns**: include the five interrogative pronouns and others that are relative (whoever, whomever, that, when, where)

- **Demonstrative pronouns**: replace something specific (this, that, those, these)

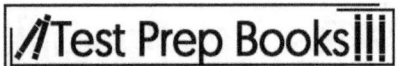

- **Reciprocal pronouns**: indicate something was done or given in return (each other, one another)
- **Indefinite pronouns**: have a nonspecific status (anybody, whoever, someone, everybody, somebody)

Indefinite pronouns such as *anybody, whoever, someone, everybody*, and *somebody* command a singular verb form, but others such as *all, none,* and *some* could require a singular or plural verb form.

An **antecedent** is the noun to which a pronoun refers; it needs to be written or spoken before the pronoun is used. For many pronouns, antecedents are imperative for clarity. In particular, many of the personal, possessive, and demonstrative pronouns need antecedents. Otherwise, it would be unclear who or what someone is referring to when they use a pronoun like *he* or *this*.

Pronoun reference means that the pronoun should refer clearly to one, clear, unmistakable noun (the antecedent).

Pronoun-antecedent agreement refers to the need for the antecedent and the corresponding pronoun to agree in gender, person, and number. Here are some examples:

The *kidneys* (plural antecedent) are part of the urinary system. *They* (plural pronoun) serve several roles.

The kidneys are part of the *urinary system* (singular antecedent). *It* (singular pronoun) is also known as the renal system.

The **subjective pronouns** —*I, you, he/she/it, we, they,* and *who*—are the subjects of the sentence.

Example: *They* have a new house.

The **objective pronouns**—*me, you* (*singular*)*, him/her, us, them,* and *whom*—are used when something is being done for or given to someone; they are objects of the action.

Example: The teacher has an apple for *us*.

The **possessive pronouns**—*mine, my, your, yours, his, hers, its, their, theirs, our,* and *ours*—are used to denote that something (or someone) belongs to someone (or something).

Example: It's *their* chocolate cake.

Even Better Example: It's *my* chocolate cake!

One of the greatest challenges and worst abuses of pronouns concerns *who* and *whom*. Just knowing the following rule can eliminate confusion. *Who* is a subjective-case pronoun used only as a subject or subject complement. *Whom* is only objective-case and, therefore, the object of the verb or preposition.

Who is going to the concert?

You are going to the concert with *whom*?

Hint: When using *who* or *whom*, think of whether someone would say *he* or *him*. If the answer is *he*, use *who*. If the answer is *him*, use *whom*. This trick is easy to remember because *he* and *who* both end in vowels, and *him* and *whom* both end in the letter *M*.

Adjective

Adjectives are words used to modify nouns and pronouns. They can be used alone or in a series and are used to further define or describe the nouns they modify.

> Mark made us a delicious, four-course meal.

The words *delicious* and *four-course* are adjectives that describe the kind of meal Mark made.

Articles are also considered adjectives because they help to describe nouns. Articles can be general or specific. The three articles in English are: a, an, and the.

Indefinite articles *(a, an)* are used to refer to nonspecific nouns. The article *a* proceeds words beginning with consonant sounds, and the article *an* proceeds words beginning with vowel sounds.

> A car drove by our house.

> An alligator was loose at the zoo.

> He has always wanted a ukulele. (The first *u* makes a *y* sound.)

Note that *a* and *an* should only proceed nonspecific nouns that are also singular. If a nonspecific noun is plural, it does not need a preceding article.

> Alligators were loose at the zoo.

The **definite article** *(the)* is used to refer to specific nouns:

> The car pulled into our driveway.

Note that *the* should proceed all specific nouns regardless of whether they are singular or plural.

> The cars pulled into our driveway.

Comparative adjectives are used to compare nouns. When they are used in this way, they take on positive, comparative, or superlative form.

> The **positive form** is the normal form of the adjective:
>
>> Alicia is tall.
>
> The **comparative form** shows a comparison between two things:
>
>> Alicia is taller than Maria.
>
> **Superlative form** shows comparison between more than two things:
>
>> Alicia is the tallest girl in her class.

Usually, the comparative and superlative can be made by adding *–er* and *–est* to the positive form, but some verbs call for the helping verbs *more* or *most*. Other exceptions to the rule include adjectives like *bad*, which uses the comparative *worse* and the superlative *worst*.

An **adjective phrase** is not a bunch of adjectives strung together, but a group of words that describes a noun or pronoun and, thus, functions as an adjective. Very happy is an adjective phrase; so are way too hungry and passionate about traveling.

Adverbs

Adverbs have more functions than adjectives because they modify or qualify verbs, adjectives, or other adverbs as well as word groups that express a relation of place, time, circumstance, or cause. Therefore, adverbs answer any of the following questions: *How, when, where, why, in what way, how often, how much, in what condition,* and/or *to what degree. How good looking is he? He is <u>very</u> handsome.*

Here are some examples of adverbs for different situations:

- how: quickly
- when: daily
- where: there
- in what way: easily
- how often: often
- how much: much
- in what condition: badly
- what degree: hardly

As one can see, for some reason, many adverbs end in *-ly*.

Adverbs do things like emphasize (*really, simply,* and *so*), amplify (*heartily, completely,* and *positively*), and tone down (*almost, somewhat,* and *mildly*).

Adverbs also come in phrases.

The dog ran as <u>though his life depended on it</u>.

Preposition

Prepositions are connecting words and, while there are only about 150 of them, they are used more often than any other individual groups of words. They describe relationships between other words. They are placed before a noun or pronoun, forming a phrase that modifies another word in the sentence. **Prepositional phrases** begin with a preposition and end with a noun or pronoun, the **object of the preposition.** *A pristine lake is <u>near the store</u> and <u>behind the bank</u>.*

Some commonly used prepositions are *about, after, anti, around, as, at, behind, beside, by, for, from, in, into, of, off, on, to,* and *with.*

Complex prepositions, which also come before a noun or pronoun, consist of two or three words such as *according to, in regards to,* and *because of.*

Prepositions show the relationship between different elements in a phrase or sentence and connect nouns or pronouns to other words in the sentence. Some examples of prepositions are words such as *after, at, behind, by, during, from, in, on, to,* and *with.*

Let's go to class.

Starry Night was painted by Vincent van Gogh in 1889.

English Language Arts and Reading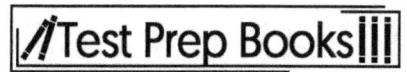

Conjunctions

Conjunctions are vital words that connect words, phrases, thoughts, and ideas. Conjunctions show relationships between components. There are two types:

Coordinating conjunctions are the primary class of conjunctions placed between words, phrases, clauses, and sentences that are of equal grammatical rank; the coordinating conjunctions are *for*, *and*, *nor*, *but*, *or*, *yet*, and *so*. A useful memorization trick is to remember that the first letter of these conjunctions collectively spell the word *fanboys*.

> I need to go shopping, *but* I must be careful to leave enough money in the bank.
> She wore a black, red, *and* white shirt.

Subordinating conjunctions are the secondary class of conjunctions. They connect two unequal parts, one **main** (or **independent**) and the other **subordinate** (or **dependent**). I must go to the store *even though* I do not have enough money in the bank.

> *Because* I read the review, I do not want to go to the movie.

Notice that the presence of subordinating conjunctions makes clauses dependent. *I read the review* is an independent clause, but *because* makes the clause dependent. Thus, it needs an independent clause to complete the sentence.

Interjection

Interjections are words used to express emotion. Examples include *wow*, *ouch*, and *hooray*. Interjections are often separate from sentences; in those cases, the interjection is directly followed by an exclamation point. In other cases, the interjection is included in a sentence and followed by a comma. The punctuation plays a big role in the intensity of the emotion that the interjection is expressing. Using a comma or semicolon indicates less excitement than using an exclamation mark.

> *Wow*! Look at that sunset!

> Was it your birthday yesterday? *Oops*! I forgot.

Agreement in Number

Subjects and verbs must agree in number. If a sentence has a singular subject, then it must use a singular verb. If there is a plural subject, then it must use a plural verb.

Singular Noun	Singular Verb	Plural Noun	Plural verb
Man	has	men	have
child	plays	children	play
basketball	bounces	basketballs	bounce

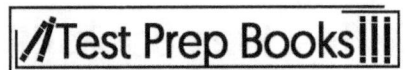

Agreement in Person

Verbs must also agree in person. A subject that uses first person must include a verb that is also in first person. The same is true for second and third person subjects and verbs.

	Noun	Verb
First person	I	am
Second person	you	are
Third person	she	is

Common Agreement Errors

Compound Subjects

Compound subjects are when two or more subjects are joined by a coordinating conjunction, such as *and*, *or*, *neither*, or *nor*. Errors in agreement sometimes occur when there is a compound subject:

Incorrect: Mike and I am in a meeting this morning.

Correct: Mike and I are in a meeting this morning.

A compound subject always uses the plural form of the verb to match with the plural subject. In the above example, readers can substitute "Mike and I" for "we" to make it easier to determine the verb: "We *are* in a meeting this morning."

Separation of Subject and Verb

Errors sometimes occur when the subject is separated from the verb by a prepositional phrase or parenthetical element:

Incorrect: The objective of the teachers are to help students learn.

Correct: The objective of the teachers is to help students learn.

The verb must agree with the singular subject *objective*, not the word *teachers*, which is the object of the preposition *of* and does not influence the subject. An easy way to determine if the subject and verb agree is to take out the middle preposition: "The objective *is* to help students learn."

Indefinite Pronouns

Indefinite pronouns refer to people or groups in a general way: *each, anyone, none, all, either, neither,* and *everyone*. Some indefinite pronouns are always singular, such as *each, everyone, someone,* and *everybody*, which affects verb choice:

Incorrect: Each of them are competing in the race.

Correct: Each of them is competing in the race.

While the word *them* can indicate that a plural verb is needed, the subject *each* is singular regardless of what it refers to, requiring the singular verb, *is*.

Other indefinite pronouns can be singular or plural, depending on what they are referring to, such as *anyone, all,* and *some.*

Some of the orders are scheduled to arrive today.

Some refers to *orders*, which is plural, so the plural verb (*are*) is needed.

> Some of the cake is left on the dining room table.

Some refers to *cake*, which is singular, so the singular verb (*is*) is needed.

Subjects Joined by Or and Nor

Compound subjects joined by *or* or *nor* rely on the subject nearest to the verb to determine conjugation and agreement:

> Neither Ben nor Jeff was in attendance at the conference.

> Pink or purple is the bride's color choice.

In each example, the subjects are both singular, so the verb should be singular.

If one subject is singular and the other plural, the subject nearest to the verb is the one that needs to agree:

> Either the shirt or pants are hanging on the clothesline.

In this example there is a singular subject (*shirt*) and a plural subject (*pants*), so the verb (*are*) should agree with the subject nearest to it (*pants*).

Collective Nouns

Collective nouns can use a singular or plural verb depending on their function in the sentence. If the collective noun is acting as a unit, then a singular verb is needed. Otherwise, it's necessary to use a plural verb.

> The staff is required to meet every third Friday of the month.

The *staff* is meeting as a collective unit, so a singular verb is needed.

> The staff are getting in their cars to go home.

The staff get into their cars separately, so a plural verb is needed.

Plural Nouns with Singular Meaning

Certain nouns end in *s*, like a plural noun, but have singular meaning, such as *mathematics, news,* and *civics*. These nouns should use a singular verb.

> The news is on at 8:00 tonight.

Nouns that are single things, but have two parts, are considered plural and should use a plural verb, such as *scissors, pants,* and *tweezers*.

> My favorite pants are in the washing machine.

There Is and There Are

There cannot be a subject, so verb agreement should be based on a word that comes after the verb.

> There is a hole in the road.

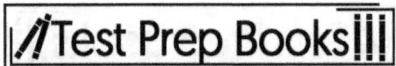

The subject in this sentence is *hole*, which is singular, so the verb should be singular (*is*).

There are kids playing kickball in the street.

The subject in this sentence is *kids*, which is plural, so the verb should be plural (*are*).

Verb Tense
Shifting verb forms entails conjugation, which is used to indicate tense, voice, or mood.

Verb tense is used to show when the action in the sentence took place. There are several different verb tenses, and it is important to know how and when to use them. Some verb tenses can be achieved by changing the form of the verb, while others require the use of helping verbs (e.g., *is, was,* or *has*).

- **Present tense** shows the action is happening currently or is ongoing:

    I walk to work every morning.

    She is stressed about the deadline.

- **Past tense** shows that the action happened in the past or that the state of being is in the past:

    I walked to work yesterday morning.

    She was stressed about the deadline.

- **Future tense** shows that the action will happen in the future or is a future state of being:

    I will walk to work tomorrow morning.

    She will be stressed about the deadline.

- **Present perfect tense** shows action that began in the past, but continues into the present:

    I have walked to work all week.

    She has been stressed about the deadline.

- **Past perfect tense** shows an action was finished before another took place:

    I had walked all week until I sprained my ankle.

    She had been stressed about the deadline until we talked about it.

- **Future perfect tense** shows an action that will be completed at some point in the future:

    By the time the bus arrives, I will have walked to work already.

Sentence Structure
Sentence Types
There are four ways in which we can structure sentences: simple, compound, complex, and compound-complex. Sentences can be composed of just one clause or many clauses joined together.

When a sentence is composed of just one clause (an independent clause), we call it a simple sentence. Simple sentences do not necessarily have to be short sentences. They just require one independent clause with a subject and a predicate. For example:

Thomas marched over to Andrew's house.

Jonah and Mary constructed a simplified version of the Eiffel Tower with Legos.

When a sentence has two or more independent clauses we call it a compound sentence. The clauses are connected by a comma and a coordinating conjunction—*and, but, or, nor, for*—or by a semicolon. Compound sentences do not have dependent clauses. For example:

We went to the fireworks stand, and we bought enough fireworks to last all night.

The children sat on the grass, and then we lit the fireworks one at a time.

When a sentence has just one independent clause and includes one or more dependent clauses, we call it a complex sentence:

Because she slept well and drank coffee, Sarah was quite productive at work.

Although Will had coffee, he made mistakes while using the photocopier.

When a sentence has two or more independent clauses and at least one dependent clause, we call it a compound-complex sentence:

It may come as a surprise, but I found the tickets, and you can go to the show.

Jade is the girl who dove from the high-dive, and she stunned the audience silent.

Sentence Fragments

Remember, a **complete sentence** must have both a subject and a verb. Complete sentences consist of at least one independent clause. Incomplete sentences are called **sentence fragments**. A sentence fragment is a common error in writing. Sentence fragments can be independent clauses that start with subordinating words, such as *but, as, so that,* or *because,* or they could simply be missing a subject or verb.

A fragment error can be corrected by adding the fragment to a nearby sentence or by adding or removing words to make it an independent clause. For example:

Dogs are my favorite animals. Because cats are too independent. (Incorrect; the word because creates a sentence fragment)

Dogs are my favorite animals because cats are too independent. (Correct; the fragment becomes a dependent clause.)

Dogs are my favorite animals. Cats are too independent. (Correct; the fragment becomes a simple sentence.)

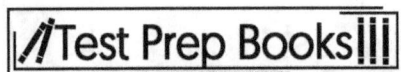

Run-on Sentences

Another common mistake in writing is the run-on sentence. A **run-on** is created when two or more independent clauses are joined without the use of a conjunction, a semicolon, a colon, or a dash. We don't want to use commas where periods belong. Here is an example of a run-on sentence:

Making wedding cakes can take many hours I am very impatient, I want to see them completed right away.

There are a variety of ways to correct a run-on sentence. The method you choose will depend on the context of the sentence and how it fits with neighboring sentences:

Making wedding cakes can take many hours. I am very impatient. I want to see them completed right away. (Use periods to create more than one sentence.)

Making wedding cakes can take many hours; I am very impatient—I want to see them completed right away. (Correct the sentence using a semicolon, colon, or dash.)

Making wedding cakes can take many hours and I am very impatient, so I want to see them completed right away. (Correct the sentence using coordinating conjunctions.)

I am very impatient because I would rather see completed wedding cakes right away than wait for it to take many hours. (Correct the sentence by revising.)

Dangling and Misplaced Modifiers

A **modifier** is a word or phrase meant to describe or clarify another word in the sentence. When a sentence has a modifier but is missing the word it describes or clarifies, it's an error called a **dangling modifier**. We can fix the sentence by revising to include the word that is being modified. Consider the following examples with the modifier italicized:

Having walked five miles, this bench will be the place to rest. (Incorrect; this version of the sentence implies that the bench walked the miles, not the person.)

Having walked five miles, Matt will rest on this bench. (Correct; in this version, *having walked five miles* correctly modifies *Matt*, who did the walking.)

Since midnight, my dreams have been pleasant and comforting. (Incorrect; in this version, the adverb clause *since midnight* cannot modify the noun *dreams*.)

Since midnight, I have had pleasant and comforting dreams. (Correct; in this version, *since midnight* modifies the verb *have had*, telling us when the dreams occurred.)

Sometimes the modifier is not located close enough to the word it modifies for the sentence to be clearly understood. In this case, we call the error a **misplaced modifier**. Here is an example with the modifier italicized and the modified word in underlined.

We gave the hot <u>cocoa</u> to the children *that was filled with marshmallows.* (Incorrect; this sentence implies that the children are what are filled with marshmallows.)

We gave the hot <u>*cocoa*</u> *that was filled with marshmallows* to the children. (Correct; here, the cocoa is filled with marshmallows. The modifier is near the word it modifies.)

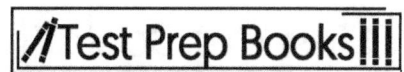

Parallelism and Subordination
Parallelism
To be grammatically correct we must use articles, prepositions, infinitives, and introductory words for dependent clauses consistently throughout a sentence. This is called **parallelism**. We use parallelism when we are matching parts of speech, phrases, or clauses with another part of the sentence. Being inconsistent creates confusion. Consider the following example.

Incorrect: Be ready for running and to ride a bike during the triathlon.

Correct: Be ready to run and to ride a bike during the triathlon.

Correct: Be ready for running and for riding a bike during the triathlon.

In the incorrect example, the gerund *running* does not match with the infinitive *to ride*. Either both should be infinitives or both should be gerunds.

Subordination
Sometimes we have unequal pieces of information in a sentence where one piece is more important than the other. We need to show that one piece of information is subordinate to the other. We can make the more important piece an independent clause and connect the other piece by making it a dependent clause. Consider this example:

Central thought: Kittens can always find their mother.

Subordinate: Kittens are blind at birth.

Complex Sentence: Despite being blind at birth, kittens can always find their mother.

The sentence "Kittens are blind at birth" is made subordinate to the sentence "Kittens can always find their mother" by placing the word "Despite" at the beginning and removing the subject, thus turning an independent clause ("kittens are blind at birth") into a subordinate phrase ("Despite being blind at birth").

Sentence Logic
Clauses
Clauses are groups of words within a sentence that have both a subject and a verb. We can distinguish a clause from a phrase because phrases do not have both a subject and a verb. There are several types of clauses; clauses can be independent or dependent and can serve as a noun, an adjective, or an adverb.

An **independent clause** could stand alone as its own sentence if the rest of the sentence were not there. For example:

The party is on Tuesday after the volleyball game is over.

I am excited to go to the party because my best friend will be there.

A **dependent clause**, or subordinating clause, is the part of the sentence that gives supportive information but cannot create a proper sentence by itself. However, it will still have both a subject and a verb; otherwise, it is a phrase. In the example above, *after the volleyball game is over* and *because my*

best friend will be there are dependent because they begin with the conjunctions *after* and *because*, and a proper sentence does not begin with a conjunction.

Noun clauses are groups of words that collectively form a noun. Look for the opening words *whether, which, what, that, who, how,* or *why.* For example:

I had fun cooking *what we had for dinner last night.*

I'm going to track down *whoever ate my sandwich.*

Adjective clauses collectively form an adjective that modifies a noun or pronoun in the sentence. If you can remove the adjective clause and the leftovers create a standalone sentence, then the clause should be set off with commas, parentheses, or dashes. If you can remove the clause it is called nonrestrictive. If it can't be removed without ruining the sentence, then it is called restrictive and does not get set off with commas.

Jenna, *who hates to get wet,* fell into the pool. (Nonrestrictive)

The girl *who hates to get wet* fell into the pool. (Restrictive; the clause tells us which girl, and if removed there is confusion)

Adverbial clauses serve as an adverb in the sentence, modifying a verb, adjective, or other adverb. Look for the opening words *after, before, as, as if, although, because, if, since, so, so that, when, where, while,* or *unless.*

She lost her wallet after she left the theme park.

Her earring fell through the crack before she could catch it.

Phrases

A **phrase** is a group of words that go together but do not include both a subject and a verb. They are used to add information, explain something, or make the sentence easier for the reader to understand. Unlike clauses, phrases can never stand alone as their own sentence. They do not form complete thoughts. There are noun phrases, prepositional phrases, verbal phrases, appositive phrases, and absolute phrases. Let's look at each of these.

Noun phrases: A noun phrase is a group of words built around a noun or pronoun that serves as a unit to form a noun in the sentence. Consider the following examples. The phrase is built around the underlined word. The entire phrase can be replaced by a noun or pronoun to test whether or not it is a noun phrase.

I like the chocolate chip ice cream. (I like it.)

I know all the shortest routes. (I know them.)

I met the best supporting actress. (I met her.)

English Language Arts and Reading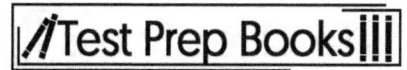

Prepositional phrases: These are phrases that begin with a preposition and end with a noun or pronoun. We use them as a unit to form the adjective or adverb in the sentence. Prepositional phrases that introduce a sentence are called introductory prepositional phrases and are set off with commas.

I found the Frisbee *on the roof peak.* (Adverb; where it was found)

The girl *with the bright red hair* was prom queen. (Adjective; which girl)

Before the sequel, we wanted to watch the first movie. (Introductory phrase)

Verbal phrases: Some phrases look like verbs but do not serve as the verb in the sentence. These are called verbal phrases. There are three types: participial phrases, gerund phrases, and infinitive phrases.

Participial phrases start with a participle and modify nouns or pronouns; therefore, they act as the adjective in the sentence.

Beaten by the sun, we searched for shade to sit in. (Modifies the pronoun *we*)

The hikers, *being eaten by mosquitoes,* longed for repellant. (Modifies the noun *hikers*)

Gerund phrases often look like participles because they end in *-ing*, but they serve as the noun, not the adjective, in the sentence. Like any noun, we can use them as the subject or as the object of a verb or preposition in the sentence.

Eating green salad is the best way to lose weight. (Subject)

Sumo wrestlers are famous for *eating large quantities of food.* (Object)

Infinitive phrases often look like verbs because they start with the word *to,* but they serve as an adjective, adverb, or noun.

To survive the chill is the goal of the Polar Bear Plunge. (Noun)

A hot tub is at the scene *to warm up after the jump.* (Adverb)

The jumpers have hot cocoa *to drink right away.* (Adjective)

Appositive phrases: We can use any of the above types of phrases to rename nouns or pronouns, and we call this an appositive phrase. Appositive phrases usually appear either just before or just after the noun or pronoun they are renaming. Appositive phrases are essential when the noun or pronoun is too general, and they are nonessential when they just add information.

The two famous brothers Orville and Wilbur Wright invented the airplane. (Essential)

Sarah Calysta, *my great grandmother,* is my namesake. (Nonessential)

Absolute phrases: When a participle comes after a noun and forms a phrase that is not otherwise part of the sentence, it's called an absolute phrase. Absolute phrases are not complete thoughts and cannot stand alone because they do not have a subject and a verb. They are not essential to the sentence in that they do not explain or add additional meaning to any other part of the sentence.

The engine roaring, Jada closed her eyes and waited for the plane to take off.

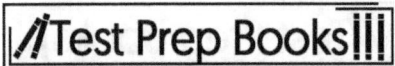

English Language Arts and Reading

The microphone crackling, the flight attendant announced the delayed arrival.

Conventions of Punctuation

End Punctuation

Periods (.) are used to end a sentence that is a statement (**declarative**) or a command (**imperative**). They should not be used in a sentence that asks a question or is an exclamation. Periods are also used in abbreviations, which are shortened versions of words.

- Declarative: The boys refused to go to sleep.
- Imperative: Walk down to the bus stop.
- Abbreviations: Joan Roberts, M.D., Apple Inc., Mrs. Adamson
- If a sentence ends with an abbreviation, it is inappropriate to use two periods. It should end with a single period after the abbreviation.

  The chef gathered the ingredients for the pie, which included apples, flour, sugar, etc.

Question marks *(?)* are used with direct questions (**interrogative**). An **indirect question** can use a period:

  Interrogative: When does the next bus arrive?

  Indirect Question: I wonder when the next bus arrives.

An **exclamation point** *(!)* is used to show strong emotion or can be used as an interjection. This punctuation should be used sparingly in formal writing situations.

  What an amazing shot!

  Whoa!

Commas

A **comma** (,) is the punctuation mark that signifies a pause—breath—between parts of a sentence. It denotes a break of flow. Proper comma usage helps readers understand the writer's intended emphasis of ideas.

In a complex sentence—one that contains a **subordinate** (dependent) clause or clauses—the use of a comma is dictated by where the subordinate clause is located. If the subordinate clause is located before the main clause, a comma is needed between the two clauses.

  I will not pay for the steak, *because I don't have that much money.*

Generally, if the subordinate clause is placed after the main clause, no punctuation is needed.

  I did well on my exam because I studied two hours the night before.

Notice how the last clause is dependent because it requires the earlier independent clauses to make sense.

Use a comma on both sides of an interrupting phrase.

> I will pay for the ice cream, *chocolate and vanilla*, and then will eat it all myself.

The words forming the phrase in italics are nonessential (extra) information. To determine if a phrase is nonessential, try reading the sentence without the phrase and see if it's still coherent.

A comma is not necessary in this next sentence because no interruption—nonessential or extra information—has occurred. Read sentences aloud when uncertain.

I will pay for his chocolate and vanilla ice cream and then will eat it all myself.

If the nonessential phrase comes at the beginning of a sentence, a comma should only go at the end of the phrase. If the phrase comes at the end of a sentence, a comma should only go at the beginning of the phrase.

Other types of interruptions include the following:

- interjections: Oh no, I am not going.
- abbreviations: Barry Potter, M.D., specializes in heart disorders.
- direct addresses: Yes, Claudia, I am tired and going to bed.
- parenthetical phrases: His wife, lovely as she was, was not helpful.
- transitional phrases: Also, it is not possible.

The second comma in the following sentence is called an **Oxford comma**.

> I will pay for ice cream, syrup, and pop.

It is a comma used after the second-to-last item in a series of three or more items. It comes before the word *or* or *and*. Not everyone uses the Oxford comma; it is optional, but many believe it is needed. The comma functions as a tool to reduce confusion in writing. So, if omitting the Oxford comma would cause confusion, then it's best to include it.

Commas are used in math to mark the place of thousands in numerals, breaking them up so they are easier to read. Other uses for commas are in dates (*March 19, 2016*), letter greetings (*Dear Sally,*), and in between cities and states (*Louisville, KY*).

Semicolons

A **semicolon** *(;)* is used to connect ideas in a sentence in some way. There are three main ways to use semicolons.

Link two independent clauses without the use of a coordinating conjunction:

> I was late for work again; I'm definitely going to get fired.

Link two independent clauses with a transitional word:

> The songs were all easy to play; therefore, he didn't need to spend too much time practicing.

Between items in a series that are already separated by commas or if necessary to separate lengthy items in a list:

> Starbucks has locations in Media, PA; Swarthmore, PA; and Morton, PA.

> Several classroom management issues presented in the study: the advent of a poor teacher persona in the context of voice, dress, and style; teacher follow-through from the beginning of the school year to the end; and the depth of administrative support, including ISS and OSS protocol.

Colons

A **colon** (:) is used after an independent clause to present an explanation or draw attention to what comes next in the sentence. There are several uses.

Explanations of ideas:

> They soon learned the hardest part about having a new baby: sleep deprivation.

Lists of items:

> Shari picked up all the supplies she would need for the party: cups, plates, napkins, balloons, streamers, and party favors.

Time, subtitles, general salutations:

> The time is 7:15.

> I read a book entitled *Pluto: A Planet No More*.

> To whom it may concern:

Parentheses and Dashes

Parentheses are half-round brackets that look like this: ( ). They set off a word, phrase, or sentence that is an afterthought, explanation, or side note relevant to the surrounding text but not essential. A pair of commas is often used to set off this sort of information, but parentheses are generally used for information that would not fit well within a sentence or that the writer deems not important enough to be structurally part of the sentence.

> The picture of the heart (see above) shows the major parts you should memorize.
> Mount Everest is one of three mountains in the world that are over 28,000 feet high (K2 and Kanchenjunga are the other two).

See how the sentences above are complete without the parenthetical statements? In the first example, *see above* would not have fit well within the flow of the sentence. The second parenthetical statement could have been a separate sentence, but the writer deemed the information not pertinent to the topic.

The **em-dash** (—) is a mark longer than a hyphen used as a punctuation mark in sentences and to set apart a relevant thought. Even after plucking out the line separated by the dash marks, the sentence will be intact and make sense.

> Looking out the airplane window at the landmarks—Lake Clarke, Thompson Community College, and the bridge—she couldn't help but feel excited to be home.

The dashes use is similar to that of parentheses or a pair of commas. So, what's the difference? Many believe that using dashes makes the clause within them stand out while using parentheses is subtler. It's advised to not use dashes when commas could be used instead.

Ellipses

An **ellipsis** (...) is used to show that there is more to the quoted text than is necessary for the current discussion. Writers use them in place of words, lines, phrases, list content, or paragraphs that might just as easily have been omitted from a passage of writing. This can be done to save space or to focus only on the specifically relevant material.

> Exercise is good for some unexpected reasons. Watkins writes, "Exercise has many benefits such as...reducing cancer risk."

In the example above, the ellipsis takes the place of the other benefits of exercise that are more expected.

The ellipsis may also be used to show a pause in sentence flow.

> "I'm wondering...how this could happen," Dylan said in a soft voice.

Quotation Marks

Double **quotation marks** are used at the beginning and end of a direct quote. They are also used with certain titles and to indicate that a term being used is slang or referenced in the sentence. Quotation marks should not be used with an indirect quote. Single quotation marks are used to indicate a quote within a quote.

> Direct quote: "The weather is supposed to be beautiful this week," she said.

> Indirect quote: One of the customers asked if the sale prices were still in effect.

> Quote within a quote: "My little boy just said 'Mama, I want cookie,'" Maria shared.

Titles: Quotation marks should also be used to indicate titles of short works or sections of larger works, such as chapter titles. Other works that use quotation marks include poems, short stories, newspaper articles, magazine articles, web page titles, and songs.

> "The Road Not Taken" is my favorite poem by Robert Frost.

> "What a Wonderful World" is one of my favorite songs.

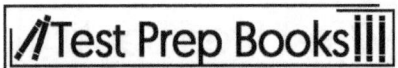

English Language Arts and Reading

Specific or emphasized terms: Quotation marks can also be used to indicate a technical term or to set off a word that is being discussed in a sentence. Quotation marks can also indicate sarcasm.

The new step, called "levigation," is a very difficult technique.

He said he was "hungry" multiple times, but he only ate two bites.

Use with other punctuation: The use of quotation marks with other punctuation varies, depending on the role of the ending or separating punctuation.

In American English, commas and periods go inside quotation marks:

"This is the last time you are allowed to leave early," his boss stated.

The newscaster said, "We have some breaking news to report."

Question marks or exclamation points go inside the quotation marks when they are part of a direct quote:

The doctor shouted, "Get the crash cart!"

When the question mark or exclamation point is part of the sentence, not the quote, it should be placed outside of the quotation marks:

Was it Jackie that said, "Get some potatoes at the store"?

Apostrophes

This punctuation mark, the **apostrophe** (') is a versatile mark. It has several different functions:

- Quotes: Apostrophes are used when a second quote is needed within a quote.
  - In my letter to my friend, I wrote, "The girl had to get a new purse, and guess what Mary did? She said, 'I'd like to go with you to the store.' I knew Mary would buy it for her."

- Contractions: Another use for an apostrophe in the quote above is a contraction. *I'd is used for I would.*

- Possession: An apostrophe followed by the letter s shows possession (Mary's purse). If the possessive word is plural, the apostrophe generally just follows the word. Not all possessive pronouns require apostrophes.
  - The trees' leaves are all over the ground.

Hyphens

The **hyphen** (-) is a small hash mark that can be used to join words to show that they are linked.

Hyphens can connect two words that work together as a single adjective (a compound adjective).

honey-covered biscuits

Some words always require hyphens even if not serving as an adjective.

>   merry-go-round

Hyphens always go after certain prefixes like *anti-* & *all-*.

Hyphens should also be used when the absence of the hyphen would cause a strange vowel combination (*semi-engineer*) or confusion. For example, *re-collect* should be used to describe something being gathered twice rather than being written as *recollect*, which means to remember.

Conventions of Spelling and Capitalization

Spelling

Both spoken and written words have rhythm that might be defined as *inflection.* This serves to help writers in their choice of words, expression, and correct spelling. When creating original works, do at least one reading aloud. Some inflection is intrinsic to the words, some are added by writers, and some will be inferred when later read. If the written words are not spelled correctly, then what the author intended is not conveyed. Use rhythm as a spelling tool.

Saying and listening to a word serves as the beginning of knowing how to spell it. Keep these subsequent guidelines in mind, remembering there are often exceptions, because the English language is replete with them.

Guideline #1: Syllables must have a vowel

Every syllable in every English word has a vowel. Examples: d*o*g, h*ay*st*a*ck, *a*nsw*e*ring, *a*bst*e*nt*iou*s (the longest word that uses the five vowels in order), and s*i*mpl*e*.

In addition to this vowel guideline is a built-in bonus: Guideline #1 helps one see whether the word looks right.

Guideline #2: The silent final -e

The final word example in Guideline #1, s*imple,* provides the opportunity to see another guideline with multiple types:

- Because every syllable has a vowel, words like *simple* require the final silent *-e*.

- In a word that has a vowel-consonant-e combination like the short, simple word at*e,* the silent –*e* at the end shapes the sound of the earlier vowel. The technical term for this is it "makes the vowel say its name." There are thousands of examples of this guideline; just for starters, look at cut*e,* mat*e,* and tot*e*.

- Let's *dance*...after we leave the *range!* Look what the final silent *–e* does for the *–c* and *–g*: each provides the word's soft sound.

- Other than to *rev* a car's engine, are there other words that ends in a *–v?* How about a word that ends in a *–u?* Well some like their cheese bl*eu,* there's one, but, while there are more (well, okay, *you*), they are few and far between, and consider words having the ending of the letter *–i.* Yes, English words generally do not end in *–v's, –u's,* and *–i's,* so silent *–e* to the rescue! Note that it does not change the pronunciation. Examples: believ*e,* lov*e,* and activ*e;* blu*e,* and tru*e;*

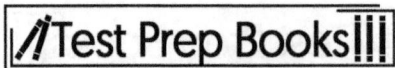

and two very important –i examples, brownie and cookie. (Exceptions to this rule are generally words from other languages.)

Guideline #3: The long and short of it
When the vowel has a short vowel sound as in *mad* or *bed,* only the single vowel is needed. If the word has a long vowel sound, add another vowel, either alongside it or separated by a consonant: bed/*bead*; mad/*made*. When the second vowel is separated by two spaces—*madder*—it does not affect the first vowel's sound.

Guideline #4: What about the –fixes (pre- and suf-)?
A *prefix* is a word, letter, or number that is placed before another. It adjusts or qualifies the root word's meaning. When written alone, prefixes are followed by a dash to indicate that the root word follows. Some of the most common prefixes are the following:

Prefix	Meaning	Example
dis-	not or opposite of	disabled
in-, im-, il-, ir-	not	illiterate
re-	again	return
un-	not	unpredictable
anti-	against	antibacterial
fore-	before	forefront
mis-	wrongly	misunderstand
non-	not	nonsense
over-	more than normal	overabundance
pre-	before	preheat
super-	above	superman

A **suffix** is a letter or group of letters added at the end of a word to form another word. The word created from the root and suffix is either a different tense of the same root (*help* + *ed* = *helped*) or a new word (*help* + *ful* = *helpful*). When written alone, suffixes are preceded by a dash to indicate that the root word comes before.

Some of the most common suffixes are the following:

Suffix	Meaning	Example
ed	makes a verb past tense	wash*ed*
ing	makes a verb a present participle verb	wash*ing*
ly	to make characteristic of	love*ly*
s/es	to make more than one	chair*s*, box*es*
able	can be done	deplor*able*
al	having characteristics of	comic*al*
est	comparative	great*est*
ful	full of	wonder*ful*
ism	belief in	commun*ism*
less	without	faith*less*
ment	action or process	accomplish*ment*
ness	state of	happi*ness*
ize, ise	to render, to make	steril*ize*, advert*ise*
cede/ceed/sede	go	con*cede*, pro*ceed*, super*sede*

Here are some helpful tips:

- When adding a suffix that starts with a vowel (for example, -*ed*) to a one-syllable root whose vowel has a short sound and ends in a consonant (for example, *stun*), double the final consonant of the root (*n*).

    stun + ed = stun*n*ed

    Exception: If the past tense verb ends in *x* such as *box*, do not double the *x*.

    box + ed = boxed

- If adding a suffix that starts with a vowel (-*er*) to a multi-syllable word ending in a consonant (*begin*), double the consonant (*n*).

    begin + er = begin*n*er

- If a short vowel is followed by two or more consonants in a word such as *i+t+c+h = itch*, do <u>not</u> double the last consonant.

    itch + ed = itched

- If adding a suffix that starts with a vowel (-*ing*) to a word ending in *e* (for example, *name*), that word's final *e* is generally (but not always) dropped.

    name + ing = naming
    exception: manage + able = manageable

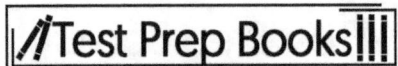

- If adding a suffix that starts with a consonant (-*ness*) to a word ending in *e* (*complete*), the *e* generally (but not always) remains.

    complete + ness = completeness
    exception: judge + ment = judgment

There is great diversity on handling words that end in *y*. For words ending in a vowel + *y*, nothing changes in the original word.

    play + ed = played

For words ending in a consonant + *y*, change the *y* to *i* when adding any suffix except for –*ing*.

    marry + ed = married
    marry + ing = marrying

Guideline #5: Which came first, the –i or the –e?

"When the letter 'c' you spy, put the 'e' before the 'i.' (Do not be) dec*ei*ved; when the letter 's' you see, put the 'i' before the 'e' (or you might be under) s*ie*ge." This old adage still holds up today regarding words where the "c" and "s" *precede* the "i." Another variation is, "'*i*' before '*e*' except after '*c*' or when sounded as '*a*' as in *neighbor* or *weigh*." Keep in mind that these are only guidelines and that there are always exceptions to every rule.

Guideline #6: Vowels in the right order

A different helpful ditty is, "When two vowels go walking, the first one does the talking." Usually, when two vowels are in a row, the first one often has a long vowel sound and the other is silent. An example is *team*.

When having difficulty spelling words, determine a strategy to help. Work on pronunciations, play word games like Scrabble or Words with Friends, and consider using phonics (sounding words out by slowly and surely stating each syllable). Try using repetition and memorization and picturing the words. Try memory aids like making up silly things. See what works best. For disorders such as dyslexia, know that there are accommodations to help.

Use computer spellcheck; however, do not *rely on* computer spellcheck.

Common Usage Mistakes

Its and It's

These pronouns are some of the most confused in the English language as most possessives contain the suffix –'s. However, for *it*, it is the opposite. *Its* is a possessive pronoun:

    The government is reassessing *its* spending plan.

It's is a contraction of the words *it is*:

    It's snowing outside.

Saw and Seen

Saw and *seen* are both conjugations of the verb *to see*, but they express different verb tenses. *Saw* is used in the simple past tense. *Seen* is the past participle form of *to see* and can be used in all perfect tenses.

> I seen her yesterday.

This sentence is incorrect. Because it expresses a completed event from a specified point in time in the past, it should use simple past tense:

> I *saw* her yesterday.

This sentence uses the correct verb tense. Here's how the past participle is used correctly:

> I *have seen* her before.

The meaning in this sentence is slightly changed to indicate an event from an unspecific time in the past. In this case, present perfect is the appropriate verb tense to indicate an unspecified past experience. Present perfect conjugation is created by combining *to have* + past participle.

Then and Than

Then is generally used as an adverb indicating something that happened next in a sequence or as the result of a conditional situation:

> We parked the car and *then* walked to the restaurant.

> If enough people register for the event, *then* we can begin planning.

Than is a conjunction indicating comparison:

> This watch is more expensive *than* that one.

> The bus departed later *than* I expected.

They're, Their, and There

They're is a contraction of the words *they are*:

> *They're* moving to Ohio next week.

Their is a possessive pronoun:

> The baseball players are training for *their* upcoming season.

There can function as multiple parts of speech, but it is most commonly used as an adverb indicating a location:

> Let's go to the concert! Some great bands are playing *there*.

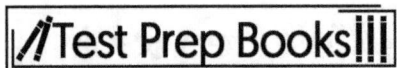

Insure and Ensure

These terms are both verbs. *Insure* means to guarantee something against loss, harm, or damage, usually through an insurance policy that offers monetary compensation:

> The robbers made off with her prized diamond necklace, but luckily it was *insured* for one million dollars.

Ensure means to make sure, to confirm, or to be certain:

> *Ensure* that you have your passport before entering the security checkpoint.

Accept and Except

Accept is a verb meaning to take or agree to something:

> I would like to *accept* your offer of employment.

Except is a preposition that indicates exclusion:

> I've been to every state in America *except* Hawaii.

Affect and Effect

Affect is a verb meaning to influence or to have an impact on something:

> The amount of rainfall during the growing season *affects* the flavor of wine produced from these grapes.

Effect can be used as either a noun or a verb. As a noun, *effect* is synonymous with a result:

> If we implement the changes, what will the *effect* be on our profits?

As a verb, *effect* means to bring about or to make happen:

> In just a few short months, the healthy committee has *effected* real change in school nutrition.

Capitalization

Here's a non-exhaustive list of things that should be capitalized:

- The first word of every sentence
- The first word of every line of poetry
- The first letter of proper nouns (World War II)
- Holidays (Valentine's Day)
- The days of the week and months of the year (Tuesday, March)
- The first word, last word, and all major words in the titles of books, movies, songs, and other creative works (In the novel, *To Kill a Mockingbird*, note that *a* is lowercase since it's not a major word, but *to* is capitalized since it's the first word of the title.)
- Titles when preceding a proper noun (President Roberto Gonzales, Aunt Judy)

When simply using a word such as president or secretary, though, the word is not capitalized.

> Officers of the new business must include a president and treasurer.

Seasons—spring, fall, etc.—are not capitalized.

North, south, east, and west are capitalized when referring to regions but are not when being used for directions. In general, if it's preceded by the it should be capitalized.

> I'm from the South.

> I drove south.

Here are some additional rules about capitalization:

- Capitalize the first word in a sentence and the first word in a quotation:

    The realtor showed them the house.

    Robert asked, "When can we get together for dinner again?"

- Capitalize proper nouns and words derived from them:

    We are visiting Germany in a few weeks.

    We will stay with our German relatives on our trip.

- Capitalize days of the week, months of the year, and holidays:

    The book club meets the last Thursday of every month.

    The baby is due in June.

    I decided to throw a Halloween party this year.

- Capitalize the main words in titles (referred to as *title case*), but not the articles, conjunctions, or prepositions:

    A Raisin in the Sun

    To Kill a Mockingbird

- Capitalize directional words that are used as names, but not when referencing a direction:

    The North won the Civil War.

    After making a left, go north on Rt. 476.

    She grew up on the West Coast.

    The winds came in from the west.

- Capitalize titles that go with names:

    Mrs. McFadden   Sir Alec Guinness   Lt. Madeline Suarez

- Capitalize familial relationships when referring to a *specific* person:

    I worked for my Uncle Steven last summer.

    Did you work for your uncle last summer?

Essay

Five-Paragraph Persuasive Essay

Brainstorming

One of the most important steps in writing an essay is prewriting. Before drafting an essay, it's helpful to think about the topic for a moment or two, in order to gain a more solid understanding of the task. Then, spending about five minutes jotting down the immediate ideas that could work for the essay is recommended. It is a way to get some words on the page and offer a reference for ideas when drafting. Scratch paper is provided for writers to use any prewriting techniques such as webbing, free writing, or listing. The goal is to get ideas out of the mind and onto the page.

Considering Opposing Viewpoints

In the planning stage, it's important to consider all aspects of the topic, including different viewpoints on the subject. There are more than two ways to look at a topic, and a strong argument considers those opposing viewpoints. Considering opposing viewpoints can help writers present a fair, balanced, and informed essay that shows consideration for all readers. This approach can also strengthen an argument by recognizing and potentially refuting opposing viewpoint(s).

Drawing from personal experience may help to support ideas. For example, if the goal for writing is a personal narrative, then the story should come from the writer's own life. Many writers find it helpful to draw from personal experience, even in an essay that is not strictly narrative. Personal anecdotes or short stories can help to illustrate a point in other types of essays as well.

Moving from Brainstorming to Planning

Once the ideas are on the page, it's time to turn them into a solid plan for the essay. The best ideas from the brainstorming results can then be developed into a more formal outline. An outline typically has one main point (the thesis) and at least three sub-points that support the main point. Here's an example:

Main Idea

- Point #1
- Point #2
- Point #3

Of course, there will be details under each point, but this approach is the best for dealing with timed writing.

Staying on Track

Basing the essay on the outline aids in both organization and coherence. The goal is to ensure that there is enough time to develop each sub-point in the essay, roughly spending an equal amount of time on each idea. Keeping an eye on the time will help. If there are fifteen minutes left to draft the essay, then it makes sense to spend about 5 minutes on each of the ideas. Staying on task is critical to success, and timing out the parts of the essay can help writers avoid feeling overwhelmed.

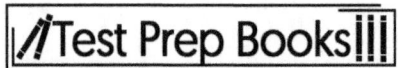

Parts of the Essay

The introduction has to do a few important things:

- Establish the topic of the essay in original wording (i.e., not just repeating the prompt)
- Clarify the significance/importance of the topic or purpose for writing (not too many details, a brief overview)
- Offer a thesis statement that identifies the writer's own viewpoint on the topic (typically one-two brief sentences as a clear, concise explanation of the main point on the topic)

Body paragraphs reflect the ideas developed in the outline. Three-four points is probably sufficient for a short essay, and they should include the following:

- A topic sentence that identifies the sub-point (e.g., a reason why, a way how, a cause or effect)
- A detailed explanation of the point, explaining why the writer thinks this point is valid
- Illustrative examples, such as personal examples or real-world examples, that support and validate the point (i.e., "prove" the point)
- A concluding sentence that connects the examples, reasoning, and analysis to the point being made

The conclusion, or final paragraph, should be brief and should reiterate the focus, clarifying why the discussion is significant or important. It is important to avoid adding specific details or new ideas to this paragraph. The purpose of the conclusion is to sum up what has been said to bring the discussion to a close.

Don't Panic!

Writing an essay can be overwhelming, and performance panic is a natural response. The outline serves as a basis for the writing and helps writers keep focused. Getting stuck can also happen, and it's helpful to remember that brainstorming can be done at any time during the writing process. Following the steps of the writing process is the best defense against writer's block.

Timed essays can be particularly stressful, but assessors are trained to recognize the necessary planning and thinking for these timed efforts. Using the plan above and sticking to it helps with time management. Timing each part of the process helps writers stay on track. Sometimes writers try to cover too much in their essays. If time seems to be running out, this is an opportunity to determine whether all of the ideas in the outline are necessary. Three body paragraphs are sufficient, and more than that is probably too much to cover in a short essay.

More isn't always better in writing. A strong essay will be clear and concise. It will avoid unnecessary or repetitive details. It is better to have a concise, five-paragraph essay that makes a clear point, than a ten-paragraph essay that doesn't. The goal is to write one to two pages of quality writing. Paragraphs should also reflect balance; if the introduction goes to the bottom of the first page, the writing may be going off-track or be repetitive. It's best to fall into the one-two page range, but a complete, well-developed essay is the ultimate goal.

TSI Practice Test #1

Math

1. If $4x - 3 = 5$, what is the value of x?
   a. 1
   b. 2
   c. 3
   d. 4

2. Write the expression for three times the sum of twice a number and one, minus six.
   a. $2x + 1 - 6$
   b. $3x + 1 - 6$
   c. $3(x + 1) - 6$
   d. $3(2x + 1) - 6$

3. On Monday, Robert mopped the floor in 4 hours. On Tuesday, he did it in 3 hours. If on Monday, his average rate of mopping was p sq. ft. per hour, what was his average rate on Tuesday?
   a. $\frac{4}{3}p$ sq. ft. per hour
   b. $\frac{3}{4}p$ sq. ft. per hour
   c. $\frac{5}{4}p$ sq. ft. per hour
   d. $p + 1$ sq. ft. per hour

4. Which of the following inequalities is equivalent to $3 - \frac{1}{2}x \geq 2$?
   a. $x \geq 2$
   b. $x \leq 2$
   c. $x \geq 1$
   d. $x \leq 1$

5. For which of the following are $x = 4$ and $x = -4$ solutions?
   a. $x^2 + 16 = 0$
   b. $x^2 + 4x - 4 = 0$
   c. $x^2 - 2x - 2 = 0$
   d. $x^2 - 16 = 0$

6. $(2x - 4y)^2 =$
   a. $4x^2 - 16xy + 16y^2$
   b. $4x^2 - 8xy + 16y^2$
   c. $4x^2 - 16xy - 16y^2$
   d. $2x^2 - 8xy + 8y^2$

7. The square and circle share a center. The circle has a radius of r. What is the area of the shaded region?

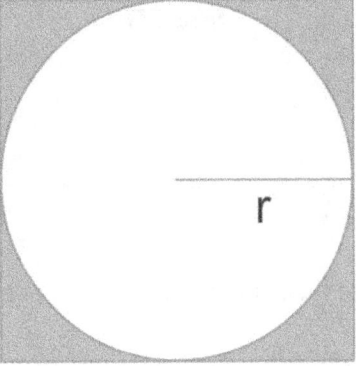

   a. $r^2 - \pi r^2$
   b. $4r^2 - 2\pi r$
   c. $(4 - \pi)r^2$
   d. $(\pi - 1)r^2$

8. Five of six numbers have a sum of 25. The average of all six numbers is 6. What is the sixth number?
   a. 8
   b. 10
   c. 11
   d. 12

9. What is the solution to the following system of equations?

$$x^2 - 2x + y = 8$$

$$x - y = -2$$

   a. $(-2, 3)$
   b. There is no solution.
   c. $(-2, 0)\ (1, 3)$
   d. $(-2, 0)\ (3, 5)$

10. A shuffled deck of 52 cards contains 4 kings. One card is drawn and is not put back in the deck. Then, a second card is drawn. What's the probability that both cards are kings?
   a. $\frac{1}{169}$
   b. $\frac{1}{221}$
   c. $\frac{1}{13}$
   d. $\frac{4}{13}$

11. The table below displays the number of three-year-olds at Kids First Daycare who are potty-trained and those who still wear diapers.

	Potty-trained	Wear diapers	
Boys	26	22	48
Girls	34	18	52
	60	40	

If a three-year-old girl is randomly selected from this school, what is the probability that she is potty-trained?
   a. 52%
   b. 34%
   c. 65%
   d. 57%

12. A shipping box has a length of 8 inches, a width of 14 inches, and a height of 4 inches. If all three dimensions are doubled, what is the relationship between the volume of the new box and the volume of the original box?
   a. The volume of the new box is double the volume of the original box.
   b. The volume of the new box is four times as large as the volume of the original box.
   c. The volume of the new box is six times as large as the volume of the original box.
   d. The volume of the new box is eight times as large as the volume of the original box.

13. What is the simplified form of the expression: $(7n + 3n^3 + 3) + (8n + 5n^3 + 2n^4)$?
   a. $9n^4 + 15n - 2$
   b. $2n^4 + 5n^3 + 15n - 2$
   c. $9n^4 + 8n^3 + 15n$
   d. $2n^4 + 8n^3 + 15n + 3$

14. What is the equation for the line passing through the origin and the point $(2, 1)$?
   a. $y = 2x$
   b. $y = \frac{1}{2}x$
   c. $y = x - 2$
   d. $2y = x + 1$

15. If $g(x) = x^3 - 3x^2 - 2x + 6$ and $f(x) = 2$, then what is $g(f(x))$?
   a. -26
   b. 6
   c. $2x^3 - 6x^2 - 4x + 12$
   d. -2

16. If the volume of a sphere is 288π cubic meters, what are the radius and surface area of the same sphere?
   a. Radius: 6 meters, surface area: 144π square meters
   b. Radius: 36 meters, surface area: 144π square meters
   c. Radius: 6 meters, surface area: 12π square meters
   d. Radius: 36 meters, surface area: 12π square meters

17. A ball is drawn at random from a ball pit containing 8 red balls, 7 yellow balls, 6 green balls, and 5 purple balls. What's the probability that the ball drawn is yellow?
   a. $\frac{1}{26}$
   b. $\frac{19}{26}$
   c. $\frac{7}{26}$
   d. 1

18. If Sarah reads at an average rate of 21 pages in 4 nights, how long will it take her to read 140 pages?
   a. 6 nights
   b. 26 nights
   c. 8 nights
   d. 27 nights

19. The phone bill is calculated each month using the equation $c = 50g + 75$. The cost of the phone bill per month is represented by c, and g represents the gigabytes of data used that month. Identify and interpret the slope of this equation.
   a. 75 dollars per day
   b. 75 gigabytes per day
   c. 50 dollars per day
   d. 50 dollars per gigabyte

20. Which equation best represents the scatter plot below?

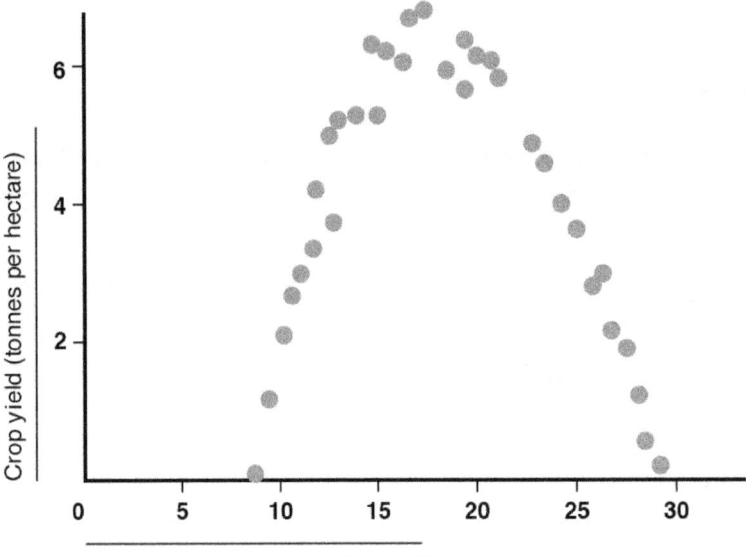

   a. $y = 3x - 4$
   b. $y = 2x^2 + 7x - 9$
   c. $y = (3)(4^x)$
   d. $y = -\frac{1}{14}x^2 + 2x - 8$

English Language Arts and Reading

Questions 1-4 are based upon the following passage:

My gentleness and good behaviour had gained so far on the emperor and his court, and indeed upon the army and people in general, that I began to conceive hopes of getting my liberty in a short time. I took all possible methods to cultivate this favourable disposition. The natives came, by degrees, to be less apprehensive of any danger from me. I, Gulliver, would sometimes lie down, and let five or six of them dance on my hand; and at last, the boys and girls would venture to come and play at hide-and-seek in my hair. I had now made a good progress in understanding and speaking the language. The emperor had a mind one day to entertain me with several of the country shows, wherein they exceed all nations I have known, both for dexterity and magnificence. I was diverted with none so much as that of the rope-dancers, performed upon a slender white thread, extended about two feet, and twelve inches from the ground. Upon which I shall desire liberty, with the reader's patience, to enlarge a little.

This diversion is only practised by those persons who are candidates for great employments, and high favour at court. They are trained in this art from their youth, and are not always of noble birth, or liberal education. When a great office is vacant, either by death or disgrace (which often happens), five or six of those candidates petition the emperor to entertain his majesty and the court with a dance on the rope; and whoever jumps the highest, without falling, succeeds in the office. Very often the chief ministers themselves are commanded to show their skill, and to convince the emperor that they have not lost their faculty. Flimnap, the treasurer, is allowed to cut a caper on the straight rope, at least an inch higher than any other lord in the whole empire. I have seen him do the summerset several times together, upon a trencher fixed on a rope which is no thicker than a common packthread in England. My friend Reldresal, principal secretary for private affairs, is, in my opinion, if I am not partial, the second after the treasurer; the rest of the great officers are much upon a par.

Excerpt adapted from Gulliver's Travels into Several Remote Nations of the World by Jonathan Swift

1. Which of the following statements best summarizes the central purpose of this text?
    a. Gulliver details his fondness for the archaic, yet interesting, practices of his captors.
    b. Gulliver conjectures about the intentions of the aristocratic sector of society.
    c. Gulliver becomes acquainted with the people and practices of his new surroundings.
    d. Gulliver's differences cause him to become penitent around new acquaintances.

2. What is the word *principal* referring to in the following text?

    My friend Reldresal, principal secretary for private affairs, is, in my opinion, if I am not partial, the second after the treasurer; the rest of the great officers are much upon a par.

    a. Primary or chief
    b. An acolyte
    c. An individual who provides nurturing
    d. One in a subordinate position

3. What can the reader infer from the following text?

> I, Gulliver, would sometimes lie down, and let five or six of them dance on my hand; and at last, the boys and girls would venture to come and play at hide-and-seek in my hair.

a. The children tortured Gulliver.
b. Gulliver traveled because he wanted to meet new people.
c. Gulliver is considerably larger than the children who are playing around him.
d. Gulliver has a genuine love and enthusiasm for people of all sizes.

4. What is the significance of the word *mind* in the following passage?

> The emperor had a mind one day to entertain me with several of the country shows, wherein they exceed all nations I have known, both for dexterity and magnificence.

a. The ability to think
b. A collective vote
c. A definitive decision
d. A mythological question

5. Annabelle Rice started having trouble sleeping. Her biological clock was suddenly amiss, and she began to lead a nocturnal schedule. She thought her insomnia was due to spending nights writing a horror story, but then she realized that even the idea of going outside into the bright world scared her to bits. She concluded she was now suffering from heliophobia.
Which of the following most accurately describes the meaning of the underlined word in the sentence above?

a. Fear of dreams
b. Fear of sunlight
c. Fear of strangers
d. Anxiety spectrum disorder

6. Which of these descriptions would give the most detailed and objective support for the claim that drinking and driving is unsafe?

a. A dramatized television commercial reenacting a fatal drinking and driving accident, including heart-wrenching testimonials from loved ones
b. The Department of Transportation's press release noting the additional drinking and driving special patrol units that will be on the road during the holiday season
c. Congressional written testimony on the number of drinking and driving incidents across the country and their relationship to underage drinking statistics, according to experts
d. A highway bulletin warning drivers of the penalties associated with drinking and driving

7. In 2015, 28 countries, including Estonia, Portugal, Slovenia, and Latvia, scored significantly higher than the United States on standardized high school math tests. In the 1960s, the United States consistently ranked first in the world. Today, the United States spends more than $800 billion on education, which exceeds the next highest country by more than $600 billion. The United States also leads the world in spending per school-aged child by an enormous margin.

If the statements above are true, which of the following statements must be correct?
   a. Outspending other countries on education has benefits beyond standardized math tests.
   b. The United States' education system is corrupt and broken.
   c. The standardized math tests are not representative of American academic prowess.
   d. Spending more money does not guarantee success on standardized math tests.

8. Raul is going to Egypt next month. He has been looking forward to this vacation all year. Since childhood, Raul has been fascinated with pyramids, especially the Great Pyramid of Giza, which is the oldest of the Seven Wonders of the Ancient World. According to religious custom, Egyptian royalty is buried in the tombs located within the pyramid's great labyrinths. Since it has been many years since Raul read about the pyramid's history, he wants to read a book describing how and why the Egyptians built the Great Pyramid thousands of years ago.

Which of the following guides would be the best for Raul?
   a. *A Beginner's Guide to Giza*, a short book describing the city's best historical sites, published by the Egyptian Tourism Bureau (2015)
   b. *The Life of Zahi Hawass*, the autobiography of one of Egypt's most famous archaeologists who was one of the first explorers at Giza (2014)
   c. *A History of Hieroglyphics*, an in-depth look at how archaeologists first broke the ancient code, published by the University of Giza's famed history department (2013)
   d. *Who Built the Great Pyramids?*, a short summary of the latest research and theories on the ancient Egyptians' religious beliefs and archaeological skills, written by a team of leading experts in the field (2015)

Question 9 is based on the following passage:

> Cynthia keeps to a strict vegetarian diet, which is part of her religion. She absolutely cannot have any meat or fish dishes. This is more than a preference; her body has never developed the enzymes to process meat or fish, so she becomes violently ill if she accidentally eats any of the offending foods.
>
> Cynthia is attending a full day event at her college next week. When at an event that serves meals, she always likes to bring a platter of vegetarian food for herself and to share with other attendees who have similar dietary restrictions. She requested a menu in advance to determine when her platter might be most useful to vegetarians. Here is the menu:
>
> Breakfast: Hazelnut coffee or English breakfast tea, French toast, eggs, and bacon strips
>
> Lunch: Assorted sandwiches (vegetarian options available), French fries, and baked beans
>
> Cocktail hour: Alcoholic beverages, fruit, and cheese
>
> Dinner: Roasted pork loin, seared trout, and bacon-bit topped macaroni and cheese

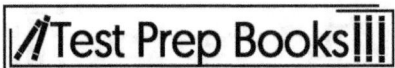

9. If Cynthia wants to pick the meal where there would be the least options for her and fellow vegetarians, during what meal should she bring the platter?
   a. Breakfast
   b. Lunch
   c. Cocktail hour
   d. Dinner

10. Emma is writing an essay about Shakespeare's *Macbeth*. She started with a detailed outline and first draft. Her ideas are her own, but she has quoted excerpts from the play to support her main points. She reworked her draft several times and revised her essay based on feedback from a writing center tutor. She asked a few classmates to read the essay and identify mistakes she missed while editing. Which of the following actions does she still need to take at this point in the writing process?
    a. Write the introduction and conclusion paragraphs.
    b. Rearrange the order of paragraphs.
    c. Insert citations where she used quotes.
    d. Organize her thoughts.

11. Jerome K. Jerome's humorous account of a boating holiday, Three Men in a Boat, was published in 1889. Originally intended as a serious travel guide, the work became a prime example of a comic novel. Read the passage below, noting the word in italics. Answer the question that follows.

    I felt rather hurt about this at first; it seemed somehow to be a sort of slight. Why hadn't I got housemaid's knee? Why this invidious reservation? After a while, however, less grasping feelings prevailed. I reflected that I had every other known malady in the pharmacology, and I grew less selfish, and determined to do without housemaid's knee. Gout, in its most malignant stage, it would appear, had seized me without my being aware of it; and *zymosis* I had evidently been suffering with from boyhood. There were no more diseases after *zymosis*, so I concluded there was nothing else the matter with me.

Which definition best fits the word *zymosis*?
   a. Discontent
   b. An infectious disease
   c. Poverty
   d. Bad luck

12. What is the meaning of the word *rookeries* in the following text?

    To-day, the plume hunters who do not dare to raid the guarded rookeries are trying to study out the lines of flight of the birds, to and from their feeding-grounds, and shoot them in transit.

   a. Houses in a slum area
   b. A place where hunters gather to trade tools
   c. A place where wardens go to trade stories
   d. A colony of breeding birds

13. There are two major kinds of cameras on the market right now for amateur photographers. Camera enthusiasts can either purchase a digital single-lens reflex (DSLR) camera or a compact system camera (CSC). The main difference between a DSLR and a CSC is that the DSLR has a full-sized sensor, which means it fits in a much larger body. The CSC uses a mirrorless system, which makes for a lighter, smaller camera. While both take quality pictures, the DSLR generally has better picture quality due to the larger sensor. CSCs still take very good quality pictures and are more convenient to carry than a DSLR. This makes the CSC an ideal choice for the amateur photographer looking to step up from a point-and-shoot camera.

What is the main difference between the DSLR and CSC?
   a. The picture quality is better in the DSLR.
   b. The CSC is less expensive than the DSLR.
   c. The DSLR is a better choice for amateur photographers.
   d. The DSLR's larger sensor makes it a bigger camera than the CSC.

14. When selecting a career path, it's important to explore the various options available. Many students entering college may shy away from a major because they don't know much about it. For example, many students won't opt for a career as an actuary because they aren't exactly sure what it entails. They would be missing out on a career that is very lucrative and in high demand. Actuaries work in the insurance field and assess risks and premiums. The average salary of an actuary is $100,000 per year. Another career option students may avoid, due to lack of knowledge of the field, is a hospitalist. This is a physician that specializes in the care of patients in a hospital, as opposed to those seen in private practices. The average salary of a hospitalist is upwards of $200,000. It pays to do some digging and find out more about these lesser-known career fields.

What is an *actuary*?
   a. A doctor who works in a hospital
   b. The same as a hospitalist
   c. An insurance agent who works in a hospital
   d. A person who assesses insurance risks and premiums

15. Hard water occurs when rainwater mixes with minerals from rock and soil. Hard water has a high mineral count, including calcium and magnesium. The mineral deposits from hard water can stain hard surfaces in bathrooms and kitchens as well as clog pipes. Hard water can stain dishes, ruin clothes, and reduce the life of any appliances it touches, such as hot water heaters, washing machines, and humidifiers.

One solution is to install a water softener to reduce the mineral content of water, but this can be costly. Running vinegar through pipes and appliances and using vinegar to clean hard surfaces can also help with mineral deposits.

From this passage, what can be concluded?
   a. Hard water can cause a lot of problems for homeowners.
   b. Calcium is good for pipes and hard surfaces.
   c. Water softeners are easy to install.
   d. Vinegar is the only solution to hard water problems.

Read the following passage and answer Questions 16-19.

1 Although many Missourians know that Harry S. Truman and Walt Disney hailed from their great state, probably far fewer know that it was also home to the remarkable George Washington Carver. (16) <u>As a child, George was driven to learn, and he loved painting.</u> At the end of the Civil War, Moses Carver, the slave owner who owned George's parents, decided to keep George and his brother and raise them on his farm.

2 He even went on to study art while in college but was encouraged to pursue botany instead. He spent much of his life helping others (17) <u>by showing them better ways to farm, his ideas improved agricultural productivity</u> in many countries. One of his most notable contributions to the newly emerging class of Black farmers was to teach them the negative effects of agricultural monoculture (i.e., (18) <u>growing the same crops in the same fields year after year, depleting the soil of much needed nutrients and results in a lesser yielding crop.)</u>

3 Carver was an innovator, always thinking of new and better ways to do things, and is most famous for his over three hundred uses for the peanut. Toward the end of his career, (19) <u>Carver returns</u> to his first love of art. Through his artwork, he hoped to inspire people to see the beauty around them and to do great things themselves. When Carver died, he left his money to help fund ongoing agricultural research. Today, people still visit and study at the George Washington Carver Foundation at Tuskegee Institute.

16. Which of the following would be the best replacement for the underlined portion of the sentence reproduced below?

   As a child, George was driven to learn, and he loved painting.

   a. Leave it as it is now.
   b. Move to the end of the first paragraph.
   c. Move to the beginning of the first paragraph.
   d. Move to the end of the second paragraph.

17. Which of the following would be the best replacement for the underlined portion of the sentence reproduced below?

   He spent much of his life helping others <u>by showing them better ways to farm, his ideas improved agricultural productivity</u> in many countries.

   a. (as it is now)
   b. by showing them better ways to farm his ideas improved agricultural productivity
   c. by showing them better ways to farm ... his ideas improved agricultural productivity
   d. by showing them better ways to farm; his ideas improved agricultural productivity

18. Which of the following would be the best replacement for the underlined portion of the sentence reproduced below?

   One of his most notable contributions to the newly emerging class of Black farmers *was to teach them the negative effects of agricultural monoculture, i.e. growing the same crops in the same fields year after year, depleting the soil of much needed nutrients and results in a lesser yielding crop.*

   a. (as it is now)
   b. growing the same crops in the same fields year after year, depleting the soil of much needed nutrients and resulting in a lesser yielding crop.
   c. growing the same crops in the same fields year after year, depletes the soil of much needed nutrients and resulting in a lesser yielding crop.
   d. grows the same crops in the same fields year after year, depletes the soil of much needed nutrients and resulting in a lesser yielding crop.

19. Which of the following would be the best replacement for the underlined portion of the sentence reproduced below?

   Toward the end of his career, Carver returns to his first love of art.

   a. (as it is now)
   b. Carver is returning
   c. Carver returned
   d. Carver was returning

20. The following sentence contains what kind of error?

   This summer, I'm planning to travel to Italy, take a Mediterranean cruise, going to Pompeii, and eat a lot of Italian food.

   a. Parallelism
   b. Sentence fragment
   c. Misplaced modifier
   d. Subject-verb agreement

21. The following sentence contains what kind of error?

   Forgetting that he was supposed to meet his girlfriend for dinner, Anita was mad when Fred showed up late.

   a. Parallelism
   b. Run-on sentence
   c. Misplaced modifier
   d. Subject-verb agreement

22. The following sentence contains what kind of error?

    Some workers use all their sick leave, other workers cash out their leave.

    a. Parallelism
    b. Comma splice
    c. Sentence fragment
    d. Subject-verb agreement

23. A student writes the following in an essay:

    Protestors filled the streets of the city. Because they were dissatisfied with the government's leadership.

Which of the following is an appropriately punctuated correction for the above?
    a. Protestors filled the streets of the city, because they were dissatisfied with the government's leadership.
    b. Protesters, filled the streets of the city, because they were dissatisfied with the government's leadership.
    c. Because they were dissatisfied with the government's leadership protestors filled the streets of the city.
    d. Protestors filled the streets of the city because they were dissatisfied with the government's leadership.

24. Which pair of words will correctly fill in the blanks?

    Increasing the price of bus fares has had a greater _____ on ridership _____ expected.

    a. affect; then
    b. affect; than
    c. effect; then
    d. effect; than

Directions for questions 25–30

Rewrite the sentence in your head following the directions given below. Keep in mind that your new sentence should be well written and should have essentially the same meaning as the original sentence.

25. Rewrite the following sentence, beginning with The author had poise and confidence while reading:

    Although she was nervous speaking in front of a crowd, the author read her narrative with poise and confidence.

    a. because she was nervous speaking in front of a crowd.
    b. but she was nervous speaking in front of a crowd.
    c. even though she was nervous speaking in front of a crowd.
    d. before she was nervous speaking in front of a crowd.

26. Rewrite the following sentence, beginning with While the hurricane occurred:

There was a storm surge and loss of electricity during the hurricane.

a. there was a storm surge after the electricity went out.
b. the storm surge caused the electricity to go out.
c. the electricity surged into the storm.
d. the electricity went out, and there was a storm surge.

27. Rewrite the following sentence, beginning with An elephant herd will:

When one elephant in a herd is sick, the rest of the herd will help it walk and bring it food.

a. be too sick and tired to walk.
b. help and support.
c. gather food when they're sick.
d. be unable to walk without food.

28. Rewrite the following sentence, beginning with They finished the soccer game:

They went out to eat after the soccer game.

a. then went out to eat.
b. after they went out to eat.
c. so they could go out to eat.
d. because they went out to eat.

29. Rewrite the following sentence, beginning with Walking through Paris,:

Armani got lost when she walked around Paris.

a. you can get lost.
b. Armani found herself lost.
c. she should have gotten lost.
d. is about getting lost.

30. If you were to rewrite the sentence below, beginning with "Phoenix buried his cat," what would the next words be?

After his cat died, Phoenix buried the cat with her favorite toys in his backyard.

a. in his backyard before she died.
b. after she died in the backyard.
c. with her favorite toys after she died.
d. after he buried her toys in the backyard.

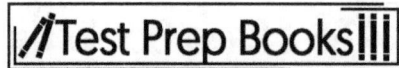

Essay

Prepare an essay of about 300-600 words on the topic below.

Some people feel that sharing their lives on social media sites such as Facebook, Instagram, and Snapchat is fine. They share every aspect of their lives, including pictures of themselves and their families, what they ate for lunch, who they are dating, and when they are going on vacation. They even say that if it's not on social media, it didn't happen. Other people believe that sharing so much personal information is an invasion of privacy and could prove dangerous. They think sharing personal pictures and details invites predators, cyberbullying, and identity theft.

Write an essay to someone who is considering whether to participate in social media. Take a side on the issue and argue whether or not he/she should join a social media network. Use specific examples to support your argument.

The following pages are provided for writing your essay.

Answer Explanations #1

Math

1. B: When solving for x, add 3 to both sides to get $4x = 8$. Then, divide both sides by 4 to get $x = 2$.

2. D: "Sum" means the result of addition, so "the sum of twice a number and one" can be written as $2x + 1$. Next, "three times the sum of twice a number and one" would be $3(2x + 1)$. Finally, "six less than three times the sum of twice a number and one" would be $3(2x + 1) - 6$.

3. A: The area of floor that he mops equals his rate of mopping multiplied by the amount of time he works: $a = rt$. (This is similar to the distance formula, $d = rt$.) On Monday, his rate was p, and his time was 4 hours, so we can use our formula to find that the floor's area is $a = p \times 4$, or $4p$. On Tuesday, the area of the floor remains the same, but the time is now $t = 3$, and the unknown rate r is what we're trying to find, so our area formula tells us that $4p = r \times 3$. Solving this equation for r, we find $r = (4/3)p$.

4. B: To simplify this inequality, subtract 3 from both sides:

$$3 - 3 - \frac{1}{2}x \geq 2 - 3$$

$$-\frac{1}{2}x \geq -1$$

Then, multiply both sides by –2 (remembering that this flips the direction of the inequality):

$$(-\frac{1}{2}x)(-2) \geq (-1)(-2)$$

$$x \leq 2.$$

5. D: Each value can be substituted into each equation. Choice *A* can be eliminated, since:

$$4^2 + 16 = 32$$

Choice *B* can be eliminated, since:

$$4^2 + 4 \times 4 - 4 = 28$$

Choice *C* can be eliminated, since:

$$4^2 - 2 \times 4 - 2 = 6$$

But, plugging in either value into $x^2 - 16$ gives:

$$(\pm 4)^2 - 16 = 16 - 16 = 0$$

Answer Explanations #1

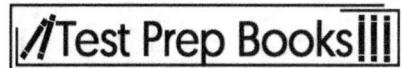

6. A: To expand a squared binomial, it's necessary to use the first, outer, inner, last (FOIL) method.

$$(2x - 4y)^2$$

$$(2x)(2x) + (2x)(-4y) + (-4y)(2x) + (-4y)(-4y)$$

$$4x^2 - 8xy - 8xy + 16y^2$$

$$4x^2 - 16xy + 16y^2$$

7. C: The area of the shaded region is the area of the square minus the area of the circle. The area of the circle is πr^2. The side of the square will be $2r$, so the area of the square will be $4r^2$. Therefore, the difference is:

$$4r^2 - \pi r^2 = (4 - \pi)r^2$$

8. C: The average is calculated by adding all six numbers, then dividing by 6. The first five numbers have a sum of 25. This scenario can be expressed by the equation $\frac{25+n}{6} = 6$, where n is the unknown number. After multiplying both sides by 6, we get $25 + n = 36$, which means $n = 11$.

9. D: This system of equations involves one quadratic equation and one linear equation. One way to solve this is through substitution.

Solving for y in the second equation yields:

$$y = x + 2$$

Plugging this equation in for the y of the quadratic equation yields:

$$x^2 - 2x + x + 2 = 8$$

Simplify the equation:

$$x^2 - x + 2 = 8$$

Set this equal to zero and factor:

$$x^2 - x - 6 = 0 = (x - 3)(x + 2)$$

Solving these two factors for x gives the zeros:

$$x = 3, -2$$

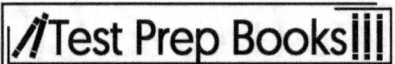

Answer Explanations #1

To find the y-value for the point, plug in each number to either original equation.

$$(3)^2 - 2(3) + y = 8$$
$$9 - 6 + y = 8$$
$$3 + y = 8$$
$$y = 5$$
$$(-2)^2 - 2(-2) + y = 8$$
$$4 + 4 + y = 8$$
$$8 + y = 8$$
$$y = 0$$

Solving each one for y yields the points $(3,5)$ and $(-2,0)$.

10. B: For the first card drawn, the probability of a king being pulled is $\frac{4}{52}$. Since this card isn't replaced, if a king is drawn first, the probability of a king being drawn second is $\frac{3}{51}$. The probability of a king being drawn in both the first and second draw is the product of the two probabilities:

$$\frac{4}{52} \times \frac{3}{51} = \frac{12}{2{,}652}$$

To reduce this fraction, divide the top and bottom by 12 to get $\frac{1}{221}$.

11. C: There are 34 girls who are potty-trained out of a total of 52 girls:

$$34 \div 52 \approx 0.65 = 65\%$$

12. D: The formula for finding the volume of a rectangular prism is $V = l \times w \times h$, where l is the length, w is the width, and h is the height. The volume of the original box is calculated:

$$V = 8 \text{ in} \times 14 \text{ in} \times 4 \text{ in} = 448 \text{ in}^3$$

The volume of the new box is calculated:

$$V = 16 \text{ in} \times 28 \text{ in} \times 8 \text{ in} = 3{,}584 \text{ in}^3$$

The volume of the new box divided by the volume of the old box equals 8.

13. D: The expression is simplified by collecting like terms. Terms with the same variable and exponent are like terms, and their coefficients can be added.

Answer Explanations #1

14. B: The origin is (0,0). The slope is given by:

$$\frac{(y_2 - y_1)}{(x_2 - x_1)} = \frac{1-0}{2-0} = \frac{1}{2}$$

The y-intercept will be 0 since it passes through the origin, (0,0). Using slope-intercept form, the equation for this line is:

$$y = \frac{1}{2}x$$

15. D: This problem involves a composition function, where one function is plugged into the other function. In this case, the $f(x)$ function is plugged into the $g(x)$ function for each x value. Since $f(x) = 2$, the composition equation becomes:

$$g(f(x)) = g(2) = (2)^3 - 3(2)^2 - 2(2) + 6$$

Simplifying the equation gives the answer:

$$g(f(x)) = 8 - 3(4) - 2(2) + 6$$

$$g(f(x)) = 8 - 12 - 4 + 6$$

$$g(f(x)) = -2$$

16. A: The volume of the sphere is 288π cubic meters. Using the formula for sphere volume, we see that:

$$\frac{4}{3}\pi r^3 = 288\pi$$

We solve this equation for r to obtain a radius of 6 meters. The formula for surface area is $4\pi r^2$, so:

$$SA = 4\pi 6^2 = 144\pi \text{ square meters}$$

17. C: The sample space is made up of $8 + 7 + 6 + 5 = 26$ balls. The probability of pulling each individual ball is $\frac{1}{26}$. Since there are 7 yellow balls, the probability of pulling a yellow ball is $\frac{7}{26}$.

18. D: This problem can be solved by setting up a proportion involving the given information and the unknown value. The proportion is:

$$\frac{21 \text{ pages}}{4 \text{ nights}} = \frac{140 \text{ pages}}{x \text{ nights}}$$

Cross-multiply to get $21x = 4 \times 140$. Solving this leaves $x \approx 26.67$. Since this is not an integer, round up to 27 nights because 26 nights would not give Sarah enough time to finish.

19. D: The slope from this equation is 50, and it is interpreted as the cost per gigabyte used. Since the g-value represents the number of gigabytes and the equation is set equal to the cost in dollars, the slope relates these two values. For every gigabyte used on the phone, the bill goes up 50 dollars.

Answer Explanations #1

20. D: The shape of the scatter plot is a parabola (U-shaped). This eliminates Choices A (a linear equation that produces a straight line) and C (an exponential equation that produces a smooth curve upward or downward). The value of a for a quadratic function in standard form ($y = ax^2 + bx + c$) indicates whether the parabola opens up (U-shaped) or opens down (upside-down U). A negative value for a produces a parabola that opens down; therefore, Choice B can also be eliminated.

English Language Arts and Reading

1. C: Choice C is the correct answer because it most extensively summarizes the entire passage. While Choices A and B are reasonable possibilities, they reference portions of Gulliver's experience, not the whole. Choice D is incorrect because Gulliver doesn't express repentance or sorrow in this particular passage.

2. A: Principal refers to *chief* or *primary* within the context of this text. Choice A is the answer that most closely aligns with this definition. Choices B and D refer to a helper or follower, while Choice C doesn't meet the description of Reldresal from the passage.

3. C: One can reasonably infer that Gulliver is considerably larger than the children who were playing around him because multiple children could fit into his hand. Choice A is incorrect because there is no indication of stress in Gulliver's tone. Choices B and D aren't the best answers because, though Gulliver seems fond of his new acquaintances, he didn't travel there with the intentions of meeting new people or to express a definite love for them in this particular portion of the text.

4. C: The emperor made a definitive decision to expose Gulliver to their native customs. In this instance, the word *mind* was not related to a vote, question, or cognitive ability.

5. B: The passage indicates that Annabelle has a fear of going outside into the daylight. Thus, *heliophobia* must refer to a fear of bright lights or sunlight. Choice B is the only answer that describes this.

6. C: The answer we seek has both the most detailed and objective information; thus, Choice C is the correct answer. The number of incidents and their relationship to a possible cause are both detailed and objective information. Choice A describing a television commercial with a dramatized reenactment is not particularly detailed. Choice B, a notice to the public informing them of additional drinking and driving units on patrol, is not detailed and objective information. Choice D, a highway bulletin, does not present the type of information required.

7. D: Outspending other countries on education could have other benefits, but there is no reference to this in the passage, so Choice A is incorrect. Choice B is incorrect because the author does not mention corruption. Choice C is incorrect because there is nothing in the passage stating that the tests are not genuinely representative. Choice D is accurate because spending more money has not brought success. The United States already spends the most money, but the country is not excelling on these tests. Choice D is the correct answer.

8. D: Raul wants a book that describes how and why ancient Egyptians built the Great Pyramid of Giza. Choice A is incorrect because it focuses more generally on Giza as a whole, rather than the Great Pyramid itself. Choice B is close but incorrect because it is an autobiography that will largely focus on the archaeologist's life. Choice C is wrong because it focuses on hieroglyphics, not the pyramids. Choice D, the book directly covering the building of the Great Pyramids, should be most helpful.

Answer Explanations #1

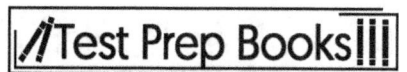

9. D: Cynthia needs to select the meal with the least vegetarian options. Although the breakfast menu, Choice *A*, includes bacon, there is also coffee, tea, French toast, and eggs available. Choice *B*, lunch, includes an option for vegetarian sandwiches along with the French fries and baked beans. The cocktail hour, Choice *C*, does not contain meat or fish. In contrast, the dinner is a vegetarian's nightmare: nothing suitable is offered. Thus, dinner, Choice *D*, is the best answer.

10. C: Because Emma quoted excerpts from the play, she needs to insert citations that give proper credit to the original work being quoted. Failing to do so would constitute plagiarism. The remaining choices are incorrect because they are steps that Emma would have completed earlier in the writing process.

11. B: The author implies that zymosis is a disease ("There were no more diseases after zymosis"), so Choice *B* is correct.

12. D: A *rookery* is a colony of breeding birds. Although *rookery* could mean Choice *A*, houses in a slum area, it does not make sense in this context. Choices *B* and *C* are both incorrect, as this is not a place for hunters to trade tools or for wardens to trade stories.

13. D: The passage directly states that the larger sensor is the main difference between the two cameras. Choices *A* and *B* may be true, but these answers do not identify the major difference between the two cameras. Choice *C* states the opposite of what the paragraph suggests is the best option for amateur photographers, so it is incorrect.

14. D: An actuary assesses risks and sets insurance premiums. While an actuary does work in insurance, the passage does not suggest that actuaries have any affiliation with hospitalists or working in a hospital, so all other choices are incorrect.

15. A: The passage focuses mainly on the problems of hard water. Choice *B* is incorrect because calcium is not good for pipes and hard surfaces. The passage does not say anything about whether water softeners are easy to install, so Choice *C* is incorrect. Choice *D* is also incorrect because the passage does offer other solutions besides vinegar.

16. B: The best place for this sentence given all the answer choices is at the end of the first paragraph. Choice *A* is incorrect; the passage is told in chronological order and leaving the sentence as-is defies that order, since we haven't been introduced to who raised George. Choice *C* is incorrect because this sentence is not an introductory sentence. It does not provide the main topic of the paragraph. Choice *D* is incorrect because again, it defies chronological order. By the end of paragraph two we have already gotten to George as an adult, so this sentence would not make sense here.

17. D: Out of these choices, a semicolon would be the best fit because there is an independent clause on either side of the semicolon, and the two sentences closely relate to each other. Choice *A* is incorrect because putting a comma between two independent clauses (i.e., complete sentences) creates a comma splice. Choice *B* is incorrect; omitting punctuation here creates a run-on sentence. Choice *C* is incorrect because an ellipsis (...) is used to designate an omission in the text.

18. B: Choice *B* is the correct answer because it uses *-ing* verbs as gerunds. Gerunds are *-ing* words that stand in for nouns. The words "growing" and "depleting" are gerunds in this example. Choice *B* also uses the conjunction "and," whereas the other answer choices have comma splices.

19. C: Choice *C* is correct because it keeps with the verb tense in the rest of the passage: past tense. Choice *A* is in present tense, which is incorrect. Choice *B* is present progressive, which means there is a

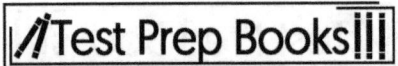

continual action, which is also incorrect. Choice *D* is incorrect because "was returning" is past progressive tense, which means that something was happening continuously at some point in the past.

20. A: Parallelism refers to consistent use of sentence structure or word form. In this case, the list within the sentence does not utilize parallelism; three of the verbs appear in their base form—*travel*, *take*, and *eat*—but one appears as a gerund—*going*. A parallel version of this sentence would be "This summer, I'm planning to travel to Italy, take a Mediterranean cruise, go to Pompeii, and eat a lot of Italian food." Choice *B* is incorrect because this description is a complete sentence. Choice *C* is incorrect, as a misplaced modifier is a modifier that is not located appropriately in relation to the word or words they modify. Choice *D* is incorrect because subject-verb agreement refers to the appropriate conjugation of a verb in relation to its subject.

21. C: In this sentence, the modifier is the phrase "Forgetting that he was supposed to meet his girlfriend for dinner." This phrase offers information about Fred's actions, but the noun that immediately follows it is Anita, creating some confusion about the "do-er" of the phrase. A more appropriate sentence arrangement would be "Forgetting that he was supposed to meet his girlfriend for dinner, Fred made Anita mad when he showed up late." Choice *A* is incorrect, as parallelism refers to the consistent use of sentence structure and verb tense, and this sentence is appropriately consistent. Choice *B* is incorrect as this sentence contains appropriate punctuation for the number of independent clauses presented; it is not a run-on sentence. Choice *D* is incorrect because subject-verb agreement refers to the appropriate conjugation of a verb relative to the subject, and all verbs have been properly conjugated.

22. B: A comma splice occurs when a comma is used to join two independent clauses together without the additional use of an appropriate conjunction. One way to remedy this problem is to replace the comma with a semicolon. Another solution is to add a conjunction: "Some workers use all their sick leave, but other workers cash out their leave." Choice *A* is incorrect, as parallelism refers to the consistent use of sentence structure and verb tense; all tenses and structures in this sentence are consistent. Choice *C* is incorrect because a sentence fragment is a phrase or clause that cannot stand alone—this sentence contains two independent clauses. Choice *D* is incorrect because subject-verb agreement refers to the proper conjugation of a verb relative to the subject, and all verbs have been properly conjugated.

23. D: The problem in the original passage is that the second sentence is a dependent clause that cannot stand alone as a sentence; it must be attached to the main clause found in the first sentence. Because the main clause comes first, it does not need to be separated by a comma. However, if the dependent clause came first, then a comma would be necessary, which is why Choice *C* is incorrect. Choices *A* and *B* also insert unnecessary commas into the sentence.

24. D: In this sentence, the first answer choice requires a noun meaning *impact* or *influence*, so *effect* is the correct answer. For the second answer choice, the sentence is drawing a comparison. *Than* shows a comparative relationship whereas *then* shows sequence or consequence. Choices *A* and *C* can be eliminated because they contain the choice *then*. Choice *B* is incorrect because *affect* is a verb while this sentence requires a noun.

25. C: The original sentence states that despite the author being nervous, she was able to read with poise and confidence, which is stated in Choice *C*. Choice *A* changes the meaning by adding *because*; however, the author didn't read with confidence *because* she was nervous, but *despite* being nervous. Choice *B* is closer to the original meaning; however, it loses the emphasis of her succeeding *despite* her

Answer Explanations #1

condition. Choice *D* adds the word *before*, which doesn't make much sense on its own, much less in relation to the original sentence.

26. D: The original sentence states that there was a storm surge and loss of electricity during the hurricane, making Choice *D* correct. Choices *A* and *B* arrange the storm surge and the loss of electricity within a cause and effect statement, which changes the meaning of the original sentence. Choice *C* changes *surge* from a noun into a verb and creates an entirely different situation.

27. B: The original sentence states that an elephant herd will help and support another herd member if it is sick, so Choice *B* is correct. Choice *A* is incorrect because it states the whole herd will be too sick and too tired to walk instead of a single elephant. Choice *C* is incorrect because the original sentence does not say that the herd gathers food when *they* are sick, but when a single member of the herd is sick. Although Choice *D* might be correct in a general sense, it does not relate to the meaning of the original sentence and is therefore incorrect.

28. A: The original sentence says that after a soccer game, they went out to eat. Choice *A* shows the same sequence: they finished the soccer game *then* went out to eat. Choice *B* is incorrect because it reverses the sequence of events. Choices *C* and *D* are incorrect because the words *so* and *because* change the meaning of the original sentence.

29. B: Choice *B* is correct because the idea of the original sentences is Armani getting lost while walking through Paris. Choice *A* is incorrect because it replaces third person with second person. Choice *C* is incorrect because the word *should* indicates an obligation to get lost. Choice *D* is incorrect because it is not specific to the original sentence but instead makes a generalization about getting lost.

30. C: Choice *C* is correct because it shows that Phoenix buried his cat with her favorite toys after she died, which is true of the original statement. Although Choices *A*, *B*, and *D* mention a backyard, the meanings of these choices are skewed. Choice *A* says that Phoenix buried his cat alive, which is incorrect. Choice *B* says his cat died in the backyard, which we do not know to be true. Choice *D* says Phoenix buried his cat after he buried her toys, which is also incorrect.

TSI Practice Test #2

Math

1. Solve for x, if $x^2 - 2x - 8 = 0$.
    a. $2 \pm \frac{\sqrt{30}}{2}$
    b. $2 \pm 4\sqrt{2}$
    c. 1 ± 3
    d. $4 \pm \sqrt{2}$

2. Which graph will be a line parallel to the graph of $y = 3x - 2$?
    a. $6x - 2y = -2$
    b. $4x - y = -4$
    c. $3y = x - 2$
    d. $2x - 2y = 2$

3. Jessica buys 10 cans of paint. Red paint costs $1 per can, and blue paint costs $2 per can. In total, she spends $16. How many red cans did she buy?
    a. 2
    b. 3
    c. 4
    d. 5

4. For a group of 20 men, the median weight is 180 pounds, and the range is 30 pounds. If each man gains 10 pounds, which of the following would be true?
    a. The median weight will increase, and the range will remain the same.
    b. The median weight and range will both remain the same.
    c. The median weight will stay the same, and the range will increase.
    d. The median weight and range will both increase.

5. A root of $x^2 - 2x - 2$ is:
    a. $1 + \sqrt{3}$
    b. $1 + 2\sqrt{2}$
    c. $2 + 2\sqrt{3}$
    d. $2 - 2\sqrt{3}$

6. What is the product of the following expression?

$$(4x - 8)(5x^2 + x + 6)$$

   a. $20x^3 - 36x^2 + 16x - 48$
   b. $6x^3 - 41x^2 + 12x + 15$
   c. $20x^3 + 11x^2 - 37x - 12$
   d. $2x^3 - 11x^2 - 32x + 20$

7. The graph shows the position of a car over a 10-second time interval. Which of the following is the correct interpretation of the graph for the interval 1 to 3 seconds?

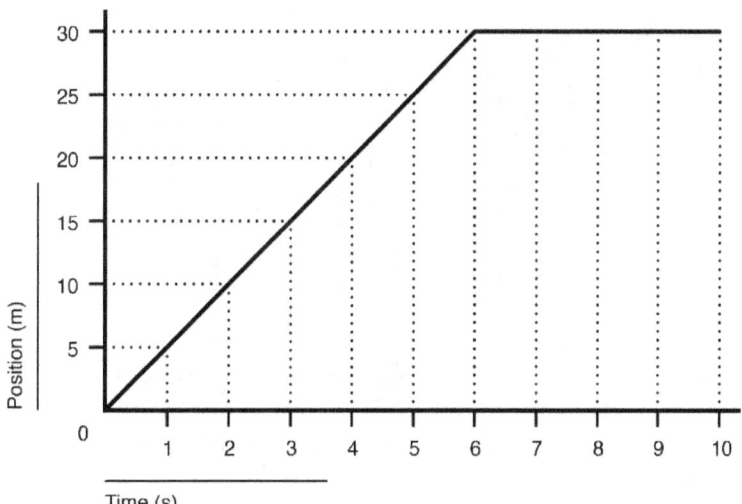

a. The car remains in the same position.
b. The car is traveling at a speed of 5 m/s.
c. The car is traveling up a hill.
d. The car is traveling at 5 mph.

8. What is the y-intercept for $y = x^2 + 3x - 4$?
  a. $y = 1$
  b. $y = -4$
  c. $y = 3$
  d. $y = 4$

9. What is the value of b in the equation: $5b - 4 = 2b + 17$?
  a. 13
  b. 24
  c. 7
  d. 21

10. Dwayne has received the following scores on his math tests: 78, 92, 83, and 97. What score must Dwayne get on his next math test to have an overall average of 90?
  a. 89
  b. 98
  c. 95
  d. 100

11. The following graph compares the various test scores of the top three students in each of these teachers' classes. Based on the graph, which teacher's students' test scores had the smallest range?

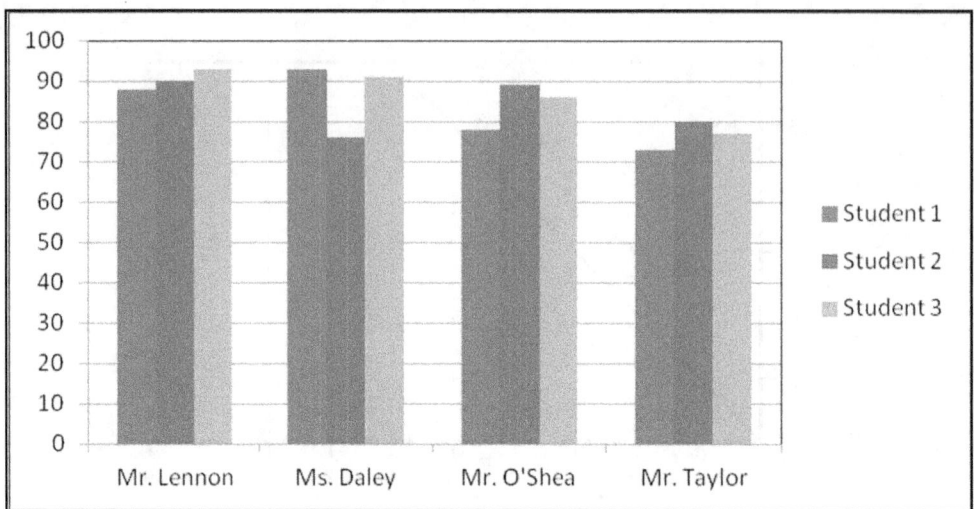

   a. Mr. Lennon
   b. Mr. O'Shea
   c. Mr. Taylor
   d. Ms. Daley

12. What's the probability of rolling a 6 at least once in two rolls of a die?
   a. $\frac{1}{3}$
   b. $\frac{1}{36}$
   c. $\frac{1}{6}$
   d. $\frac{5}{18}$

13. If the point $(-3, -4)$ is reflected over the x-axis, what new point does it make?
   a. $(-3, -4)$
   b. $(3, -4)$
   c. $(3, 4)$
   d. $(-3, 4)$

14. If $-3(x + 4) \geq x + 8$, what is the value of x?
   a. $x = 4$
   b. $x \geq 2$
   c. $x \geq -5$
   d. $x \leq -5$

15. Karen gets paid a weekly salary and a commission for every sale that she makes. The table below shows the number of sales and her pay for different weeks.

Sales	2	7	4	8
Pay	$380	$580	$460	$620

Which of the following equations represents Karen's weekly pay?
- a. $y = 90x + 200$
- b. $y = 90x - 200$
- c. $y = 40x + 300$
- d. $y = 40x - 300$

16. Which of the ordered pairs below is a solution to the following system of inequalities?

$$y > 2x - 3$$

$$y < -4x + 8$$

- a. $(4, 5)$
- b. $(-3, -2)$
- c. $(3, -1)$
- d. $(5, 2)$

17. The area of a given rectangle is 24 cm^2. If the measure of each side is multiplied by 3, what is the area of the new figure?
- a. 48 cm^2
- b. 72 cm^2
- c. 216 cm^2
- d. $13,824 \text{ cm}^2$

18. What is the perimeter of the figure below? Note that the solid outer line is the perimeter.

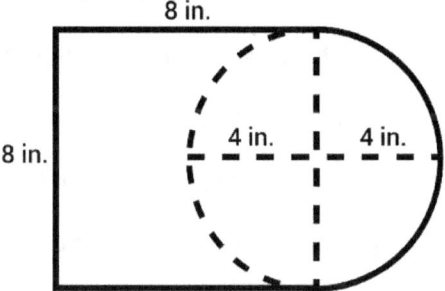

- a. 48.565 in
- b. 36.565 in
- c. 39.78 in
- d. 39.565 in

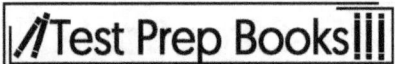

19. The graph of which function has an x-intercept of -2?
    a. $y = 2x - 3$
    b. $y = 4x + 2$
    c. $y = x^2 + 5x + 6$
    d. $y = 2x^2 + 3x - 1$

20. In Jim's school, there are a total of 650 students. There are three girls for every two boys. How many students are girls?
    a. 260 girls
    b. 130 girls
    c. 65 girls
    d. 390 girls

English Language Arts and Reading

The next article is for questions 1-4:

The Old Man and His Grandson

There was once a very old man, whose eyes had become dim, his ears dull of hearing, his knees trembled, and when he sat at table he could hardly hold the spoon, and spilt the broth upon the table-cloth or let it run out of his mouth. His son and his son's wife were disgusted at this, so the old grandfather at last had to sit in the corner behind the stove, and they gave him his food in an earthenware bowl, and not even enough of it. And he used to look towards the table with his eyes full of tears. Once, too, his trembling hands could not hold the bowl, and it fell to the ground and broke. The young wife scolded him, but he said nothing and only sighed. Then they brought him a wooden bowl for a few half-pence, out of which he had to eat.

They were once sitting thus when the little grandson of four years old began to gather together some bits of wood upon the ground. 'What are you doing there?' asked the father. 'I am making a little trough,' answered the child, 'for father and mother to eat out of when I am big.'

The man and his wife looked at each other for a while, and presently began to cry. Then they took the old grandfather to the table, and henceforth always let him eat with them, and likewise said nothing if he did spill a little of anything.

(Grimms' Fairy Tales, p. 111)

1. Which of the following most accurately represents the theme of the passage?
   a. Respect your elders.
   b. Children will follow their parents' example.
   c. You reap what you sow.
   d. Loyalty will save your life.

2. How is the content in this selection organized?
   a. Chronologically
   b. Problem and solution
   c. Compare and contrast
   d. Order of importance

3. Which character trait most accurately reflects the son and his wife in this story?
   a. Compassion
   b. Understanding
   c. Cruelty
   d. Impatience

4. Where does the story take place?
   a. In the countryside
   b. In America
   c. In a house
   d. In a forest

Below, there is a blank in each question. Choose the word or phrase in the answer choice that best fits the meaning of the sentence as a whole.

5. Before she put a down payment on the house, the would-be buyer had to make sure the house was properly _____ first.
   a. Vacated
   b. Dilapidated
   c. Inspected
   d. Insulated

6. The time had come when Deirdre knew she had to _____ her position at her company in order to go back to school and earn a degree.
   a. Relinquish
   b. Rearrange
   c. Reciprocate
   d. Receive

Directions for questions 7–12: After reading the passage, choose the best answer to the question based on what is stated in the passage.

7. Coaches of kids' sports teams are increasingly concerned about the behavior of parents at games. Parents are screaming and cursing at coaches, officials, players, and other parents. Physical fights have even broken out at games. Parents need to be reminded that coaches are volunteers, giving up their time and energy to help kids develop in their chosen sport. The goal of kids' sports teams is to learn and develop skills, but it's also to have fun. When parents are out of control at games and practices, it takes the fun out of the sport.

From this passage, what can be concluded?
   a. Coaches are modeling good behavior for kids.
   b. Organized sports are not good for kids.
   c. Parents' behavior at their kids' games needs to change.
   d. Parents and coaches need to work together.

8. While scientists aren't entirely certain why tornadoes form, they have some clues about the process. Tornadoes are dangerous funnel clouds that occur during a large thunderstorm. When warm, humid air near the ground meets cold, dry air from above, a column of the warm air can be drawn up into the clouds. Winds at different altitudes blowing at different speeds make the column of air rotate. As the spinning column of air picks up speed, a funnel cloud is formed. This funnel cloud moves rapidly and haphazardly. Rain and hail inside the cloud cause it to touch down, creating a tornado. Tornadoes move in a rapid and unpredictable pattern, making them extremely destructive and dangerous. Scientists continue to study tornadoes to improve radar detection and warning times.

The main purpose of this passage is to do which of the following?
   a. Show why tornadoes are dangerous.
   b. Explain how a tornado forms.
   c. Compare thunderstorms to tornadoes.
   d. Explain what to do in the event of a tornado.

9. Many people are unsure of exactly how the digestive system works. Digestion begins in the mouth where teeth grind up food and saliva breaks it down, making it easier for the body to absorb. Next, the food moves to the esophagus, and it is pushed into the stomach. The stomach is where food is stored and broken down further by acids and digestive enzymes, preparing it for passage into the intestines. The small intestine is where the nutrients are taken from food and passed into the blood stream. Other essential organs like the liver, gall bladder, and pancreas aid the stomach in breaking down food and absorbing nutrients. Finally, food waste is passed into the large intestine where it is eliminated by the body.

The purpose of this passage is to do which of the following?
   a. Explain how the liver works.
   b. Show why it is important to eat healthy foods.
   c. Explain how the digestive system works.
   d. Show how nutrients are absorbed by the small intestine.

10. Osteoporosis is a medical condition that occurs when the body loses bone or makes too little bone. This can lead to brittle, fragile bones that easily break. Bones are already porous, and when osteoporosis sets in, the spaces in bones become much larger, causing them to weaken. Both men and women can contract osteoporosis, though it is most common in women over age 50. Loss of bone can be silent and progressive, so it is important to be proactive in prevention of the disease.

The main purpose of this passage is to do which of the following?
a. Discuss some of the ways people contract osteoporosis.
b. Describe different treatment options for those with osteoporosis.
c. Explain how to prevent osteoporosis.
d. Define osteoporosis.

11. Vacationers looking for a perfect experience should opt out of Disney parks and try a trip on Disney Cruise Lines. While a park offers rides, characters, and show experiences, it also includes long lines, often very hot weather, and enormous crowds. A Disney cruise, on the other hand, is a relaxing, luxurious vacation that includes many of the same experiences as the parks, minus the crowds and lines. The cruise has top-notch food, maid service, water slides, multiple pools, Broadway-quality shows, and daily character experiences for kids. There are also many activities, such as bingo, trivia contests, and dance parties that can entertain guests of all ages. The cruise even stops at Disney's private island for a beach barbecue with characters, water slides, and water sports. Those looking for the Disney experience without the hassle should book a Disney cruise.

The main purpose of this passage is to do which of the following?
a. Explain how to book a Disney cruise.
b. Show what Disney parks have to offer.
c. Show why Disney parks are expensive.
d. Compare Disney parks to a Disney cruise.

12. As summer approaches, drowning incidents will increase. Drowning happens very quickly and silently. Most people assume that drowning is easy to spot, but a person who is drowning doesn't make noise or wave their arms. Instead, they will have their head back and their mouth open, with just the face out of the water. A person who is truly in danger of drowning is not able to wave their arms in the air or move much at all. Recognizing these signs of drowning can prevent tragedy.

The main purpose of this passage is to do which of the following?
a. Explain the dangers of swimming
b. Show how to identify the signs of drowning
c. Explain how to be a lifeguard
d. Compare the signs of drowning

The next question is based on the following conversation between a scientist and a politician.

> Scientist: Last year was the warmest ever recorded in the last 134 years. During that time period, the 10 warmest years have all occurred since 2000. This correlates directly with the recent increases in carbon dioxide as large countries like China, India, and Brazil continue developing and industrializing. No longer do just a handful of countries burn massive amounts of carbon-based fossil fuels; it is quickly becoming the case throughout the whole world as technology and industry spread.

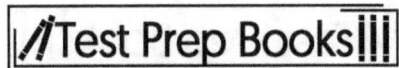

Politician: Yes, but there is no causal link between increases in carbon emissions and increasing temperatures. The link is tenuous and nothing close to certain. We need to wait for all of the data before drawing hasty conclusions. For all we know, the temperature increase could be entirely natural. I believe the temperatures also rose dramatically during the dinosaurs' time, and I do not think they were burning any fossil fuels back then.

13. What is one point on which the scientist and politician agree?
    a. Burning fossil fuels causes global temperatures to rise.
    b. Global temperatures are increasing.
    c. Countries must revisit their energy policies before it's too late.
    d. Earth's climate naturally goes through warming and cooling periods.

The next question is based on the following passage.

A famous children's author recently published a historical fiction novel under a pseudonym; however, it did not sell as many copies as her children's books. In her earlier years, she had majored in history and earned a graduate degree in Antebellum American History, which is the time frame of her new novel. Critics praised this newest work far more than the children's series that made her famous. In fact, her new novel was nominated for the prestigious Albert J. Beveridge Award but still isn't selling like her children's books, which fly off the shelves because of her name alone.

14. Which one of the following statements might be accurately inferred based on the above passage?
    a. The famous children's author produced an inferior book under her pseudonym.
    b. The famous children's author is the foremost expert on Antebellum America.
    c. The famous children's author did not receive the bump in publicity for her historical novel that it would have received if it were written under her given name.
    d. People generally prefer to read children's series over historical fiction.

The next article is for question 15.

The Myth of Head Heat Loss

It has recently been brought to my attention that most people believe that 75% of your body heat is lost through your head. I had certainly heard this before, and I'm not going to attempt to say I didn't believe it when I first heard it. It is natural to be gullible to anything said with enough authority. But the "fact" that the majority of your body heat is lost through your head is a lie.

Let me explain. Heat loss is proportional to surface area exposed. An elephant loses a great deal more heat than an anteater because it has a much greater surface area than an anteater. Each cell has mitochondria that produce energy in the form of heat, and it takes a lot more energy to run an elephant than an anteater.

So, each part of your body loses its proportional amount of heat in accordance with its surface area. The human torso probably loses the most heat, though the legs lose a significant amount as well. Some people have asked, "Why does it feel so much warmer when you cover your head than when you don't?" Well, that's because your head loses a lot of heat when it is not clothed, while the clothing on the rest of your body provides insulation. If you went outside with a hat and pants but no shirt, not only would you look silly, but your heat loss would be significantly greater because so much more of you would be exposed. So, if given the choice to cover your chest or your head in the cold, choose the chest. It could save your life.

15. The author appeals to which branch of rhetoric to prove their case?
    a. Factual evidence
    b. Emotion
    c. Ethics and morals
    d. Author qualification

Read the following section about Fred Hampton and answer Questions 16-19.

1 (16) <u>As the Black Panther Party's popularity and influence grew, the Federal Bureau of Investigation (FBI) placed the group under constant surveillance.</u> In an attempt to neutralize the party, the FBI launched several harassment campaigns against the BPP, raided its headquarters in Chicago three times, and arrested over 100 of the group's members. Hampton was shot during such a raid that occurred on the morning of December 4th 1969.

2 (17) <u>In 1976; seven years after the event,</u> it was revealed that William O'Neal, Hampton's trusted bodyguard, was an undercover FBI agent. (18) <u>O'Neal will provide</u> the FBI with detailed floor plans of the BPP's headquarters, identifying the exact location of Hampton's bed. It was because of these floor plans that the police were able to target and kill Hampton.

3 The assassination of Hampton fueled outrage amongst the African American community. It was not until years after the assassination that the police admitted wrongdoing. (19) <u>The Chicago City Council now are commemorating December 4th as Fred Hampton Day.</u>

16. Which of the following would be the best replacement for the underlined portion of the sentence reproduced below?

    As the Black Panther Party's popularity and influence grew, the Federal Bureau of Investigation (FBI) placed the group under constant surveillance.

    a. (as it is now)
    b. The Federal Bureau of Investigation (FBI) placed the group under constant surveillance as the Black Panther Party's popularity and influence grew.
    c. Placing the group under constant surveillance, the Black Panther Party's popularity and influence grew.
    d. As their influence and popularity grew, the FBI placed the group under constant surveillance.

17. Which of the following would be the best replacement for the underlined portion of the sentence reproduced below?

> *<u>In 1976; seven years after the event,</u> it was revealed that William O'Neal, Hampton's trusted bodyguard, was an undercover FBI agent.*

   a. (as it is now)
   b. In 1976, seven years after the event,
   c. In 1976 seven years after the event,
   d. In 1976. Seven years after the event,

18. Which of the following would be the best replacement for the underlined portion of the sentence reproduced below?

> *<u>O'Neal will provide</u> the FBI with detailed floor plans of the BPP's headquarters, identifying the exact location of Hampton's bed.*

   a. (as it is now)
   b. O'Neal provides
   c. O'Neal provided
   d. O'Neal, providing

19. Which of the following would be the best replacement for the underlined portion of the sentence reproduced below?

> *<u>The Chicago City Council now are commemorating December 4th as Fred Hampton Day.</u>*

   a. (as it is now)
   b. Fred Hampton Day by the Chicago City Council, December 4, is now commemorated.
   c. Now commemorated December 4th is Fred Hampton Day.
   d. The Chicago City Council now commemorates December 4th as Fred Hampton Day.

20. Which of the following sentences uses correct punctuation?
    a. Carole is not currently working; her focus is on her children at the moment.
    b. Carole is not currently working and her focus is on her children at the moment.
    c. Carole is not currently working, her focus is on her children at the moment.
    d. Carole is not currently working her focus is on her children at the moment.

21. Which of these examples shows INCORRECT use of subject-verb agreement?
    a. Neither of the cars are parked on the street.
    b. Both of my kids are going to camp this summer.
    c. Any of your friends are welcome to join us on the trip in November.
    d. Each of the clothing options is appropriate for the job interview.

22. When it gets warm in the spring, _____ and _____ like to go fishing at Cobbs Creek.

   Which of the following word pairs should be used in the blanks above?

   a. me, him
   b. he, I
   c. him, I
   d. he, me

23. Which of the following examples uses correct punctuation?
   a. Recommended supplies for the hunting trip include the following: rain gear, a large backpack, hiking boots, a flashlight, and non-perishable foods.
   b. I left the store, because I forgot my wallet.
   c. As soon as the team checked into the hotel; they met in the lobby for a group photo.
   d. None of the furniture came in on time: so they weren't able to move into the new apartment.

24. Which of the following sentences uses correct subject-verb agreement?
   a. There is two constellations that can be seen from the back of the house.
   b. At least four of the sheep needs to be sheared before the end of summer.
   c. Lots of people were auditioning for the singing competition on Saturday.
   d. Everyone in the group have completed the assignment on time.

Directions for questions 25–30

Rewrite each sentence, following the directions given below. Your new sentence should be well written and should fundamentally have the same meaning as the original sentence.

25. If you were to rewrite the sentence below, beginning with "Tears streamed down my eyes," what would the next words be?

While I was in the helicopter, I saw the sunset, and tears streamed down my eyes.
   a. while I watched the helicopter fly into the sunset.
   b. because the sunset flew up into the sky.
   c. because the helicopter was facing the sunset.
   d. when I saw the sunset from the helicopter.

26. I won't go to the party unless some of my friends go.

Rewrite, beginning with

<u>I will go the party</u>

The next words will be
   a. if I want to.
   b. if my friends go.
   c. since a couple of my friends are going.
   d. unless people I know go.

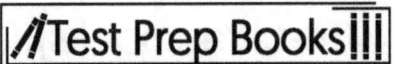

27. He had a broken leg before the car accident, so it took him a long time to recover.

Rewrite, beginning with

He took a long time to recover from the car accident

The next words will be
   a. from his two broken legs.
   b. after he broke his leg.
   c. because he already had a broken leg.
   d. since he broke his leg again afterward.

28. We had a party the day after Halloween to celebrate my birthday.

Rewrite, beginning with

It was my birthday

The next words will be
   a. , so we celebrated with a party the day after Halloween.
   b. the day of Halloween so we celebrated with a party.
   c. , and we celebrated with a Halloween party the day after.
   d. a few days before Halloween, so we threw a party.

29. There are many risks in firefighting, including smoke inhalation, exposure to hazardous materials, and oxygen deprivation, so firefighters are outfitted with many items that could save their lives, including a self-contained breathing apparatus.

Rewrite, beginning with

so firefighters

The next words will be which of the following?
   a. are exposed to lots of dangerous situations.
   b. need to be very careful on the job.
   c. wear life-saving protective gear.
   d. have very risky jobs.

30. Though social media sites like Facebook, Instagram, and Snapchat have become increasingly popular, experts warn that teen users are exposing themselves to many dangers such as cyberbullying and predators.

Rewrite, beginning with

Experts warn that

The next words will be which of the following?
   a. Facebook is dangerous.
   b. they are growing in popularity.
   c. teens are using them too much.
   d. they can be dangerous for teens.

144

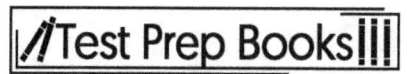

Essay

Please read the prompt below and answer in an essay format in 300–600 words.

Coaches of kids' sports teams are increasingly concerned about the behavior of parents at games. Parents are screaming and cursing at coaches, officials, players, and other parents. Physical fights have even broken out at games. Parents need to be reminded that coaches are volunteers, giving up their time and energy to help kids develop in their chosen sport. The goal of kids' sports teams is to learn and develop skills, but it's also to have fun. When parents are out of control at games and practices, it takes the fun out of the sport.

1. Analyze and evaluate the passage given.

2. State and develop your own perspective.

3. Explain the relationship between your perspective and the one given.

The following pages are provided for writing your essay.

Answer Explanations #2

Math

1. C: The quadratic formula can be used to solve this problem. Given the equation, use the values $a = 1$, $b = -2$, and $c = -8$.

$$x = \frac{-b \pm \sqrt{b^2 - 4ac}}{2a} = \frac{-(-2) \pm \sqrt{(-2)^2 - 4(1)(-8)}}{2(1)}$$

From here, simplify to solve for x.

$$x = \frac{2 \pm \sqrt{4 + 32}}{2} = \frac{2 \pm \sqrt{36}}{2} = \frac{2 \pm 6}{2} = 1 \pm 3$$

2. A: Parallel lines have the same slope. The slope of the given equation is 3. The slope of Choice C can be seen to be $\frac{1}{3}$ by dividing both sides by 3. The other choices are in standard form $Ax + By = C$, for which the slope is given by $\frac{-A}{B}$. For Choice A, the equation can be written as $6x - 2y = -2$. Therefore, the slope is:

$$\frac{-A}{B} = \frac{-6}{-2} = 3$$

This is the same as the given equation. The slope of Choice B is:

$$\frac{-A}{B} = \frac{-4}{-1} = 4$$

The slope of Choice B is 4. The slope of Choice D is:

$$\frac{-A}{B} = \frac{-2}{-2} = 1$$

Therefore, the only equation with a parallel slope of 3 is $6x - 2y = -2$

3. C: The question states that red cans are $1 each and blue cans are $2 each. Since the total cost is $16, use the equation $r \times 1 + b \times 2 = 16$, where r is the number of red cans and b is the number of blue cans. It can be written more simply as $r + 2b = 16$.

Because Jessica buys 10 cans total, $r + b = 10$, so $b = 10 - r$. Substituting in $10 - r$ for b in the original equation ($r + 2b = 16$), gives the equation $r + 2(10 - r) = 16$. Simplifying and solving for r gives the answer:

$$r + 20 - 2r = 16$$

$$20 - r = 16$$

$$r = 4$$

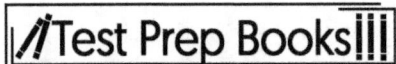

Answer Explanations #2

4. A: If each man gains 10 pounds, every original data point will increase by 10 pounds. Therefore, the man with the original median will still have the median value, but that value will increase by 10. The smallest value and largest value will also increase by 10, so the difference between the two (the range) will remain the same.

5. A: You can put each answer choice into the expression as an x value and see which value makes it equal zero. Or you can use the quadratic formula, which gives:

$$x = \frac{2 \pm \sqrt{(-2)^2 - 4(1)(-2)}}{2} = = \frac{2}{2} \pm \frac{\sqrt{12}}{2} = 1 \pm \frac{\sqrt{12}}{2}$$

$$1 \pm \frac{\sqrt{4}\sqrt{3}}{2} = 1 \pm \frac{2\sqrt{3}}{2} = 1 \pm \sqrt{3}$$

The only one of these which appears as an answer choice is $1 + \sqrt{3}$.

6. A: Finding the product means distributing one polynomial over the other so that each term in the first is multiplied by each term in the second. Then, like terms can be collected. Multiplying the factors yields the expression:

$$20x^3 + 4x^2 + 24x - 40x^2 - 8x - 48$$

Collecting like terms means adding the x^2 terms and adding the x terms. The final answer after simplifying the expression is:

$$20x^3 - 36x^2 + 16x - 48$$

7. B: The car is traveling at a speed of 5 meters per second. On the interval from 1 to 3 seconds, the position changes by 10 meters. This is 10 meters in 2 seconds, or 5 meters in each second.

8. B: The y-intercept of an equation is found where the x-value is zero. Plugging zero into the equation for x, the first two terms cancel out, leaving -4 as the correct answer:

$$y = 0^2 + 3(0) - 4 = -4$$

9. C: To solve for the value of b, isolate the variable b on one side of the equation.

Start by moving the lower value of -4 to the other side by adding 4 to both sides:

$$5b - 4 = 2b + 17$$

$$5b - 4 + 4 = 2b + 17 + 4$$

$$5b = 2b + 21$$

Then subtract $2b$ from both sides:

$$5b - 2b = 2b + 21 - 2b$$

$$3b = 21$$

150

Then, divide both sides by 3 to get the value of b:

$$\frac{3b}{3} = \frac{21}{3}$$

$$b = 7$$

10. D: To find the average of a set of values, add the values together and then divide by the total number of values. In this case, include the unknown value, x, of what Dwayne needs to score on his next test. The average must equal 90. Set up the equation and solve:

First, combine like terms:

$$\frac{78 + 92 + 83 + 97 + x}{5} = 90$$

$$\frac{350 + x}{5} = 90$$

Next, multiply both sides by 5:

$$(5)\left(\frac{350 + x}{5}\right) = (90)(5)$$

$$350 + x = 450$$

Lastly, subtract 350 from both sides:

$$350 + x - 350 = 450 - 350$$

$$x = 100$$

11. A: To calculate the range in a set of data, subtract the lowest value from the highest value. In this graph, the range of Mr. Lennon's students is 5, which can be seen physically in the graph as having the smallest difference between the highest value and the lowest value compared with the other teachers.

12. D: If we roll a die twice, there are six possibilities for the first roll and six for the second roll, which gives $6 \times 6 = 36$ total possibilities. Now, how many ways are there to roll exactly one 6? We could get a 6 & 1, or 6 & 2, or 6 & 3, or 6 & 4, or 6 & 5. Furthermore, the 6 could come on the second roll; we could get a 1 & 6, or 2 & 6, or 3 & 6, or 4 & 6, or 5 & 6. Counting these up, we find a total of 10 different ways to roll exactly one 6. That means the event could happen in 10 out of 36 possible rolls, so the probability is $\frac{10}{36}$, which simplifies to $\frac{5}{18}$.

13. D: When a point is reflected over an axis, the sign of at least one of the coordinates must change. When it's reflected over the x-axis, the sign of the y coordinate must change. The x-value remains the same. Therefore, the new point is $(-3, 4)$.

14. D: Solve a linear inequality in a similar way to solving a linear equation. First, start by distributing the -3 on the left side of the inequality.

$$-3x - 12 \geq x + 8$$

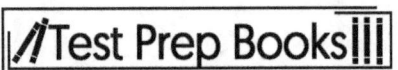

Answer Explanations #2

Then, add 12 to both sides.

$$-3x \geq x + 20$$

Next, subtract x from both sides.

$$-4x \geq 20$$

Finally, divide both sides of the inequality by -4. Don't forget to flip the inequality sign because you are dividing by a negative number.

$$x \leq -5$$

15. C: In this scenario, the variables are the number of sales and Karen's weekly pay. The weekly pay depends on the number of sales. Therefore, weekly pay is the dependent variable (y), and the number of sales is the independent variable (x). All four answer choices are in slope-intercept form, $y = mx + b$, so we just need to find m (the slope) and b (the y-intercept). We can calculate both by picking any two points, for example, (2, 380) and (4, 460).

The slope is given by $m = \frac{y_2 - y_1}{x_2 - x_1}$, so $m = \frac{460 - 380}{4 - 2} = 40$. This gives us the equation $y = 40x + b$. Now we can plug in the x and y values from our first point to find b. Since $380 = 40(2) + b$, we find $b = 300$. This means the equation is $y = 40x + 300$.

16. B: For an ordered pair to be a solution to a system of inequalities, it must make a true statement for both inequalities when substituting its values for x and y. Substituting $(-3, -2)$ into the inequalities produces:

$$(-2) > 2(-3) - 3,$$

which becomes $-2 > -9$,

and

$$(-2) < -4(-3) + 8,$$

which becomes $-2 < 20$

Both are true statements.

17. C: The area of a rectangle is $A = lw$. We don't know the length or width of this rectangle, but the area is 24, so we can say that $lw = 24$. Length and width are each multiplied by 3, so the area of our new rectangle is $3l \times 3w$, or $9lw$. Since we know that $lw = 24$, the area of the new rectangle is $9lw = 9 \times 24 = 216$ cm^2.

18. B: The figure is composed of three sides of a square and a semicircle. The sides of the square are simply added:

$$8 \text{ in} + 8 \text{ in} + 8 \text{ in} = 24 \text{ in}$$

Answer Explanations #2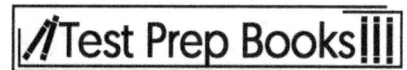

The circumference of a circle is found by the equation $C = 2\pi r$. The radius is 4 in, so the circumference of the circle is approximately 25.13 in. Only half of the circle makes up the outer border of the figure (part of the perimeter), and half of 25.13 in is 12.565 in. Therefore, the total perimeter is:

$$24 \text{ in} + 12.565 \text{ in} = 36.565 \text{ in}$$

The other answer choices use the incorrect formula or fail to include all of the necessary sides.

19. C: An x-intercept is a point where the graph crosses the x-axis. At this point, the value of y is 0. To determine if an equation has an x-intercept of -2, substitute -2 for x, and calculate the value of y. If the value of -2 for x corresponds with a y-value of 0, then the equation has an x-intercept of -2. The only answer choice that produces this result is Choice C.

$$0 = (-2)^2 + 5(-2) + 6$$

20. D: Three girls for every two boys can be expressed as a ratio, $3:2$. This can be visualized as splitting the school into five groups: three girl groups and two boy groups. The number of students that are in each group can be found by dividing the total number of students by five:

$$\frac{650 \text{ students}}{5 \text{ groups}} = \frac{130 \text{ students}}{\text{group}}$$

To find the total number of girls, multiply the number of students per group (130) by the number of girl groups in the school (3). This equals 390, Choice D.

English Language Arts and Reading

1. B: Choice B fits most appropriately with the primary purpose because the son and wife realize that, when they grow old, their child is planning on treating them the same cruel way that they treat the grandfather. Choice A is incorrect because even though the parents are treating the grandfather with disrespect, the purpose of the passage is more about how children respond to their parents' actions. Choice C, to "reap what you sow," means that there are repercussions for every action, yet the parents receive no punishment other than their own sorrow. Choice D is incorrect because, even though it may be argued that the boy is being loyal to his grandfather, this does not fit with the primary purpose.

2. A: Choice A is correct because it follows a series of events that happen in order, one right after the other. First the grandfather spills his food, then his son puts him in a corner, then the child makes a trough for his parents to eat out of when he's older, and finally the parents welcome the old man back to the table. Choice B is incorrect as even though it could be argued that the way they treat the old man is a problem, there really isn't a solution to the problem, even though they stop treating him badly. Also, problem and solution styles generally do not follow a chronological timeline. Choice C is incorrect because events in the passage are not compared and contrasted; this is not a primary organizational structure of the passage. Choice D is incorrect because there is no language to indicate that one person or event is more important than the other.

3. C: Choice C is correct because it condenses the terrible actions of the son and his wife into a single, appropriate word. Choice A is incorrect because although they show him compassion in the end, it is only out of a selfish realization that they will be treated the same way when they are older. Choice B is incorrect because the son and his wife neither understand nor care about the grandfather's aging

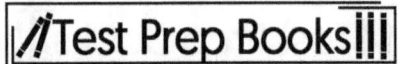

troubles. Choice D may be tempting to pick as they are impatient with him, but it is not the best answer. People can be impatient without being cruel.

4. C: Choice A is incorrect as there is no descriptive language to indicate that they are in the countryside. Choice B is incorrect because the passage has no language or descriptions to indicate they are in America. Choice C is correct because the setting contains elements of a house: a table, a stove, and a corner. Choice D may be tempting as there is mention of "bits of wood upon the ground," but as there are no other elements of a forest in the story, this is not the correct answer.

5. C: The best word here is *inspected*, which means *approved* or *investigated*. Choice A, *vacated*, means to leave empty. While this is a possible choice, it is not the best choice because it is assumed that the house would be vacated before it was bought. Choice B, *dilapidated*, means decayed. Someone buying a house does not want the house to be decayed, so this is incorrect. Choice D, *insulated*, means that the house would be properly enclosed against the loss of heat or the intrusion of sound. Although this is a possible answer, this would be included in an inspection. Therefore, Choice D is incorrect.

6. A: *Relinquish. Relinquish* most closely means to give up or let go. Deirdre knew she had to give up her position in order to go back to school. Choice B, *rearrange*, means to shift or change. Choice C, *reciprocate*, means to exchange or swap. Choice D, *receive*, means to accept.

7. C: The main point of this paragraph is that parents need to change their poor behavior at their kids' sporting events. Choice A is incorrect because the coaches' behavior is not mentioned in the paragraph. Choice B suggests that sports are bad for kids, but the paragraph is about parents' behavior, so it is incorrect. While Choice D may be true, it offers a specific solution to the problem, which the paragraph does not discuss.

8. B: The main point of this passage is to show how a tornado forms. Choice A is off base because while the passage does mention that tornadoes are dangerous, it is not the main focus of the passage. While thunderstorms are mentioned, they are not compared to tornadoes, so Choice C is incorrect. Choice D is incorrect because the passage does not discuss what to do in the event of a tornado.

9. C: The purpose of this passage is to explain how the digestive system works. Choice A focuses only on the liver, which is a small part of the process and not the focus of the paragraph. Choice B is off-track because the passage does not mention healthy foods. Choices D and E each only focus on one part of the digestive system.

10. D: The main point of this passage is to define osteoporosis. Choice A is incorrect because the passage does not list ways that people contract osteoporosis. Choice B is incorrect because the passage does not mention any treatment options. While the passage does briefly mention prevention, it does not explain how, so Choice C is incorrect.

11. D: The passage compares Disney cruises with Disney parks. It does not discuss how to book a cruise, so Choice A is incorrect. Choice B is incorrect because, though the passage does mention some of the park attractions, it is not the main point. The passage does not mention the cost of either option, so Choice C is incorrect.

12. B: The point of this passage is to show what drowning looks like. Choice A is incorrect because while drowning is a danger of swimming, the passage doesn't mention any other dangers. The passage is for a general audience, not lifeguards specifically, so Choice C is incorrect. There are a few signs of drowning, but the passage does not compare them; thus, Choice D is incorrect.

13. B: The scientist and politician largely disagree, but the question asks for a point where the two are in agreement. The politician would not concur that burning fossil fuels causes global temperatures to rise; thus, Choice *A* is wrong. The politician also would not agree with Choice *C* suggesting that countries must revisit their energy policies. By inference from the given information, the scientist would likely not concur that earth's climate naturally goes through warming and cooling cycles; so Choice *D* is incorrect. However, both the scientist and politician would agree that global temperatures are increasing. The reason for this is in dispute. The politician thinks it is part of the earth's natural cycle; the scientist thinks it is from the burning of fossil fuels. However, both acknowledge an increase, so Choice *B* is the correct answer.

14. C: We are looking for an inference—a conclusion that is reached on the basis of evidence and reasoning—from the passage that will likely explain why the famous children's author did not achieve her usual success with the new genre (despite the book's acclaim). Choice *A* is wrong because the statement is false according to the passage. Choice *B* is wrong because, although the passage says the author has a graduate degree on the subject, it would be an unrealistic leap to infer that she is the foremost expert on Antebellum America. Choice *D* is wrong because there is nothing in the passage to lead us to infer that people generally prefer a children's series to historical fiction. In contrast, Choice *C* can be logically inferred since the passage speaks of the great success of the children's series and the declaration that the fame of the author's name causes the children's books to "fly off the shelves." Thus, we can infer that she did not receive any bump from her name since she published the historical novel under a pseudonym, which makes Choice *C* correct.

15. A: The author gives logical examples and reasons in order to prove that most of one's heat is not lost through their head, therefore Choice *A* is correct. Choice *B* is incorrect because there is not much emotionally charged language in this selection, and even the small amount present is greatly outnumbered by the facts and evidence. Choice *C* is incorrect because there is no mention of ethics or morals in this selection. Choice *D* is incorrect because the author never qualifies himself as someone who has the authority to be writing on this topic.

16. A: Choice *A* is correct because it provides the most clarity. Choice *B* is incorrect because it doesn't name the group until the end, so the phrase "the group" is vague. Choice *C* is incorrect because it indicates that the BPP's popularity grew as a result of placing the group under constant surveillance, which is incorrect. Choice *D* is incorrect because there is a misplaced modifier; this sentence actually says that the FBI's influence and popularity grew, which is incorrect.

17. B: Choice *B* is correct. Choice *A* is incorrect because there should be an independent clause on either side of a semicolon, and the phrase "In 1976" is not an independent clause. Choice *C* is incorrect because there should be a comma after introductory phrases in general, such as "In 1976," and Choice *C* omits a comma. Choice *D* is incorrect because the sentence "In 1976." is a fragment.

18. C: Choice *C* is correct because the past tense verb "provided" fits in with the rest of the verb tense throughout the passage. Choice *A*, "will provide," is future tense. Choice *B*, "provides," is present tense. Choice *D*, "providing," is a present participle, which means the action is continuous.

19. D: The correct answer is Choice *D* because this statement provides the most clarity. Choice *A* is incorrect because the noun "Chicago City Council" acts as one, so the verb "are" should be singular, not plural. Choice *B* is incorrect because it is perhaps the most confusingly worded out of all the answer choices; the phrase "December 4" interrupts the sentence without any indication of purpose. Choice *C* is incorrect because it is too vague and leaves out *who* does the commemorating.

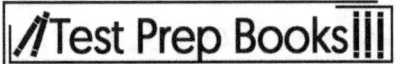

20. A: Choice A is correct because it uses a semicolon to join the two independent clauses (clauses that could function as independent sentences). Choice B is incorrect because the conjunction is not preceded by a comma. A comma and conjunction should be used together to join independent clauses. Choice C is incorrect because a comma should only be used to join independent sentences when it also includes a coordinating conjunction such as *and* or *so*. Choice D does not use punctuation to join the independent clauses, so it is considered a fused (same as a run-on) sentence.

21. A: Choice A uses incorrect subject-verb agreement because the indefinite pronoun *neither* is singular and must use the singular verb form *is*. In Choice B, the pronoun *both* is plural and uses the plural verb form of *are*. The pronoun *any* can be either singular or plural. In Choice C, it is plural, so the plural verb form *are* is used. The pronoun *each* is singular and uses the singular verb form *is*, as seen in Choice D.

22. B: Choice B is correct because the pronouns *he* and *I* are in the subjective case. *He* and *I* are the subjects of the verb *like* in the independent clause of the sentence. Choices A, C, and D are incorrect because they all contain at least one objective pronoun (*me* and *him*). Objective pronouns should not be used as the subject of the sentence, but rather, they should come as an object of a verb. To test for correct pronoun usage, try reading the pronouns as if they were the only pronoun in the sentence. For example, *he* and *me* may appear to be the correct answer choices, but try reading them as the only pronoun.

> He like[s] to go fishing...
>
> Me like to go fishing...
>
> When looked at that way, *me* is an obviously incorrect choice.

23. A: In this example, a colon is correctly used to introduce a series of items. Choice B places an unnecessary comma before the word *because*. A comma is not needed before the word *because* when it introduces a dependent clause at the end of a sentence and provides necessary information to understand the sentence. Choice C is incorrect because it uses a semi-colon instead of a comma to join a dependent clause and an independent clause. Choice D is incorrect because it uses a colon in place of a comma and coordinating conjunction to join two independent clauses.

24. C: The simple subject of this sentence, the word *lots*, is plural. It agrees with the plural verb form *were*. Choice A is incorrect, because the simple subject *there*, referring to the two constellations, is considered plural. It does not agree with the singular verb form *is*. In Choice B, the singular subject *four*, does not agree with the plural verb form *needs*. In Choice D, the plural subject *everyone* does not agree with the singular verb form *have*.

25. D: Choice D is correct because it expresses the sentiment of a moment of joy bringing tears to one's eyes as one sees a sunset while in a helicopter. Choice A is incorrect because it implies that the person was outside of the helicopter watching it from afar. Choice B is incorrect because the original sentence does not portray the sunset flying up into the sky. Choice C is incorrect because, while the helicopter may have been facing the sunset, this is not the reason that tears were in the speaker's eyes.

26. B: Choice B is correct because like the original sentence, it expresses their plan to go to the party if friends also go. Choice A is incorrect because it does not follow the meaning of the original sentence. Choice C is incorrect because it states that their friends are going, even though that is not known. Choice D is incorrect because it would make the new sentence mean the opposite of the original sentence.

27. C: Choice C is correct because the original sentence states that his recovery time was long because his leg was broken before the accident. Choice A is incorrect because there is no indication that the man had two broken legs. Choice B is incorrect because it indicates that he broke his leg during the car accident, not before. Choice D is incorrect because there is no indication that he broke his leg after the car accident.

28. A: Choice A is correct because it expresses the fact that the birthday and the party were both after Halloween. Choice B is incorrect because it says that the birthday was on Halloween, even though that was not stated in the original sentence. Choice C is incorrect because it says the party was specifically a Halloween party and not a birthday party. Choice D is incorrect because the party was after Halloween, not before.

29. C: The original sentence states that firefighting is dangerous, making it necessary for firefighters to wear protective gear. The portion of the sentence that needs to be rewritten focuses on the gear, not the dangers, of firefighting. Choices A, B, and D all discuss the danger, not the gear, so C is the correct answer.

30. D: The original sentence states that though the sites are popular, they can be dangerous for teens, so D is the best choice. Choice A does state that there is danger, but it doesn't identify teens and limits it to just one site. Choice B repeats the statement from the beginning of the sentence, and Choice C says the sites are used too much, which is not the point made in the original sentence.

TSI Practice Test #3

Math

1. If $6t + 4 = 16$, what is t?
   a. 1
   b. 2
   c. 3
   d. 4

2. The variable y is directly proportional to x. If $y = 3$ when $x = 5$, then what is y when $x = 20$?
   a. 10
   b. 12
   c. 14
   d. 16

3. A line passes through the point $(1, 2)$ and crosses the y-axis at $y = 1$. Which of the following is an equation for this line?
   a. $y = 2x$
   b. $y = x + 1$
   c. $x + y = 1$
   d. $y = \frac{x}{2} - 2$

4. There are $4x + 1$ treats in each party favor bag. If a total of $60x + 15$ treats are distributed, how many bags are given out?
   a. 15
   b. 16
   c. 20
   d. 22

5. Apples cost $2 each, while bananas cost $3 each. Maria purchased a total of 10 pieces of fruit and spent $22. How many apples did she buy?
   a. 5
   b. 6
   c. 7
   d. 8

6. What are the roots of the polynomial $x^2 + x - 2$?
   a. 1 and −2
   b. −1 and 2
   c. 2 and −2
   d. 9 and 13

TSI Practice Test #3

7. What is the y-intercept of $y = x^{5/3} + (x-3)(x+1)$?
    a. 3.5
    b. 7.6
    c. −3
    d. −15.1

8. $x^4 - 16$ can be simplified to which of the following?
    a. $(x^2 - 4)(x^2 + 4)$
    b. $(x^2 + 4)(x^2 + 4)$
    c. $(x^2 - 4)(x^2 - 4)$
    d. $(x^2 - 2)(x^2 + 4)$

9. $(4x^2y^4)^{\frac{3}{2}}$ can be simplified to which of the following?
    a. $8x^3y^6$
    b. $4x^{\frac{5}{2}}y$
    c. $4xy$
    d. $32x^{\frac{7}{2}}y^{\frac{11}{2}}$

10. If $\sqrt{1+x} = 4$, what is x?
    a. 10
    b. 15
    c. 20
    d. 25

11. Suppose $\frac{x+2}{x} = 2$. What is x?
    a. -1
    b. 0
    c. 2
    d. 4

12. A ball is thrown from the top of a high hill so that the height of the ball as a function of time is $h(t) = -16t^2 + 4t + 6$, in feet. What is the maximum height of the ball in feet?
    a. 6
    b. 6.25
    c. 6.5
    d. 6.75

13. A rectangle has a length that is 5 feet longer than 3 times its width. If the perimeter is 90 feet, what is the length in feet?
    a. 10
    b. 20
    c. 25
    d. 35

14. Five students take a test. The scores of the first four students are 80, 85, 75, and 60. If the median score is 80, which of the following could NOT be the score of the fifth student?
   a. 60
   b. 80
   c. 85
   d. 100

15. In an office, there are 50 workers. A total of 60% of the workers are women, and 50% of the women are wearing skirts. If no men are wearing skirts, how many workers are wearing skirts?
   a. 12 workers
   b. 15 workers
   c. 16 workers
   d. 20 workers

16. Ten students take a test. Five students get a 50. Four students get a 70. If the average score is 55, what was the last student's score?
   a. 20
   b. 40
   c. 50
   d. 60

17. A company invests $50,000 in a building where they can produce saws. If the cost of producing one saw is $40, then which function expresses the total amount of money the company spends on producing saws? The variable y is the money paid, and x is the number of saws produced.
   a. $y = 50,000x + 40$
   b. $y + 40 = x - 50,000$
   c. $y = 40x - 50,000$
   d. $y = 40x + 50,000$

18. A six-sided die is rolled. What is the probability that the roll is 1 or 2?
   a. $\frac{1}{6}$
   b. $\frac{1}{4}$
   c. $\frac{1}{3}$
   d. $\frac{1}{2}$

19. For the following similar triangles, what are the values of x and y (rounded to the nearest tenth)?

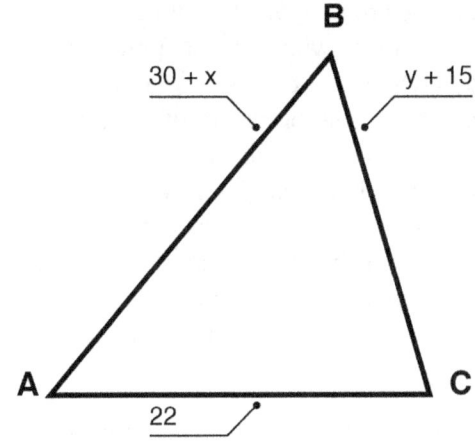
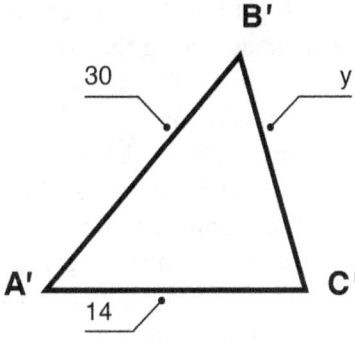

a. $x = 16.5, y = 25.1$
b. $x = 19.5, y = 24.1$
c. $x = 17.1, y = 26.3$
d. $x = 26.3, y = 17.1$

20. An equilateral triangle has a perimeter of 18 feet. The sides of a square have the same length as the triangle's sides. What is the area of the square?
  a. 6 square feet
  b. 36 square feet
  c. 256 square feet
  d. 1,000 square feet

English Language Arts and Reading

Questions 1-4 are based upon the following passage:

This excerpt is an adaptation from Charles Dickens' speech in Birmingham in England on December 30, 1853 on behalf of the Birmingham and Midland Institute.

> My Good Friends,—When I first imparted to the committee of the projected Institute my particular wish that on one of the evenings of my readings here the main body of my audience should be composed of working men and their families, I was animated by two desires; first, by the wish to have the great pleasure of meeting you face to face at this Christmas time, and accompany you myself through one of my little Christmas books; and second, by the wish to have an opportunity of stating publicly in your presence, and in the presence of the committee, my earnest hope that the Institute will, from the beginning, recognize one great principle—strong in reason and justice—which I believe to be essential to the very life of such an Institution. It is, that the working man shall, from the first unto the last, have a share in the management of an Institution which is designed for his benefit, and which calls itself by his name.
>
> I have no fear here of being misunderstood—of being supposed to mean too much in this. If there ever was a time when any one class could of itself do much for its own

good, and for the welfare of society—which I greatly doubt—that time is unquestionably past. It is in the fusion of different classes, without confusion; in the bringing together of employers and employed; in the creating of a better common understanding among those whose interests are identical, who depend upon each other, who are vitally essential to each other, and who never can be in unnatural antagonism without deplorable results, that one of the chief principles of a Mechanics' Institution should consist. In this world a great deal of the bitterness among us arises from an imperfect understanding of one another. Erect in Birmingham a great Educational Institution, properly educational; educational of the feelings as well as of the reason; to which all orders of Birmingham men contribute; in which all orders of Birmingham men meet; wherein all orders of Birmingham men are faithfully represented—and you will erect a Temple of Concord here which will be a model edifice to the whole of England.

Contemplating as I do the existence of the Artisans' Committee, which not long ago considered the establishment of the Institute so sensibly, and supported it so heartily, I earnestly entreat the gentlemen—earnest I know in the good work, and who are now among us,—by all means to avoid the great shortcoming of similar institutions; and in asking the working man for his confidence, to set him the great example and give him theirs in return. You will judge for yourselves if I promise too much for the working man, when I say that he will stand by such an enterprise with the utmost of his patience, his perseverance, sense, and support; that I am sure he will need no charitable aid or condescending patronage; but will readily and cheerfully pay for the advantages which it confers; that he will prepare himself in individual cases where he feels that the adverse circumstances around him have rendered it necessary; in a word, that he will feel his responsibility like an honest man, and will most honestly and manfully discharge it. I now proceed to the pleasant task to which I assure you I have looked forward for a long time.

1. Which word is most closely synonymous with the word patronage as it appears in the following statement:

"... that I am sure he will need no charitable aid or condescending patronage ..."

a. Auspices
b. Aberration
c. Acerbic
d. Adulation

2. Which term is most closely aligned with the definition of the term *working man* as it is used in the following quotation?

> "You will judge for yourselves if I promise too much for the working man, when I say that he will stand by such an enterprise with the utmost of his patience, his perseverance, sense, and support ..."

a. Athlete
b. Viscount
c. Entrepreneur
d. Bourgeois

3. Which of the following statements most closely correlates with the definition of the term *working man* as it is defined in the previous question?
a. A working man is not someone who works for institutions or corporations but rather someone who is well versed in the workings of the soul.
b. A working man is someone who is probably not involved in social activities because the physical demand for work is too high.
c. A working man is someone who works for wages among the middle class.
d. The working man has historically taken to the field, to the factory, and now to the screen.

4. Based upon the contextual evidence provided in the passage above, what is the meaning of the term *enterprise* in the third paragraph?
a. Company
b. Courage
c. Game
d. Cause

The next question is based on the following passage.

Smoking is Terrible

Smoking tobacco products is terribly destructive. A single cigarette contains over 4,000 chemicals, including 43 known carcinogens and 400 deadly toxins. Some of the most dangerous ingredients include tar, carbon monoxide, formaldehyde, ammonia, arsenic, and DDT. Smoking can cause numerous types of cancer, including throat, mouth, nasal cavity, esophageal, gastric, pancreatic, renal, bladder, and cervical cancer.

Cigarettes contain a drug called nicotine, one of the most addictive substances known. Addiction is defined as a compulsion to seek the substance despite negative consequences. According to the National Institute on Drug Abuse, nearly 35 million smokers expressed a desire to quit smoking in 2015; however, more than 85 percent of those who struggle with addiction will not achieve their goal. Almost all smokers regret picking up that first cigarette. You would be wise to learn from their mistake if you have not yet started smoking.

According to the US Department of Health and Human Services, 16 million people in the United States presently suffer from a smoking-related condition, and nearly nine million suffer from a serious smoking-related illness. According to the Centers for Disease Control and Prevention (CDC), tobacco products cause nearly six million deaths per year.

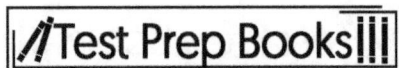

This number is projected to rise to over eight million deaths by 2030. Smokers, on average, die ten years earlier than their nonsmoking peers.

In the United States, local, state, and federal governments typically tax tobacco products, which leads to high prices. Nicotine users who struggle with addiction sometimes pay more for a pack of cigarettes than for a few gallons of gas. Additionally, smokers tend to stink. The smell of smoke is all-consuming and creates a pervasive nastiness. Smokers also risk staining their teeth and fingers with yellow residue from the tar.

Smoking is deadly, expensive, and socially unappealing. Clearly, smoking is not worth the risks.

5. The author would be most likely to agree with which of the following statements?
    a. Smokers should only quit cold turkey and should avoid all nicotine cessation devices.
    b. Other substances are more addictive than tobacco.
    c. Smokers should quit for whatever reason gets them to stop smoking.
    d. People who want to continue smoking should advocate for a reduction in tobacco product taxes.

The next question is based on the following passage.

Christopher Columbus is often credited with discovering America. This is a matter of perspective; America was unknown to fifteenth-century Europe, but bear in mind that the places he "discovered" were already filled with people who had been living there for centuries. What's more, Christopher Columbus was not the first European explorer to reach the Americas! Rather, it was Leif Erikson who first came to the New World and contacted the natives nearly 500 years before Christopher Columbus.

Leif Erikson, the son of Erik the Red (a famous Viking outlaw and explorer in his own right), was born in either 970 or 980, depending on which historian you read. His own family, though, did not raise Leif, which was a Viking tradition. Instead, one of Erik's prisoners taught Leif reading and writing, languages, sailing, and weaponry. At age 12, Leif was considered a man and returned to his family. He killed a man during a dispute shortly after his return, and the council banished the Erikson clan to Greenland.

In 999, Leif left Greenland and traveled to Norway, where he would serve as a guard to King Olaf Tryggvason. It was there that he became a convert to Christianity. Leif later tried to return home with the intention of taking supplies and spreading Christianity to Greenland, but his ship was blown off course and he arrived in a strange new land: present-day Newfoundland, Canada.

When he finally returned to his adopted homeland of Greenland, Leif consulted with a merchant who had also seen the shores of this previously unknown land. The son of the legendary Viking explorer then gathered a crew of 35 men and set sail. Leif became the first European to set foot in the New World as he explored present-day Baffin Island and Labrador, Canada. His crew called the land Vinland since it was plentiful with grapes.

During their time in present-day Newfoundland, Leif's expedition made contact with the natives, whom they referred to as Skraelings (which translates to "wretched ones" in Norse). There are several secondhand accounts of their meetings. Some contemporaries described trade between the peoples. Other accounts describe clashes where the Skraelings defeated the Viking explorers with long spears, while still others claim the Vikings dominated the natives. Regardless of the circumstances, it seems that the Vikings made contact of some kind. This happened around 1000, nearly 500 years before Columbus famously sailed the ocean blue.

Eventually, in 1003, Leif set sail for home and arrived at Greenland with a ship full of timber. In 1020, 17 years later, the legendary Viking died. Many believe that Leif Erikson should receive more credit for his contributions in exploring the New World.

6. Which of the following is an opinion, rather than a historical fact, expressed by the author?
    a. Leif Erikson was definitely the son of Erik the Red; however, historians debate the year of his birth.
    b. Leif Erikson's crew called the land Vinland since it was plentiful with grapes.
    c. Leif Erikson deserves more credit for his contributions in exploring the New World.
    d. Leif Erikson explored the Americas nearly 500 years before Christopher Columbus.

This article discusses the famous poet and playwright William Shakespeare. Read it and answer question 7.

People who argue that William Shakespeare is not responsible for the plays attributed to his name are known as anti-Stratfordians (from the name of Shakespeare's birthplace, Stratford-upon-Avon). The most common anti-Stratfordian claim is that William Shakespeare simply was not educated enough or from a high enough social class to have written plays overflowing with references to such a wide range of subjects like history, the classics, religion, and international culture. William Shakespeare was the son of a glove-maker, he only had a basic grade-school education, and he never set foot outside of England—so how could he have produced plays of such sophistication and imagination? How could he have written in such detail about historical figures and events, or about different cultures and locations around Europe? According to anti-Stratfordians, the depth of knowledge contained in Shakespeare's plays suggests a well-traveled writer from a wealthy background with a university education, not a countryside writer like Shakespeare. But in fact, there is not much substance to such speculation, and most anti-Stratfordian arguments can be refuted with a little background about Shakespeare's time and upbringing.

First of all, those who doubt Shakespeare's authorship often point to his common birth and brief education as stumbling blocks to his writerly genius. Although it is true that Shakespeare did not come from a noble class, his father was a very *successful* glove-maker and his mother was from a very wealthy landowning family—so while Shakespeare may have had a country upbringing, he was certainly from a well-off family and would have been educated accordingly. Also, even though he did not attend university, grade-school education in Shakespeare's time was actually quite rigorous and exposed students to classic drama through writers like Seneca and Ovid. It is not unreasonable to believe that Shakespeare received a very solid foundation in poetry and literature from his early schooling.

Next, anti-Stratfordians tend to question how Shakespeare could write so extensively about countries and cultures he had never visited before. For instance, several of his most famous works like *Romeo and Juliet* and *The Merchant of Venice* were set in Italy, which is located on the opposite side of Europe from England. But again, this criticism does not hold up under scrutiny. For one thing, Shakespeare was living in London, a bustling metropolis of international trade, the most populous city in England, and a political and cultural hub of Europe. In the daily crowds of people, Shakespeare would certainly have been able to meet travelers from other countries and hear firsthand accounts of life in their home country. And, in addition to the influx of information from world travelers, this was also the age of the printing press. This jump in technology made it possible to print and circulate books much more easily than in the past. This also facilitated a freer flow of information across different countries, allowing people to read about life and ideas from all over Europe. One needn't travel the continent in order to learn and write about its different cultures.

7. Which sentence contains the author's thesis?
   a. People who argue that William Shakespeare is not responsible for the plays attributed to his name are known as anti-Stratfordians.
   b. But in fact, there is not much substance to such speculation, and most anti-Stratfordian arguments can be refuted with a little background about Shakespeare's time and upbringing.
   c. It is not unreasonable to believe that Shakespeare received a very solid foundation in poetry and literature from his early schooling.
   d. Next, anti-Stratfordians tend to question how Shakespeare could write so extensively about countries and cultures he had never visited before.

Question 8 refers to the following paragraph.

The Brookside area is an older part of Kansas City, developed mainly in the 1920s and '30s, and is considered one of the nation's first "planned" communities with shops, restaurants, parks, and churches all within a quick walk. A stroll down any street reveals charming two-story Tudor and Colonial homes with smaller bungalows sprinkled throughout the beautiful tree-lined streets. It is common to see lemonade stands on the corners and baseball games in the numerous "pocket" parks tucked neatly behind rows of well-manicured houses. The Brookside shops on 63rd street between Wornall Road and Oak Street are a hub of commerce and entertainment where residents freely shop and dine with their pets (and children) in tow. This is also a common "hangout" spot for younger teenagers because it is easily accessible by bike for most. In short, it is an idyllic neighborhood just minutes from downtown Kansas City.

8. Which of the following states the main idea of this paragraph?
   a. The Brookside shops are a popular hangout for teenagers.
   b. There are a number of pocket parks in the Brookside neighborhood.
   c. Brookside is a great place to live.
   d. Brookside has a high crime rate.

Use the following excerpt for question 9.

Evidently, our country has overlooked both the importance of learning history and the appreciation of it. But why is this a huge problem? Other than historians, who really cares how the War of 1812 began or who Alexander the Great's tutor was? Well, not many, as it turns out. So, *is* history really that important? Yes! History is *critical* for understanding the underlying forces that shape decisive events, preventing us from making the same mistakes twice, and giving us context for current events.

9. The above is an example of which type of writing?
    a. Expository
    b. Persuasive
    c. Narrative
    d. Poetry

10. Which of the following would be a good topic sentence if you were writing a paragraph about the effects of education on crime rates?
    a. Crime statistics are difficult to verify for a number of reasons.
    b. Educated people do not commit crimes.
    c. Education is an important factor in lowering crime rates.
    d. Education has been proven to lower crime rates by as much as 20% in some urban areas.

11. Which of the following is not an example of a good thesis statement for an essay?
    a. Animals in danger of becoming extinct come from a wide range of countries.
    b. Effective leadership requires specific qualities that anyone can develop.
    c. Industrial waste poured into Lake Michigan has killed 27 percent of marine life in the past decade.
    d. In order to fully explore the wreck of the *Titanic*, scientists must address several problems.

12. Which of the following sentences contains an opinion statement?
    a. In 1819, the Supreme Court ruled that Congress could create a national bank.
    b. Marshall also ruled that the states did not have the right to tax the bank or any other agency created by the federal government.
    c. John Marshall was one of the most intelligent chief justices of the United States.
    d. The chief justice is the head of the judicial branch of the government.

13. Which of the following sentences is a factual statement?
    a. Many nutritionists believe a low-carbohydrate, high-protein diet is the healthiest diet.
    b. Legislation should be passed mandating that cell phones be banned in all public-school classrooms.
    c. Spanish is an easier language to learn than Japanese.
    d. College students would benefit greatly from participating in intramural sports on their campuses.

Question 14 refers to the following quote from Martin Luther King Jr.'s Nobel Peace Prize acceptance speech in Oslo on December 10, 1964.

"I refuse to accept the view that mankind is so tragically bound to the starless midnight of racism and war that the bright daybreak of peace and brotherhood can never become a reality ... I believe that unarmed truth and unconditional love will have the final word."

14. Which of the following statements is NOT accurate based on this quote?
    a. Martin Luther King Jr. felt that the fight against racism was ultimately hopeless due to mankind's primitive instincts.
    b. Martin Luther King Jr. was eternally optimistic about mankind's ability to overcome racism.
    c. Martin Luther King Jr. believed that the war against racism could be won with truth and love.
    d. Martin Luther King Jr. believed that the goodness of mankind would prevail.

Question 15 is based upon the following passage:

Insects as a whole are preeminently creatures of the land and the air. This is shown not only by the possession of wings by a vast majority of the class, but by the mode of breathing to which reference has already been made, a system of branching air-tubes carrying atmospheric air with its combustion-supporting oxygen to all the insect's tissues. The air gains access to these tubes through a number of paired air-holes or spiracles, arranged segmentally in series.

It is of great interest to find that, nevertheless, a number of insects spend much of their time under water. This is true of not a few in the perfect winged state, as for example aquatic beetles and water-bugs ('boatmen' and 'scorpions') which have some way of protecting their spiracles when submerged, and, possessing usually the power of flight, can pass on occasion from pond or stream to upper air. But it is advisable in connection with our present subject to dwell especially on some insects that remain continually under water till they are ready to undergo their final molt and attain the winged state, which they pass entirely in the air. The preparatory instars of such insects are aquatic; the adult instar is aerial. All mayflies, dragonflies, and caddisflies, many beetles and two-winged flies, and a few moths thus divide their life-story between the water and the air. For the present we confine attention to the stoneflies, the mayflies, and the dragonflies, three well-known orders of insects respectively called by systematists the Plecoptera, the Ephemeroptera, and the Odonata.

In the case of many insects that have aquatic larvae, the latter are provided with some arrangement for enabling them to reach atmospheric air through the surface-film of the water. But the larva of a stonefly, a dragonfly, or a mayfly is adapted more completely than these for aquatic life; it can, by means of gills of some kind, breathe the air dissolved in water.

This excerpt is adapted from *The Life-Story of Insects*, by Geo H. Carpenter.

15. What is the purpose of the first paragraph in relation to the second paragraph?
    a. The first paragraph serves as a cause, and the second paragraph serves as an effect.
    b. The first paragraph serves as a contrast to the second.
    c. The first paragraph is a description for the argument in the second paragraph.
    d. The first and second paragraphs are merely presented in a sequence.

Read the selection and answer questions 16-19.

I have to admit that when my father bought an RV, I thought he was making a huge mistake. In fact, I even thought he might have gone a little bit crazy. I did not really know anything about recreational vehicles, but I knew that my dad was as big a "city slicker" as there was. On trips to the beach, he preferred to swim at the pool, and whenever he went hiking, he avoided touching any plants for fear that they might be poison ivy. Why would this man, with an almost irrational fear of the outdoors, want a 40-foot camping behemoth?

The RV was a great purchase for our family and brought us all closer together. Every morning we would wake up, eat breakfast, and broke camp. We laughed at our own comical attempts to back The Beast into spaces that seemed impossibly small. We rejoiced when we figured out how to "hack" a solution during a difficult situation. When things inevitably went wrong and we couldn't solve the problems on our own, we discovered the incredible helpfulness and friendliness of the RV community. We even made some new friends in the process.

Above all, owning the RV allowed us to share adventures travelling across America that we could not have experienced in cars and hotels. Enjoying a campfire on a chilly summer evening with the mountains of Glacier National Park in the background, or waking up early in the morning to see the sun rising over the distant spires of Arches National Park are memories that will always stay with me and our entire family. Those are also memories that my siblings and I have now shared with our own children.

16. Which of the following examples would make a good addition to the selection after this sentence?

    On trips to the beach, he preferred to swim at the pool, and whenever he went hiking, he avoided touching any plants for fear that they might be poison ivy.

    a. My father is also afraid of seeing insects.
    b. My father is surprisingly good at starting a campfire.
    c. My father negotiated contracts for a living.
    d. My father isn't even bothered by pigeons.

17. What transition word could be added to the beginning of this sentence?

    The RV was a great purchase for our family and brought us all closer together.

    a. Not surprisingly,
    b. Furthermore,
    c. As it turns out,
    d. Of course,

18. Which of the following would correct the error in this sentence?

    Every morning we would wake up, eat breakfast, and broke camp.

    a. Every morning we would wake up, ate breakfast, and broke camp.
    b. Every morning we would wake up, eat breakfast, and broke camp.
    c. Every morning we would wake up, eat breakfast, and break camp.
    d. Every morning we would wake up, ate breakfast, and break camp.

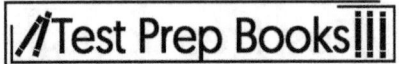

19. Which of the following choices offers the best phrasing for this sentence?

   <u>Above all, owning the RV allowed us to share adventures travelling across America that we could not have experienced in cars and hotels.</u>

   a. Above all, owning the RV allowed us to share adventures travelling across America that we could not have experienced in cars and hotels.
   b. Above all, owning the RV will allow us to share adventures travelling across America that we could not have experienced in cars and hotels.
   c. Above all, it allows you to share adventures travelling across America that you could not have experienced in cars and hotels.
   d. Above all, it allows them to share adventures travelling across America that they could not have experienced in cars and hotels.

20. Which of the following is a clearer way to describe the following phrase?

   "employee-manager relations improvement guide"

   a. A guide to employing better managers
   b. A guide to improving relations between managers and employees
   c. A relationship between employees, managers, and improvement
   d. An improvement in employees' and managers' use of guides

Read the sentences, and then answer the following question.

21. Polls show that more and more people in the US distrust the government and view it as dysfunctional and corrupt. Every election, the same people are voted back into office.

Which word or words would best link these sentences?
   a. Not surprisingly,
   b. Understandably,
   c. And yet,
   d. Therefore,

22. Which of the following statements would make the best conclusion to an essay about civil rights activist Rosa Parks?
   a. On December 1, 1955, Rosa Parks refused to give up her bus seat to a white passenger, setting in motion the Montgomery bus boycott.
   b. Rosa Parks was a hero to many and came to symbolize the way that ordinary people could bring about real change in the civil rights movement.
   c. Rosa Parks died in 2005 in Detroit, having moved from Montgomery shortly after the bus boycott.
   d. Rosa Parks' arrest was an early part of the civil rights movement and helped lead to the passage of the Civil Rights Act of 1964.

Directions for questions 23-30: Choose the best version of the underlined segment of the sentence. If you feel the original sentence is correct, then choose the first answer choice.

23. Since none of the furniture were delivered on time, we have to move in at a later date.
    a. none of the furniture were delivered
    b. none of the furniture was delivered
    c. all of the furniture were delivered
    d. all of the furniture was delivered

24. An important issues stemming from this meeting is that we won't have enough time to meet all of the objectives.
    a. An important issues stemming from this meeting
    b. Important issue stemming from this meeting
    c. An important issue stemming from this meeting
    d. Important issues stemming from this meeting

25. There were many questions about what causes the case to have gone cold, but the detective wasn't willing to discuss it with reporters.
    a. about what causes the case to have gone cold
    b. about why the case is cold
    c. about what causes the case to go cold
    d. about why the case went cold

26. The fact the train set only includes four cars and one small track was a big disappointment to my son.
    a. the train set only includes four cars and one small track was a big disappointment
    b. that the trains set only include four cars and one small track was a big disappointment
    c. that the train set only includes four cars and one small track was a big disappointment
    d. that the train set only includes four cars and one small track were a big disappointment

27. The rising popularity of the clean eating movement can be attributed to the fact that experts say added sugars and chemicals in our food are to blame for the obesity epidemic.
    a. to the fact that experts say added sugars and chemicals in our food are to blame for the obesity epidemic.
    b. in the facts that experts say added sugars and chemicals in our food are to blame for the obesity epidemic.
    c. to the fact that experts saying added sugars and chemicals in our food are to blame for the obesity epidemic.
    d. with the facts that experts say added sugars and chemicals in our food are to blame for the obesity epidemic.

28. She's looking for a suitcase that can fit all of her clothes, shoes, accessory, and makeup.
    a. clothes, shoes, accessory, and makeup.
    b. clothes, shoes, accessories, and makeup.
    c. clothes, shoes, accessories, and makeups.
    d. clothes, shoe, accessory, and makeup.

29. Shawn started taking guitar lessons if he wanted to become a better musician.
    a. if he wanted to become a better musician.
    b. so that he wanted to become a better musician.
    c. even though he wanted to become a better musician.
    d. because he wanted to become a better musician.

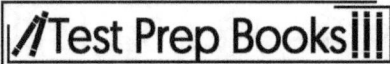

30. <u>Considering the recent rains we have had, it's a wonder</u> the plants haven't drowned.
   a. Considering the recent rains we have had, it's a wonder
   b. Consider the recent rains we have had, it's a wonder
   c. Considering for how much recent rain we have had, its a wonder
   d. Considering, the recent rains we have had, its a wonder

Essay

Please read the prompt below and answer in an essay format in 300–600 words.

> Technology has been invading cars for the last several years, but there are some new high tech trends that are pretty amazing. It is now standard in many car models to have a rear-view camera, hands-free phone and text, and a touch screen digital display. Music can be streamed from a paired cell phone, and some displays can even be programmed with a personal photo. Sensors beep to indicate there is something in the driver's path when reversing and changing lanes. Rain-sensing windshield wipers and lights are automatic, leaving the driver with little to do but watch the road and enjoy the ride. The next wave of technology will include cars that automatically parallel park, and a self-driving car is on the horizon. These technological advances make it a good time to be a driver.

1. Analyze and evaluate the passage given.

2. State and develop your own perspective.

3. Explain the relationship between your perspective and the one given.

The following pages are provided for writing your essay.

Answer Explanations #3

Math

1. B: First, subtract 4 from each side:

$$6t + 4 = 16$$

$$6t + 4 - 4 = 16 - 4$$

$$6t = 12$$

Now, divide both sides by 6:

$$\frac{6t}{6} = \frac{12}{6} t = 2$$

2. B: The variable y is directly proportional to x, which means that whenever x is multiplied by a number, y is multiplied by that same number. When x changes from 5 to 20, it is multiplied by 4, so the original y value must also be multiplied by 4. That means $y = 3 \times 4 = 12$.

3. B: We can use slope-intercept form, $y = mx + b$. We are told that the y-intercept (b) is 1, which gives us $y = mx + 1$. Now we can plug in the x and y values from our point, $(1,2)$, to find the slope: $2 = m(1) + 1$, so $m = 1$. This gives us $y = x + 1$.

4. A: Each bag has $4x + 1$ treats. The total number of treats is $60x + 15$, which means that $60x + 15$ must be divided by $4x + 1$.

$$\frac{60x + 15}{4x + 1} = 15$$

5. D: Let a represent the number of apples and b the number of bananas. The total number of fruits is $a + b = 10$, and the total cost is $2a + 3b = 22$. To solve this pair of equations, we can multiply the first equation by -3:

$$-3(a + b) = -3(10)$$

$$-3a - 3b = -30$$

When we add this to the other equation, the b terms cancel out:

$$(-3a - 3b = -30)$$

$$+(2a + 3b = 22)$$

$$= (-a = -8)$$

This simplifies to $a = 8$.

6. A: Finding the roots means finding the values of x that make the polynomial equal zero. The quadratic formula could be used, but in this case, it is possible to factor by hand since the numbers -1 and 2 add to 1 and multiply to -2. So, factor:

$$x^2 + x - 2 = (x - 1)(x + 2) = 0$$

Then, set each factor equal to zero. Solving for each value gives the values $x = 1$ and $x = -2$.

7. C: To find the y-intercept, substitute zero for x, which gives us:

$$y = 0^{5/3} + (0 - 3)(0 + 1) = 0 + (-3)(1) = -3$$

8. A: This has the form $t^2 - y^2$, with $t = x^2$ and $y = 4$. It's also known that:

$$t^2 - y^2 = (t + y)(t - y)$$

Substitute the values for t and y into the right-hand side:

$$(x^2 - 4)(x^2 + 4)$$

9. A: Simplify this to:

$$(4x^2 y^4)^{\frac{3}{2}} = 4^{\frac{3}{2}}(x^2)^{\frac{3}{2}}(y^4)^{\frac{3}{2}}$$

Now,

$$4^{\frac{3}{2}} = (\sqrt{4})^3 = 2^3 = 8$$

For the rest, recall that the exponents must be multiplied, so this yields:

$$8x^{2 \times \frac{3}{2}} y^{4 \times \frac{3}{2}} = 8x^3 y^6$$

10. B: Start by squaring both sides to get $1 + x = 16$. Then, subtract 1 from both sides to get $x = 15$.

11. C: Multiply both sides by x to get $x + 2 = 2x$. Then, subtract x from both sides: $-x = -2$, or $x = 2$.

12. B: The independent variable's coordinate at the vertex of a parabola (which is the highest point when the coefficient of the squared independent variable is negative) is given by $x = -\frac{b}{2a}$. Substitute and solve for x to get:

$$x = -\frac{4}{2(-16)} = \frac{1}{8}$$

Using this value of x, the maximum height of the ball (y), can be calculated. Substituting $\frac{1}{8}$ into the equation for x yields:

$$h(t) = -16\left(\frac{1}{8}\right)^2 + 4\frac{1}{8} + 6 = 6.25$$

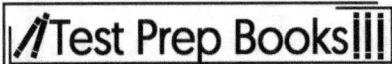

Answer Explanations #3

13. D: Denote the width as w and the length as l. Then, $l = 3w + 5$. The perimeter is $2w + 2l = 90$. Substituting the first expression for l into the second equation yields:

$$2(3w + 5) + 2w = 90$$

$$6w + 10 + 2w = 90$$

$$8w = 80$$

$$w = 10$$

Putting this into the first equation, it yields:

$$l = 3(10) + 5 = 35$$

14. A: Putting the scores in order from least to greatest, we have 60, 75, 80, and 85, as well as one unknown. The median is 80, so 80 must be the middle data point out of these five. Therefore, the unknown data point must be the fourth or fifth data point, meaning it must be greater than or equal to 80. The only answer that fails to meet this condition is 60.

15. B: If 60% of 50 workers are women, then there are 30 women working in the office. If half of them are wearing skirts, then that means 15 women wear skirts. Since nobody else wears skirts, this means there are 15 people wearing skirts.

16. A: Let the unknown score be x. The average will be:

$$\frac{5 \times 50 + 4 \times 70 + x}{10} = \frac{530 + x}{10} = 55$$

Multiply both sides by 10 to get:

$$530 + x = 550$$

or

$$x = 20$$

17. D: The total amount the company pays, y, equals the cost of the building ($50,000) plus the cost of the saws. Since the saws cost $40 each, the overall cost of the saws is $40 times x, where x is the number of saws. Putting all this together, we have $y = 50{,}000 + 40x$, which is equivalent to Choice D.

18. C: When a die is rolled, each outcome is equally likely. Since it has six sides, each outcome has a probability of $\frac{1}{6}$. The chance of a 1 or a 2 is therefore $\frac{1}{6} + \frac{1}{6} = \frac{1}{3}$.

19. C: Because the triangles are similar, the lengths of the corresponding sides are proportional. Therefore, these two relationships exist:

$$\frac{30 + x}{30} = \frac{22}{14}$$

$$\frac{y + 15}{y} = \frac{22}{14}$$

Answer Explanations #3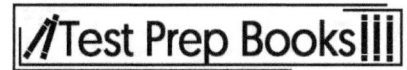

Using cross multiplication on the first proportion results in the equation:

$$14(30 + x) = 22 \times 30$$

When solved, this gives:

$$x \approx 17.1$$

Using cross multiplication on the second proportion results in the equation:

$$14(y + 15) = 22y$$

When solved, this gives:

$$y \approx 26.3$$

20. B: An equilateral triangle has 3 sides of equal length, so if the total perimeter is 18 feet, each side must be 6 feet long. A square with sides of 6 feet will have an area of $6^2 = 36$ square feet.

English Language Arts and Reading

1. A: The word *patronage* most nearly means auspices, which means protection or support. Choice *B*, *aberration*, means abnormality and does not make sense within the context of the sentence. Choice *C*, *acerbic*, means sour or sharply critical, and it also does not make sense in the sentence. Choice *D*, *adulation*, is a positive word meaning *praise*, and thus does not fit with the word *condescending* in the sentence.

2. D: *Working man* is most closely aligned with Choice *D*, *bourgeois.* In the context of the speech, the word *bourgeois* means working or middle class. Choice *A*, *athlete*, does suggest someone who works hard, but it does not make sense in this context. Choice *B*, *viscount*, is a European title used to describe a specific degree of nobility. Choice *C*, *entrepreneur*, is a person who operates their own business.

3. C: In the context of the speech, the term *working man* most closely correlates with Choice *C*. Choice *A* is not mentioned in the passage and is off-topic. Choice *B* may be true in some cases, but it does not reflect the sentiment described for the term *working man* in the passage. Choice *D* is not a definition, and the topics of the field, factory, and screen are not mentioned in the passage.

4. D: *Enterprise* most closely means cause. Choices *A*, *B*, and *C* are all related to the term *enterprise*. However, Dickens speaks of a *cause* here, not a *company*, *courage*, or a *game*. "He will stand by such an enterprise" is a call to stand by a cause to enable the working man to have a certain autonomy over his own economic standing. The very first paragraph ends with the statement that the working man "shall ... have a share in the management of an institution which is designed for his benefit."

5. C: We are looking for something the author would agree with, so it should be anti-smoking or an argument in favor of quitting smoking. Choice *A* is incorrect because the author does not speak against means of cessation. Choice *B* is incorrect because the author does not reference other substances but does speak of how addictive nicotine, a drug in tobacco, is. Choice *D* is incorrect because the author would not encourage reducing taxes to encourage a reduction of smoking costs, thereby helping smokers to continue the habit. Choice *C* is correct because the author is attempting to persuade smokers to quit smoking.

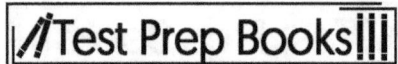

6. C: Choice A is incorrect because it describes facts: Leif Erikson was the son of Erik the Red and historians debate Leif's date of birth. These are not opinions. Choice B is incorrect; Erikson calling the land Vinland is a verifiable fact, as is Choice D, because he did contact the natives almost 500 years before Columbus. Choice C is the correct answer because it is the author's opinion that Erikson deserves more credit. Another person could argue that Columbus or another explorer deserves more credit, which makes it an opinion rather than a historical fact.

7. B: The thesis is a statement that contains the author's topic and main idea. The main purpose of this article is to use historical evidence to provide counterarguments to anti-Stratfordians. Choice A is simply a definition; Choice C is a supporting detail, not a main idea; and Choice D represents an idea of anti-Stratfordians, not the author's opinion.

8. C: All the details in this paragraph suggest that Brookside is a great place to live, plus the last sentence states that it is an *idyllic neighborhood*, meaning it is perfect, happy, and blissful. Choices A and B are incorrect, because although they do contain specific details from the paragraph that support the main idea, they are not the main idea. Choice D is incorrect because there is no reference in the paragraph to the crime rate in Brookside.

9. B: Persuasive is the correct answer because the author is clearly trying to convey the point that history education is very important. Choice A is incorrect because expository writing is more informational and less emotional. Choice C is incorrect because narrative writing involves storytelling. Choice D is incorrect because this is a piece of prose, not poetry.

10. C: Choice C is correct because it states the fact that education has a positive impact on lowering crime rates, and it tells your reader what you will cover in that paragraph without providing specific details yet. That's what the remainder of the paragraph is for. Choice A is incorrect because the paragraph is not about the verification of crime statistics. Choice B is incorrect because it is a broad generalization that is simply not true. Choice D, while it is on topic, is too specific to be a topic sentence, but it would be an excellent supporting detail.

11. C: This sentence would not be a good thesis statement because it conveys one very specific detail. All the other answer choices would be good thesis statements because they are general enough for an entire essay but specific enough that the reader knows exactly what the essay will cover.

12. C: This answer choice is correct because "one of the most intelligent" "is a matter of opinion, not a quantifiable fact. All the other answer choices are factual statements.

13. A: This answer choice is correct because it is the only statement that is" not based on opinion. Nutritionists' belief in one certain diet might be a matter of opinion, but the statement that many do believe in the health benefits of this particular diet is a fact.

14. A: This is the correct answer choice because there is evidence to the contrary that Martin Luther King Jr. refused to believe that mankind would be bound to the darkness of racism.

15. B: Notice how the first paragraph goes into detail describing how insects are able to breathe air. The second paragraph acts as a contrast to the first by stating, "[i]t is of great interest to find that, nevertheless, a number of insects spend much of their time under water." Watch for transition words such as *nevertheless* to help find what type of passage you're dealing with.

16. A: Choices B and D go against the point the author is trying to make—that the father is not comfortable in nature. Choice C is irrelevant to the topic. Choice A is the only choice that emphasizes the father's discomfort with spending time in nature.

17. C: In paragraph 2, the author surprises the reader by asserting that the opposite of what was expected was in fact true—the city slicker father actually enjoyed the RV experience. Only Choice C indicates this shift in expected outcome, while the other choices indicate a continuation of the previous expectation.

18. C: This sentence uses verbs in a parallel series, so each verb must follow the same pattern. In order to fit with the helping verb *would*, each verb must be in the present tense. In Choices A, B, and D, one or more of the verbs switches to past tense. Only Choice C remains in the same tense, maintaining the pattern.

19. A: The sentence should be in the same tense and person as the rest of the selection. The rest of the selection is in past tense and first person. Choice B is in future tense. Choice C is in second person. Choice D is in third person. While none of these sentences are incorrect by themselves, they are written in a tense that is different from the rest of the selection. Choices C and D additionally begin the third paragraph with a pronoun. Ideally, since a paragraph introduces separate ideas, it should reintroduce its nouns. Only Choice A, the original sentence, maintains tense and voice consistent with the rest of the selection.

20. B: Stacked modifying nouns such as this example are untangled by starting from the end and adding words as necessary to provide meaning. In this case, a *guide* to *improving relations* between *managers* and *employees*. Choices C and D do not define the item first as a guide. Choice A does identify the item as a guide, but confuses the order of the remaining descriptors. Choice B is correct, as it unstacks the nouns in the correct order and also makes logical sense.

21. C: The second sentence tells of an unexpected outcome of the first sentence. Choice A, Choice B, and Choice D indicate a logical progression, which does not match this surprise. Only Choice C indicates this unexpected twist.

22. B: Choices A, C, and D all relate facts but do not present the kind of general statement that would serve as an effective summary or conclusion. Choice B is correct.

23. B: Choice A uses the plural form of the verb, when the subject is the pronoun *none*, which needs a singular verb. Choice C also uses the wrong verb form and uses the word *all* in place of *none*, which doesn't make sense in the context of the sentence. Choice D uses *all* again, and is missing the comma, which is necessary to set the dependent clause off from the independent clause.

24. C: In this answer, the article and subject agree, and the subject and predicate agree. Choice A is incorrect because the article *an* and *issues* do not agree in number. Choice B is incorrect because an article is needed before *important issue*. Choice D is incorrect because the plural subject *issues* does not agree with the singular verb *is*.

25. D: Choices A and C use additional words and phrases that aren't necessary. Choice B is more concise but uses the present tense of *is*. This does not agree with the rest of the sentence, which uses past tense. The best choice is Choice D, which uses the most concise sentence structure and is grammatically correct.

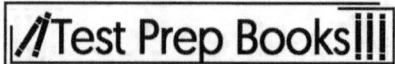

Answer Explanations #3

26. C: Choice *A* is missing the word *that*. Choice *B* uses the plural verb *include*, which does not agree with the word *set*. Choice *D* changes *was* to *were*, which is in plural form and does not agree with the singular subject, *fact*.

27. A: Choices *B* and *D* both use the expression *attributed to the fact* incorrectly. It can only be attributed *to* the fact, not *with* or *in* the fact. Choice *C* incorrectly uses a gerund, *saying,* when it should use the present tense of the verb *say*.

28. B: Choice *B* is correct because it uses correct parallel structure of plural nouns. Choice *A* is incorrect because the word *accessory* is in singular form. Choice *C* is incorrect because it pluralizes *makeup*, which is already in plural form. Choice *D* is incorrect because it again uses the singular *accessory*, and it uses the singular *shoe*.

29. D: In a cause/effect relationship, it is correct to use the word "because" in the clausal part of the sentence. This can eliminate both Choices *A* and *C* which don't clearly show the cause/effect relationship. Choice *B* is incorrect because it uses the present tense, when the first part of the sentence is in the past tense. It makes grammatical sense for both parts of the sentence to be in past tense.

30. A: In Choice *B*, the present tense form of the verb *consider* creates an independent clause joined to another independent clause with only a comma, which is a comma splice and grammatically incorrect. Choices *C* and *D* use the possessive form of *its*, when it should be the contraction *it's* for *it is*. Choice *D* also includes incorrect comma placement.

TSI Practice Tests #4, #5, and #6

To keep the size of this book manageable, save paper, and provide a digital test-taking experience, the 4th, 5th, and 6th practice tests can be found online. Scan the QR code or go to this link to access it:

testprepbooks.com/online387/tsi

The first time you access the tests, you will need to register as a "new user" and verify your email address.

If you have any issues, please email support@testprepbooks.com.

Index

Absolute Phrases, 91
Abstract Noun, 79
Active Voice, 78, 79
Addition Rule for Probabilities, 56
Adjective Clauses, 90
Adjective Phrase, 82
Adjectives, 81
Adverbial Clauses, 90
Adverbs, 62, 82
Algebraic Expressions, 20
Alliteration, 60
Anaphora, 60
Anecdotes, 64, 68, 105
Angle, 37, 38, 40, 43, 47
Antecedent, 80
Antimetabole, 60
Antiphrasis, 60
Apostrophe, 96
Appositive Phrases, 91
Arc Length, 37
Area of a Polygon, 43
Articles, 81
Assonance, 60
Circumference, 37, 153
Clauses, 89
Coefficients, 22, 30, 126
Collective Noun, 79, 85
　Collective Nouns, 85
Colon, 88, 94, 156
Comma, 83, 87, 92, 93, 129, 130, 155, 156, 181, 182
Common Noun, 79
Comparative Adjectives, 81
Comparative Form, 81
Complete Sentence, 64, 87, 129, 130
Complex Prepositions, 82
Compound Subjects, 84, 85
Concrete Noun, 79
Conditional Probability, 54
Congruent Figures, 40
Conjugation, 78, 85, 86, 101, 130
Conjunctions, 83
Coordinating Conjunctions, 83
Correlated, 52
Counterargument, 69

Credible, 70, 75
Cube Root, 30, 49
Cubing, 29
Dangling Modifier, 88
Declarative, 92
Definite Article, 81
Degree of the Polynomial, 22
Demonstrative Pronouns, 79
Dependent, 14, 20, 52, 53, 83, 87, 89, 92, 130, 156, 181
Dependent Clause, 87, 89, 130, 156, 181
Dependent Variable, 14, 20, 52, 53
Descriptive Statistics, 49
Descriptive Writing, 63
Dilation, 40, 41
Discriminant, 26, 28
Domain, 13, 14
Ellipsis, 95, 129
Em-Dash, 95
Epiphora, 60
Equilateral Triangle, 38, 179
Ethos, 68
Exclamation Point, 83, 92, 96
Exponent, 22, 29, 30, 126
Exponential Expression, 29
Expository Writing, 58
Factors for Polynomials, 23
First Person, 79, 84
First Quartile, 51
FOIL, 23
Fourth Quartile, 51
Function, 13, 14, 15, 16, 20, 22, 26, 29, 34, 54, 77, 85, 101, 127, 128, 136, 159, 160
Function Notation, 13
Future Perfect Tense, 78, 86
Future Tense, 78, 86
Gerund Phrases, 91
Helping (Auxiliary) Verbs, 77
Horizontal, 17, 34
Hyphen, 95, 96, 97
Hypotenuse, 47, 49
Image, 38, 39, 40
Imperative, 80, 92
Indefinite Articles, 81
Indefinite Pronouns, 80, 84

Index

Independent, 14, 20, 52, 53, 55, 56, 83, 87, 88, 89, 92, 93, 94, 129, 130, 155, 156, 177, 181, 182
Independent Clause, 83, 87, 88, 89, 92, 93, 94, 129, 130, 155, 156, 181, 182
Independent Variable, 14, 20, 52, 53, 177
Indirect Question, 92
Inferences, 49, 59, 60
Inferential Statistics, 49
Infinitive Phrases, 91
Informative Writing, 63
Intercept Form, 17
Interior Angles, 38, 47
Interjections, 83
Interrogative, 79, 92
Interrogative Pronouns, 79
Irregular, 78
Isosceles Triangle, 38
Jargon, 59, 61
Line of Reflection, 38, 39
Line Segment, 36, 38, 43
Line Symmetry, 42
Linear, 14, 15, 16, 17, 18, 19, 21, 53, 128, 151
Linear Correlation, 53
Linear System of Equations, 19
Logos, 68
Main, 45, 63, 64, 65, 66, 67, 68, 70, 74, 75, 76, 77, 83, 92, 93, 103, 105, 106, 114, 115, 129, 130, 138, 139, 154, 161, 166, 180
Main Idea, 63, 64, 65, 66, 67, 68, 70, 74, 75, 76, 166, 180
Mean, 16, 20, 49, 50, 51, 52, 53, 71, 129, 156, 161
Meanings, 60, 61, 71, 73, 76, 131
Median, 50, 51, 52, 132, 150, 160
Misplaced Modifier, 88, 130, 155
Mode, 51, 52, 168
Modifier, 88, 117, 130
Monomial, 22, 23
Mood, 61, 62
Multiplication Rule for Probabilities, 57
Narrative Writing, 58
Neutral Tone, 62
Noun, 77, 79, 80, 81, 82, 85, 88, 89, 90, 91, 102, 130, 131, 155
Noun Clauses, 90
Noun Phrases, 90

n^{th} Percentile, 51
Object of the Preposition, 82, 84
Objective Pronouns, 80
Onomatopoeia, 61
Origin, 16, 40, 109, 127
Outliers, 50, 52
Outline, 66, 67, 105, 106, 114
Oxford Comma, 93
Parabola, 26, 128, 177
Parallel, 37, 38, 130, 132, 181, 182
Parallelism, 89, 130
Parallelogram, 38
Paraphrasing, 67, 68
Parentheses, 31, 94
Particles, 77
Passive Voice, 78, 79
Past Perfect Tense, 78, 86
Past Tense, 78, 86
Pathos, 68
PEMDAS, 31
Percentiles, 51
Perimeter, 43, 48, 135, 153, 159, 178, 179
Periods, 92
Perpendicular, 37
Personal Pronouns, 79
Persuasive Writing, 59, 63, 68
Phrase, 31, 53, 71, 74, 75, 76, 77, 82, 84, 88, 89, 90, 91, 93, 94, 130, 137, 155, 170
Plane, 15, 16, 36, 38, 40, 45, 91
Points, 15, 16, 17, 36, 37, 38, 39, 40, 41, 45, 46, 50, 51, 52, 64, 70, 74, 75, 105, 106, 114
Point-Slope Form, 17
Polygon, 38, 43, 44
Polynomial, 22, 23, 25, 26, 32, 150
Polynomial Function, 22
Positive Form, 81
Positive Root, 30
Possessive Pronouns, 79
Pre-Image, 38, 39
Prepositional Phrases, 82, 91
Prepositions, 82
Present Perfect Tense, 78, 86
Present Tense, 78, 86
Probability Distribution, 54
Pronoun, 79, 80, 82, 90, 91, 100, 101, 156, 181
Pronoun Reference, 80
Pronoun-Antecedent Agreement, 80

Index

Proper Name, 79
Proper Noun, 79, 102, 103
Pun, 61
Pythagorean Theorem, 47
   Pythagorean Formula, 36
Quadratic, 26, 27, 28, 29, 125, 128, 149, 177
Quadratic Equation, 27, 28, 29, 125
Quadrilateral, 38, 44
Question Marks, 92, 96
Quotation Marks, 68, 70, 95, 96
Radical, 30
Range, 13, 49, 54, 56, 60, 97, 106, 132, 134, 151, 165, 167
Rational Equation, 33
Rational Expression, 32, 33
Rational Function, 34, 35
Rays, 36
Reciprocal Pronouns, 80
Rectangle, 33, 38, 43, 44, 45, 46, 48, 135, 159
Rectangular Prism, 45, 126
Rectangular Pyramid, 46, 49
Reduction, 40, 164, 179
Reflection, 38, 40, 41
Regular, 38, 78
Regular Polygon, 38
Relation, 13, 16, 20, 21, 82, 130, 131, 168
Relative Pronouns, 79
Rhetorical Devices, 60
Rhetorical Questions, 69
Right Triangle, 38, 47, 48, 49
Rotation, 38, 40, 41
Rotational Symmetry, 42, 43
Rotations, 38
Run-on, 88, 129, 130, 156
Scale Factor, 40, 41, 47
Second Person, 79, 84
Second Quartile, 51
Semicolon, 83, 87, 88, 93, 129, 130, 155
Sentence Fragments, 87
Slope, 17, 21, 22, 110, 127, 149

Slope-Intercept Form, 17
SOAP, 24
Sphere, 46, 109
Square, 23, 28, 30, 31, 38, 45, 47, 48, 49, 52, 108, 109, 125, 127, 152, 161, 179
Square Root, 28, 30, 31, 49, 52
Squaring, 29, 31, 177
Standard Deviation, 52
Standard Form, 17
Statistics, 49, 70
Stereotypes, 69
Style, 61
Subjective Pronouns, 80
Subordinate, 83, 89, 92, 111
Subordinating Conjunctions, 83
Suffix, 78, 98, 99, 100
Summarizing, 67, 68
Superlative Form, 81
Systems of Equations, 19
Technical Writing, 59, 61
Terms of the Polynomial, 22
Text Evidence, 70
Third Person, 79, 84
Third Quartile, 51
Tone, 61
Topic, 59, 61, 62, 63, 64, 65, 69, 94, 105, 106, 120, 129, 155, 167, 179, 181
Translation, 38, 40, 41
Triangle, 38, 39, 41, 43, 44, 45, 46, 47, 48
Two-Point Form, 17
Uniform Probability Distribution, 54, 55
Variance, 51, 52
Verb, 75, 77, 78, 80, 83, 84, 85, 86, 87, 88, 89, 90, 91, 99, 101, 102, 117, 118, 129, 130, 131, 142, 143, 155, 156, 181, 182
Verb Tense, 78, 86
Verbal Phrases, 91
Vertex, 26, 37, 40, 46, 177
Vertical Line Test, 16
Vertical Lines, 17

Dear TSI Test Taker,

Thank you for purchasing this study guide for your TSI exam. We hope that we exceeded your expectations.

Our goal in creating this study guide was to cover all of the topics that you will see on the test. We also strove to make our practice questions as similar as possible to what you will encounter on test day. With that being said, if you found something that you feel was not up to your standards, please send us an email and let us know.

We would also like to let you know about other books in our catalog that may interest you.

ACCUPLACER

This can be found on Amazon: amazon.com/dp/1637756356

SAT

amazon.com/dp/1637754051

ACT

amazon.com/dp/1637758596

AP Biology

amazon.com/dp/1628456221

We have study guides in a wide variety of fields. If the one you are looking for isn't listed above, then try searching for it on Amazon or send us an email.

Thanks Again and Happy Testing!
Product Development Team
info@studyguideteam.com

Online Resources

Included with your purchase are multiple online resources. This includes the practice tests in an interactive format and a convenient study timer to help you manage your time.

Scan the QR code or go to this link to access this content:

testprepbooks.com/online387/tsi

The first time you access the page, you will need to register as a "new user" and verify your email address.

If you have any issues, please email support@testprepbooks.com.

Thank you for letting us be a part of your studying journey!